LONGMAN LINGUISTICS LIBRARY
General editors
R. H. Robins, University of London
G. N. Leech, University of Lancaster
Title no :

LONGMAN LINGUISTICS LIBRARY
Title no 17
SPATIAL AND TEMPORAL USES OF ENGLISH PREPOSITIONS
AN ESSAY IN STRATIFICATIONAL SEMANTICS

Spatial and Temporal Uses of English Prepositions

An Essay in Stratificational Semantics

David C. Bennett
Lecturer in Linguistics
School of Oriental and African Studies
University of London

LONGMAN

LONGMAN GROUP LIMITED LONDON

Associated companies, branches and representatives throughout the world

© **Longman Group Ltd 1975**

First published 1975

ISBN 0 582 52453 9

Made and printed in Great Britain by
William Clowes & Sons, Limited, London, Beccles and Colchester

Spatial and Temporal Uses of English Prepositions

An Essay in Stratificational Semantics

David C. Bennett
Lecturer in Linguistics
School of Oriental and African Studies
University of London

LONGMAN

LONGMAN GROUP LIMITED LONDON

Associated companies, branches and representatives throughout the world

© **Longman Group Ltd 1975**

First published 1975

ISBN 0 582 52453 9

Made and printed in Great Britain by
William Clowes & Sons, Limited, London, Beccles and Colchester

To the memory of my mother

Preface

This book is based on a Yale University PHD thesis. I am grateful to the English-Speaking Union for sponsoring my application for admission to Yale University; to Yale Graduate School for the award of a Fellowship for the years 1965–67 and a Sterling Fellowship for 1967–68; and to the American Council of Learned Societies for the award of a Fellowship for Advanced Study in Linguistics for the year 1967–68. The work was also partially supported by the National Science Foundation under a grant to Yale University, and by the Central Research Fund of the University of London.

While writing the original thesis and subsequently revising it, I have benefited considerably from discussions with a large number of scholars; and a number of former teachers and colleagues have earned my special gratitude by commenting on earlier versions of the book. Faced with the choice of (a) acknowledging no one, or (b) mentioning only those to whom I owe the greatest debt, or (c) listing the names of all those to whom I feel in one way or another indebted, I have opted for (c). My thanks go to: Edward N. Adams, Michael Ashby, Emmon Bach, C. E. Bazell, Guy Carden, Fred Castro, Harold C. Conklin, Ian R. H. Dale, Isidore Dyen, Robin Fawcett, Charles J. Fillmore, Ilah Fleming, Howard B. Garey, M. A. K. Halliday, Jorge Hankamer, Dick Hayward, Roger Higgins, Dick Hudson, Yoshihiko Ikegami, Phil Johnson-Laird, John Kelly, Ruth Kempson, Jay Keyser, William Labov, Sydney M. Lamb, Floyd G. Lounsbury, Samuel E. Martin, Hazel Phillips, Nigel Phillips, Paul M. Postal, Randolph Quirk, Peter A. Reich, R. H. Robins, John R. Ross, Geoffrey Sampson, Alexander M. Schenker, Neil Smith, William J. Sullivan, Rulon S. Wells, Huw Williams and Hans-Christoff

Wolfart; and also to students at S.O.A.S., on whom much of the material discussed in the book has been tried out. I am particularly grateful to Sydney Lamb, who was my thesis supervisor at Yale. Needless to say, none of the above can be held responsible for any of the shortcomings of the book.

Finally, I must mention the contribution of my immediate family. My wife has been a source of constant encouragement and much valuable criticism. And for a long time there was a section of the children's prayers that ran: 'please let Daddy write his book faster and please let elephants run faster'. It is nice that they can now concentrate on the elephants.

University of London   DCB
June 1974

Contents

Acknowledgments

We are grateful to the following for permission to reproduce copyright material:

Oxford University Press for an extract from 'Concerning the Present Tense' by R. A. Close from *English Language Teaching* 13, 1959, published by Oxford University Press in association with the British Council; the author and University Microfilms for an extract from 'A Relational Network Model of Language Behavior', a PHD dissertation submitted to the University of Michigan in 1970 by P. A. Reich; the author for an extract from a paper 'Six performances in search of a competence' by P. A. Reich, presented at a Seminar on the Construction of Complex Grammars at Harvard University in 1970; and the author and the Ohio State University for an extract from 'The Pathological Case' by Charles R. Stratton from *Working Papers in Linguistics* 10.

Introduction

0.1 The Topic

English prepositions serve a wide variety of functions. In classifying their functions it is customary to distinguish between 'grammatical' uses and 'local' uses. In this book we shall be concerned only with local, *ie* spatial and temporal, uses. Not all prepositions that have spatial or temporal uses will be considered; however, the number investigated is sufficiently large to ensure that a clear picture emerges of the way in which English handles spatial and temporal relations. To be specific, thirty-seven prepositions are considered (thirty-eight if we include *in back of*, which does not occur in my own dialect – standard British English – but is briefly discussed in connection with *behind*). The thirty-seven (or thirty-eight) items are listed in *Table 1*.

above	beyond	into	through
across	by	off	throughout
after	down	on	till
along	during	onto	to
(a)round	for	out of	towards
at	from	outside	under
away from	in	over	until
before	[in back of]	past	up
behind	in front of	since	via
below	inside		

Table 1 The prepositions considered

In the case of some prepositions, not all spatial and temporal uses are discussed. Sometimes it is specifically stated in the text that a particular use is being ignored. On other occasions there is no such warning. The primary aim of the book is to characterize the overall structure of this area of the semantics of English, rather than to be exhaustive on any given preposition.

There is a further important distinction that needs to be made in relation to prepositions, namely the distinction between 'determined' and 'non-determined' uses. A preposition is fully determined in a particular position if there is no other preposition with which it contrasts, *eg: on* in *rely on*, or *at* in *at least*. Several other terms are available for this distinction. A determined preposition occurs in what may be referred to as a 'tight' construction, *cf* Bugarski 1968: 253 *ff* and references cited there. A non-determined preposition occurs in a 'loose' construction. Also, one may speak of the degree of 'cohesion' that exists between a preposition and the items with which it is in construction, *cf* Chomsky 1965: 101. To allow the possibility of 'various degrees of cohesion', as Chomsky does, implies that a given construction is not simply either tight or loose, but rather more or less tight. This question of degrees of cohesion is investigated in detail by Quirk and Mulholland (1963), Bugarski (1968) and Carvell and Svartvik (1969). They propose an extensive list of criteria that may be applied in determining the degree of cohesion within particular instances of a given construction-type. The following two examples illustrate three degrees of cohesion – going from tight to loose – in two construction-types (the first is taken from Quirk and Mulholland 1963, and the second from Bugarski 1968):

in spite of the hotel – at the sight of the hotel – in the lounge of the
    hotel
beside himself – beside the point – beside the ash-tray

As soon as one considers the distinction between prepositional phrases 'inside the verb phrase' and 'outside the verb phrase' – *eg: John keeps his car in the garage* versus *John washes his car in the garage* (Fillmore 1968: 26) – one is necessarily concerned with different degrees of cohesion. To this extent the notion of cohesion will come up for discussion below. However, a detailed investigation of the gradient separating tight and loose constructions, such as is found in Quirk and Mulholland 1963 and Bugarski 1968, is beyond the scope of the present work.

The dialect of English on which the analysis is based, as already indicated, is standard British English. But from time to time there will be some discussion of American English, namely at points at which I was aware of a particular difference between the two varieties that seemed, in addition, to be of special interest.

0.2 The Approach

Spatial uses of English prepositions are discussed in Part I, and temporal uses in Part II. The semantic structure of specific sentences is represented there by means of phrase markers, or tree diagrams. Otherwise, however, the discussion is informal. Then in Part III we turn to the question of formalizing the analysis, using for this purpose the theory of language known as 'stratificational grammar'. It is here that I shall indicate how the semantic structures proposed in Parts I and II can be generated, and also how they can be mapped onto surface structures. I do not regard the semantic structures themselves as being in any way exclusively 'stratificational'. The stratificational nature of the analysis emerges only at the point where we relate the semantic structures to surface structures. Accordingly, the subtitle of the book – *An Essay in Stratificational Semantics* – should be interpreted as meaning 'an essay in semantics within the framework of stratificational grammar'.

The approach that I adopt in Parts I and II derives from accepting three particular points of view, namely those of (1) case grammar, (2) componential analysis, and (3) the 'Gesamtbedeutung' ('general meaning') method of describing the meaning of lexical and grammatical items. Each of the three is a theoretical standpoint, but they are of a sufficiently general nature as to be capable of being incorporated into the framework of any of the specific theories of language. Fillmore's brand of case grammar – *cf* Fillmore 1968, 1971a – has developed within the framework of transformational grammar, but Halliday (1967–68) has evolved another version of case grammar within the framework of systemic grammar. Similarly, components of meaning are invoked by both transformationalists and stratificationalists, and the fact that they are called 'semantic markers' by one group and 'sememes' by the other is of minor importance.

In analysing the meaning of the prepositions in *Table* 1 it is necessary to invoke five cases. They are: 'locative', 'source', 'path', 'goal' and 'extent'. In addition, we need to refer to Fillmore's (1971a) 'object' case; and one example discussed in Part I requires an 'ergative' case. The main way in which the version of case grammar developed here differs from earlier versions is that it allows the possibility of case phrases being embedded inside other case phrases, and on quite a

considerable scale. It is only by adopting this innovation that we are able
to give a satisfactory account of the data.

The technique of componential analysis of meaning provides a very
straightforward method of expressing the semantic relationship between
different vocabulary items. For instance, the component 'interior' is
part of the meaning of the prepositions *in*, *into* and *through*, and also the
verbs *enter* and *contain*, but absent from the componential definition of,
say, *behind*. The main emphasis in this book will in general be on intra-
linguistic semantic relationships, rather than on the relationship between
linguistic items and the world in which we live. When particular semantic components are posited in the course of the analysis, they will usually
be accompanied by a definition, and to that extent we shall be concerned
with the physical world, but the definitions will be couched in informal
terms rather than, say, in precise geometrical phraseology. Wherever the
label chosen for some semantic component is self-explanatory, *eg* 'interior', not even an informal definition will be given.

The remainder of this section is devoted to indicating the policy we
shall adopt on the question of polysemy. This will entail referring to the
notion of a 'Gesamtbedeutung' ('general meaning'), *cf* Jakobson 1932,
1936. At the outset we need to make a three-way distinction between
'lexemes', 'senses (of a lexeme)' and 'occurrences (of a lexeme)'.

The way in which the term 'lexeme' is used in stratificational grammar will become clear in the course of Part III. At this stage it will suffice
to say that each of the items in *Table* 1 is a lexeme. (The term 'morpheme' is inappropriate since several of the items are polymorphemic,
eg: throughout, inside, in front of. Nor is 'word' any more appropriate,
since some of the entries consist of more than one word, *eg: in front of*.)
Our task, then, is to describe the meaning of a particular set of English
lexemes.

'Occurrences' means exactly what one would expect it to mean. Thus
the sentences [1a–c] contain three separate occurrences of the lexeme
by:

She was sitting by the fire   [1a]
She was sitting by the window   [1b]
Return it to me by Monday   [1c]

Now it is generally assumed – and I see no reason for rejecting this assumption – that a lexeme may or may not have the same meaning on two
separate occurrences. There would presumably be general agreement
that the meaning of *by* is the same in [1a and b], but different in [1a and

c]. We may say, then, that the lexeme *by* has at least two distinct 'senses'. One sense occurs in [1a and b], and another sense occurs in [1c]. The task of describing the meaning of the lexeme *by* now becomes that of describing the meaning of the various senses of *by*. Each sense will need to be assigned a separate componential definition.

One of the most difficult problems in an analysis such as the present one is that of deciding how many senses to ascribe to a given lexeme. For almost any preposition there is considerable discrepancy in the number of senses listed by different dictionaries. The situation is no better if one compares Lindkvist 1950, which describes the spatial meanings of *in*, *at*, *on* and *to*, or Sandhagen 1956, which describes the temporal meanings of *at*, *on*, *in*, *by* and *for*, with Wood 1967, which provides a general account of approximately 100 prepositions. What these three works have in common, however, is that they postulate relatively many senses of the prepositions they analyse. For instance, Wood recognizes twenty-one senses of the preposition *to*; and Lindkvist recognizes eight purely spatial senses of the same preposition. Relatively many senses are postulated also in the larger dictionaries, *eg* the Oxford English Dictionary.

Lindkvist 1950, Sandhagen 1956 and Wood 1967 are also similar in so far as they present an informal account of the meaning of English prepositions intended primarily for the use of non-native speakers of English. The approach they have adopted is quite possibly the best for their purposes. On the other hand, when one sets out to present a rather more formalized account of the meaning of English prepositions within the framework of an explicit theory of the structure of language, it soon becomes clear that it is both unnecessary and undesirable to postulate as many senses of each preposition as are listed by Lindkvist, Sandhagen and Wood, and in the larger dictionaries.

Ultimately one would like a linguistic description to reflect the psychological facts, but at the present time we have only a very rudimentary understanding of the way in which language is stored and processed in the brain. It would seem, *a priori*, that the notion of separate senses of a lexeme might well have psychological validity, since we presumably do not store every single occurrence of a given lexeme that we have ever encountered. But I know of no psycholinguistic technique for determining how many senses a given lexeme has for a particular speaker, and so am obliged to rely on the methodology of linguistics.

The first way in which we reduce the number of senses recognized is by excluding all cases of alleged differences in meaning which depend in fact on 'vagueness' (*cf* Weinreich 1966a: 178–9, 203, 1966b: 411–12; Lakoff 1970a). Much of the polysemy represented in dictionaries is of this kind. In the words of Weinreich (1966a: 203):

> Most dictionaries vastly exaggerate the incidence of polysemy at the expense of vagueness or generality, e.g., in listing separate meanings for *fair* as in *fair chance* and *fair* as in *fair health*.

A number of tests have been proposed for distinguishing between ambiguity and vagueness, *eg* by Weinreich (1966b: 411–12) and Lakoff (1970a). The aim of such tests is to match the intuition of linguists, who tend to agree quite well on whether a given sentence is genuinely ambiguous or merely vague. Of the two tests mentioned, the one proposed by Lakoff is clearly to be preferred (for some discussion of Weinreich's test, see Bennett 1970: 51 *ff*). Lakoff considers examples such as *Selma likes visiting relatives*, which it is generally agreed is ambiguous (meaning either that she likes to visit relatives or that she likes relatives who are visiting), and *Harry kicked Sam*, which is felt to be vague rather than ambiguous on the question of which foot Harry used. He points out that *Selma likes visiting relatives and so does Sam* has only two possible interpretations, whereas *Harry kicked Sam and so did Pete* has four. Either Selma and Sam both like to visit relatives or else they both like relatives who are visiting – *ie: likes visiting relatives* has to be interpreted in the same way on either side of *and so does*; a mixed interpretation is not possible. With regard to the other example, Sam may have been kicked by two right feet, by two left feet, by Harry's right foot and Pete's left, or by Harry's left foot and Pete's right. Here a mixed interpretation is possible. The test thus consists in extending the original sentence by adding *and so does* (*do*, *did*, etc) *X*, and then asking whether the right-hand side and the left-hand side of the resulting sentence have to be interpreted in the same way or not. If the answer to this question is yes, the original sentence was ambiguous; if the answer is no, it was vague.

Let us now consider an example involving a preposition. It is appropriate to use the sentence *John has gone to the study* under two different circumstances. On the one hand, John may now be inside the study; on the other hand, he may be waiting at the entrance to the study. I regard this as a case of vagueness rather than ambiguity. The sentence simply does not specify whether it was the interior or the exterior of the study that John reached. Lakoff's test confirms this judgment. It would be appropriate to say *John has gone to the study and so has James* if one of them were now inside the study and the other were at the entrance to the

study – *ie* it is not necessary for each side of the sentence to be interpreted in the same way, which implies that the original sentence was
merely vague. It would be a mistake, therefore, to posit two senses of *to*
(one of them meaning the same as *into*) and to suggest that *to* can have
either one of these meanings in the sentence in question. Thus when
Lindkvist (1950) sets up a sense of *to* that he glosses as 'motion reaching
a goal' and another one glossed as 'motion entering into the interior of
an object', it seems to me that he is guilty of identifying polysemy where
none exists.

Such examples can be multiplied indefinitely. By weeding out cases of
vagueness, we achieve a considerable reduction in the number of senses
it is necessary to ascribe to English prepositions.

We need to consider one other way in which a considerable amount of
apparent polysemy is eliminated. Let us suppose that some lexeme L
seems to have two distinct senses. Initially we represent the facts as:

$$L \ [s_1 \ V \ s_2] \tag{2}$$

– in which s stands for *sense* and V means 'or' (*cf* Weinreich 1966a: 178).
We then carry out a componential analysis of the meaning of the two
senses, on the basis of the set of contrasts the lexeme enters into in each
case, and reach the conclusion (we will assume) that s_1 contains the components c_1, c_2 and c_3, whereas s_2 contains c_1, c_2 and c_4. We therefore replace [2] first of all by:

$$L \ [(c_1 \cdot c_2 \cdot c_3) \ V \ (c_1 \cdot c_2 \cdot c_4)] \tag{3}$$

– in which a raised dot means 'and'. Since the components c_1 and c_2
are present in L whichever of the two senses occurs, it is more econo-
mical to refer to them only once in stating the meaning of the lexeme,
giving us:

$$L \ [c_1 \cdot c_2 \cdot (c_3 \ V \ c_4)] \tag{4}$$

instead of [3]. So far, nothing that we have done has brought about a
reduction in the amount of polysemy recognized. L has two alternative
meanings according to [2], [3] and [4]. We turn now to a closer examina-
tion of the semantic components c_3 and c_4. Suppose that whenever L
has the meaning s_1, the component c_3 is present not only in L but also in
some neighbouring lexeme; and that when L has the meaning s_2, the
component c_4 is present in some neighbouring lexeme as well as in L. In
such a situation there is an obvious way in which the analysis can be
simplified. s_1 is the meaning that L appears to have when it occurs in the

environment of a lexeme containing the component c_3, and s_2 is the
meaning it appears to have in the environment of a lexeme containing
c_4. Since we are in any case recognizing a distinction between c_3 and c_4 in
the environment of L, it is unnecessary to regard L itself as containing
either c_3 or c_4. Thus we eliminate the disjunction from [4] and are left
with:

$$L [c_1 \cdot c_2] \tag{5}$$

L is now no longer analysed as being polysemous.

Let us turn now from this hypothetical example to a real example.
Wood (1967: 44–5) identifies two separate senses of the preposition *in* in:

Brighton is in Sussex	[6a]
Some people have their main meal . . . in the evening	[6b]

The first sense is said to express 'position or enclosure within a particular
place, area or object . . .' and the second 'a period of time . . . within
which something takes place'. In other words, *in* is supposed to have a
spatial meaning in [6a] and a temporal meaning in [6b]. Notice, however,
that the environment of *in* is spatial in [6a] (*Sussex*) and temporal in [6b]
(*the evening*). Rather than saying that *in* has a spatial meaning in a spatial
context and a temporal meaning in a temporal context, I prefer to say
that *in* itself is neutral as between space and time. In both [6a] and [6b]
it indicates simply that something is at the interior of something else,
and we are dealing with only one sense rather than two.

Elsewhere Wood's analysis is more in keeping with the policy I am
advocating here. For instance, in the sentences *There is not another
house for two miles* and *We have been waiting for twenty minutes* he identifies only one sense of the preposition *for*, glossing it as 'denoting distance or length of time'.

We will consider one further example illustrating the same general
principle, but involving the meaning of the perfect tenses – taken,
specifically, from Allen's criticism (1966: 55) of Millington-Ward's
(1954) account of the present perfect. According to Millington-Ward, the
present perfect has a 'finished' meaning in *Jones has written a new book*
but an 'unfinished' meaning in *Jones has lived in New York for several
years*. Allen points out that an end or termination of activity is implied
by *to write a book*, irrespective of whether it occurs in the present perfect, whereas *to live in New York* carries with it no such implication.
Thus the difference in meaning that Millington-Ward locates in the
present perfect is more appropriately treated as residing elsewhere. Ex-

pressing a similar point in more general terms, Allen writes (1966: 25):

> Several studies of English verb forms which the writer had read in-
> cluded generalizations about one or another verb form which seemed
> based not so much on the actual grammatical meaning signaled by
> that verb form as upon some meaning to which other elements in the
> sentence had contributed.

Allen is by no means unique in adopting such a standpoint – *cf*, for instance, Ota 1963: 41–58, 63, and Bauer 1970 – but it is surprising how
often the principle in question is overlooked.

The fewer senses of a given lexeme one recognizes, the more general
is the meaning of those senses that are recognized. According to the
approach adopted here, the same sense of *from* and *to* occurs in each of
the following sentences:

> We drove from London to Oxford
> The film lasted from seven o'clock to nine o'clock
> Jean converted from Protestant to Catholic
> The lights changed from red to green

From marks the beginning of any sort of movement or transition, and *to*
marks the end. Information on what kind of movement or transition is
involved in a given instance is supplied by other lexemes in the environment of *from* and *to*.

The rather abstract view of the meaning of lexemes at which we have
arrived can be compared with the abstract view of phonemes to which
Bloomfield subscribed. Bloomfield wrote (1933: 79–80):

> distinctive features occur in lumps or bundles, each one of which we
> call a phoneme . . .
>
> It would be useless to try to produce the distinctive features in a
> pure state, free from non-distinctive accompaniments . . . The pho-
> nemes of a language are not sounds, but merely features of sound
> which the speakers have been trained to produce and recognize in the
> current of actual speech-sound – just as motorists are trained to stop
> before a red signal, be it an electric signal-light, a lamp, a flag, or what
> not, although there is no disembodied redness apart from these actual
> signals.

This view of the phoneme is abstract in so far as only a selection of the
sound-features present in a segment belong to the phoneme occurring in
that segment. The other features are redundant features, determined by

the environment of the phoneme in a given instance. By comparison, any view of phonemes which defines them as classes of actually occurring sounds (allophones) is more concrete.

Notions such as 'end', which I have suggested is the meaning of *to*, or 'interior', are relatively hard to envisage divorced from specific situations. Inevitably we find ourselves contextualizing them – *eg* we think of the end of a journey, or the end of some more abstract transition. Contextualizing a notion in this way is like making a phoneme pronounceable by clothing it in a particular selection of non-distinctive features. The dictionary approach to defining the meanings of English prepositions entails listing a set of specific, contextualized senses. It is analogous to defining a phoneme by listing a set of (pronounceable) allophones.

It seems to me that the rather general senses of English prepositions that I shall be invoking in Parts I and II are essentially similar to the 'Gesamtbedeutungen' of Jakobson 1932 and 1936. The Gesamtbedeutung of an item – *cf*, for instance, Jakobson 1936: 60 – is the general meaning that it has in isolation, or that is independent of the context when the item occurs in a particular utterance. In a given context the item appears to have a specific meaning ('Sonderbedeutung') but this results from the contribution of the meanings of neighbouring items.

As was indicated above, it is not feasible to ascribe the same meaning to the preposition *by* in *She was sitting by the fire* and *Return it to me by Monday*. Certainly one can attempt to attribute the spatial meaning of the first sentence and the temporal meaning of the second to the context of *by* rather than to the preposition itself. However, the remainder that one is left with in each case is not the same. In applying the label 'Gesamtbedeutung' to the present approach, I have assumed that the Gesamtbedeutung standpoint does not preclude one from attributing more than one sense to some lexemes. If this is an incorrect assumption, then it would have been more appropriate to apply some other label to the present approach. Of course, the details of the analysis itself are far more important than the question of how to label the approach adopted. On a separate but comparable issue, it should perhaps be stated explicitly that there is no conflict between the Gesamtbedeutung approach and componential analysis. Jakobson defines the meaning of the Russian cases in terms of bundles of distinctive semantic features – see, for instance, 1936: 68. On the other hand, the Gesamtbedeutung of a lexeme does not have to be semantically complex, *ie* we allow the special case of a bundle of distinctive features which consists of only one feature.

Finally, it should be pointed out why the word 'uses' occurs in the title of the book, rather than 'senses'. It seemed to me that 'spatial and temporal senses' would imply that a general distinction is drawn between spatial senses and temporal senses. Yet in many cases a general sense is posited which is not specifically spatial or temporal – *eg* the same sense of *in* occurs in both *in Sussex* and *in the evening*. Wherever I speak of different uses of some preposition, this formulation leaves open the question of whether or not distinct senses are involved.

Part One

Spatial uses of English prepositions

1.1 Overall structure of the analysis

1.1.1 Locative and directional sentences

Any comprehensive account of spatial uses of English prepositions must assign a prominent place to the distinction between locative sentences, such as *Gwyneth is at the supermarket*, and directional sentences, such as *Trevor went to the post office (a few minutes ago)*. The function of a locative sentence is to specify where something is located. A directional sentence, on the other hand, describes a change of position. These two types of sentences are discussed in some detail in the present subsection. Then in 1.1.2 a third type is introduced – referred to as 'extent sentences'. Finally, in 1.1.3, we return to a consideration of certain rather complex locative and directional sentences.

Let us begin by considering three relatively simple locative sentences:

Gwyneth is here	[7a]
Gwyneth is at the supermarket	[7b]
Gwyneth is in the supermarket	[7c]

In *Figs* 1–3 semantic representations are proposed for these three sentences. (The abbreviations used there are explained in *Table* 2.) The following paragraphs – up to the point at which we begin to discuss directional sentences – constitute a detailed commentary on specific features of *Figs* 1–3.

We note first of all that there is an occurrence of the 'locative' case in each of *Figs* 1–3, reflecting the fact that each of the sentences in [7] specifies Gwyneth's location. The constituents with which 'locative' is

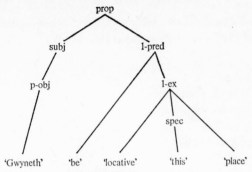

Fig 1 Semantic representation of [7a]

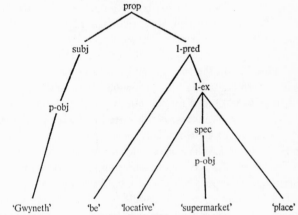

Fig 2 Semantic representation of [7b]

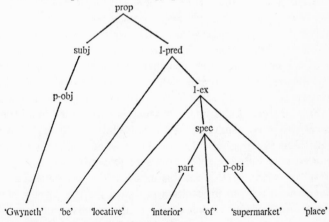

Fig 3 Semantic representation of [7c]

directly in construction in each instance provide information concerning the nature of the location in question (see below).

prop: proposition
subj: subject
l-pred: locative predicate
l-ex: locative expression
spec: specifier
p-obj: physical object

Table 2 List of abbreviations used in *Figs* 1–3

Secondly, it is necessary to explain why there is no case directly associated with the constituent 'Gwyneth' in *Figs* 1–3; and what is understood by the notion of a semantic subject. According to the versions of case grammar presented in Fillmore 1971a and Anderson 1971 'Gwyneth' would be in the 'object' and the 'nominative' case (respectively), and according to Halliday 1967–68 'Gwyneth' would be the 'affected' participant. One of the objectives of case grammar has been to determine how many distinct ways there are in which a participant may be related to an event or state of affairs, *ie* how many distinct functions a participant may have. Let us assume that we have decided to recognize *n* possible functions. Then it is necessary to employ some means of distinguishing them. One possibility – adopted in Fillmore 1971a, Anderson 1971 and Halliday 1967–68 – entails positing *n* cases and showing each participant in a given proposition as being in one or other of these cases. Another possibility – adopted here – is to posit one fewer cases, *ie: n*−1. According to this analysis, one function is identified by virtue of the fact that there is no case associated with the participant in question. This possibility suggests itself in particular because of the unique status of one of the generally recognized functions, namely the one to which Fillmore, Anderson and Halliday apply the case-label 'object', 'nominative' or 'affected'. Its unique status manifests itself in two main ways. First, if there is any function which is represented in all types of sentences, this is it (*cf* Anderson 1971: 50, Halliday 1968: 195). Secondly, this particular function is said to be the most neutral from a semantic point of view (*cf* Fillmore 1968: 25, 1971: 42; Anderson 1971: 37; and also Halliday 1968: 195). What this means is that the participant with this function in a given proposition is shown thereby merely to be in some way involved. The exact nature of the involvement depends on whatever other functions are represented, *ie* on the type of sentence.

Thus, according to Halliday's analysis, the 'affected' participant takes on the specific role of an 'attribuand' in an ascriptive sentence and a 'thing to be identified' in an equative sentence (1968: 195). To this we may add that it takes on the role of a 'thing to be located' in a locative sentence. It should be emphasized, however, that it is essentially a notational matter whether or not we decide to invoke an 'object'/'nominative'/'affected' case. On the one hand, we say that 'Gwyneth' in [7] is in a case which happens to be the semantically most neutral. On the other hand, we say that there is no case at all directly associated with 'Gwyneth'. The important thing is that 'Gwyneth' does not fulfil any of the specific functions designated by case-labels such as 'locative'. This is true of either analysis.

That participant in a locative proposition which, according to the analysis adopted here, has no case directly associated with it will be referred to as the semantic subject. As already indicated, it is the thing whose location is specified. It will not necessarily be the surface structure subject. Thus in *This box contains pencils* the surface structure subject is *this box*, but the semantic subject is *pencils*. Directional and extent sentences also contain a semantic subject. In a directional sentence it is the thing which undergoes a change of position; in an extent sentence it is the thing whose extent is specified. The remainder of a proposition will be referred to as the predicate, and we shall therefore distinguish between locative, directional and extent predicates.

Sentence [7a] contains an adverb (*here*), whereas [7b and c] contain a prepositional phrase (*at the supermarket, in the supermarket*). Thus [7a] differs syntactically from [7b and c]. Semantically, however, all three sentences are parallel in structure. They each contain a constituent which will be referred to as a locative expression, consisting of the element 'locative', a 'specifier' and the element 'place'. We need to comment on several points relating to the internal structure of locative expressions.

It is necessary, first of all, to justify positing a semantic element 'place' in addition to the case 'locative'. Consider in this connection the two sentences *I saw Gwyneth at the supermarket* and *I saw Gwyneth at 10 o'clock*. Each of these sentences contains an embedded proposition, expressed in surface structure as *I saw Gwyneth* (*cf* Lakoff 1970b: 154–7). The first sentence locates the event of 'my seeing Gwyneth' in space, whereas the second sentence locates it in time. The phrases LOCATE IN SPACE and LOCATE IN TIME imply that there is a general notion of location which is neither specifically spatial nor temporal. It is this general notion of location that is designated by the element 'locative' in *Figs* 1–3. The element 'place' is included to distinguish spatial locative expressions from temporal locative expressions (the latter contain the element 'time' as their third constituent, rather than 'place', *cf* Part II). This analysis is suggested also by the fact that words such as *here* and *now* can be paraphrased as *at this place* and *at this time* (in which *at* represents the general notion of location).

An alternative analysis involves ascribing a purely spatial meaning to the 'locative' case, and then invoking in addition a 'time' case (see, for instance, Fillmore 1971a). The disadvantage of such an analysis is that it implies that the occurrence of the same preposition in *at the supermarket* and *at 10 o'clock* is merely a coincidence. This follows from the fact that *at* would be attributed a different meaning in these two phrases. According to the analysis adopted here, on the other hand, it is certainly not coincidental that *at* occurs in these two phrases, since it is regarded as expressing the same notion in each instance. From the present standpoint, the 'locative' and 'time' cases of Fillmore 1971a are semantically complex. Each contains the general notion of location, combined with either 'place' or 'time'.

The constituent that fills the 'specifier' slot in a locative expression has the function of specifying the place (or time) in question. Three kinds of specifiers are illustrated by *Figs* 1–3. In *Fig* 1 the specifier is a deictic element: 'this'; in *Fig* 2 it is a physical object: 'the supermarket'; and in *Fig* 3 it is a part of a physical object: 'the interior of the supermarket'. In *Gwyneth is at the supermarket*, the supermarket as such (rather than any specific part of it) functions as Gwyneth's location. Consequently nothing in the sentence itself tells us whether she is inside or outside the supermarket. On the other hand, [7c] is more specific, and the possibility of her being outside the supermarket is excluded.

Since the definiteness or indefiniteness of noun phrases has no bearing on the meaning of any preposition, all the semantic representations proposed here will be simplified by the omission of such details. If we were giving explicit recognition to definiteness, the item 'this' would not occur as a constituent of semantic representations (as in *Fig* 1). Its place would be taken by the separate components of the meaning of the word *this*, one of which is the notion 'definite'.

A semantic category of 'parts' will feature prominently in the componential definitions presented in **1.2**. Two members of this category are 'interior' – one component of the meaning of *in* – and 'surface', which will be invoked in defining *on*. The other members of the category are parts of the space surrounding something, rather than parts of the thing itself. For instance, 'anterior' – one component of the meaning of *in front of* – may be loosely defined as that part of the space surrounding something which is adjacent to its front. Similarly, 'posterior' may be defined as that part of the space surrounding something which is adjacent to its back (or rear). There is good evidence to suggest that notions such as 'posterior' are in fact semantically complex. It has been shown, for instance, in psycholinguistic experiments (*eg* Clark 1968: 430) that antonymous prepositions are very closely related in meaning. Now if we define *in, in front of* and *behind* as meaning 'at the interior of', 'at the anterior of' and 'at the posterior of' (respectively), we fail to show that *in front of* and *behind* are closer to each other semantically than either is to *in*. On the other hand, the special relationship between *in front of* and *behind* can be reflected if the notions 'anterior' and 'posterior' are analysed into still more elementary components of meaning, in such a way as to show that they share some part of their meaning and differ in another respect. Nevertheless, in the present book notions such as 'interior', 'anterior' and 'posterior' are treated as though they were not further analysable. For a treatment which goes further on this issue, see Leech 1969: 166 *ff.*

The semantic representations shown in *Figs* 1–3 contain a constituent labelled 'be'. A number of scholars have suggested that the verb *be* is a semantically empty 'dummy verb', introduced into surface structures as a 'carrier' of tense, and other, distinctions (*cf* Bach 1967 and Lyons 1968: 322–3). Anticipating our discussion of directional sentences, it is relevant to note also that a similar treatment has been proposed for *go* (Bach 1967: 484, Lyons 1968: 397–8). The most convenient place at which to state our own position on this question is in Part III. In the meantime 'be' and 'go' will be included in the semantic representations proposed below, without further comment.

The item 'of', which features in *Fig* 3, will be discussed in **1.2.1** and **1.2.5** and then again in Part III. Tenses will be omitted from the semantic representations until they become relevant in Part II. Finally, a brief comment is appropriate on our use of the terms 'physical object' and 'proposition'. These terms will be restricted to semantic representations. On the other hand, 'noun' and 'sentence' will be restricted to surface structures. There is need for a separate set of terminology for the categories of semantic representations and surface structures, because there is not a one-to-one correspondence between the two levels. For instance, many nouns represent physical objects, but there are many others which do not – *eg: happiness*. Similarly, *I saw Gwyneth at the supermarket* contains two propositions (one embedded inside the other), but at the level of surface structure it is only one sentence. However, at places where there is no possibility of confusion I shall also use the term 'sentence' in a more general way; thus the occurrence of this term will not necessarily imply that we are talking specifically about surface structures.

We turn now to directional sentences. The present analysis has two main distinguishing characteristics. First, three directional cases are posited: 'source', 'path' and 'goal'. Secondly, all directional expressions are analysed as containing a locative expression – which means that, for instance, the semantic structure of *to the church* would be more accurately reflected if we could say in English *to at the church. These two aspects of the analysis are described in some detail in the following paragraphs, after which we shall briefly consider certain alternative analyses that have been proposed elsewhere.

A sentence such as *We went from Waterloo Bridge along the Embankment to Westminster* is considered to contain three directional expressions in its semantic representation: a source expression, a path expression and a goal expression. The source expression, realized in surface structure as *from Waterloo Bridge*, specifies the starting-point of the change of position described by the sentence. The goal expression, realized as *to Westminster*, specifies the end-point. And the path expression, realized as *along the Embankment*, provides information about the route taken. It is rather obvious that any change of position involves an earlier location and a later location, and not surprising therefore that a distinction between source and goal expressions has often been invoked in the past. On the other hand, the need to recognize path expressions in addition has frequently been overlooked. I will therefore mention two kinds of evidence which support our decision to posit path expressions.

First, it should be noted that many sentences of the kind *The boy ran behind the tree* are ambiguous, depending on whether something travels VIA or TO a particular location. Either the boy ran past the back of the tree on his way to some other, unspecified location; or alternatively, behind the tree was where his journey ended. Similarly, *The dog ran under the table* may mean that the dog passed under the table on its way to some other location, or that it ran to a position under the table and then remained there. Finally, in my own dialect (but apparently not in all dialects of English) *Please put the lamp over the counter* can mean either 'please put the lamp via a position directly above the counter (to some unspecified position on the other side of the counter)' or 'please put the lamp to a position directly above the counter'. Positing three directional cases – 'source', 'path' and 'goal' – gives us a very natural way of describing the ambiguity of the above examples. Each of the sentences has two alternative semantic representations, one containing a path expression and the other a goal expression – *ie: behind the tree, under the table* and *over the counter* realize either a path or a goal expression. (The further possibility that the first two examples might also have a purely locative interpretation in no way affects the point at issue.) Secondly, it is very revealing to compare the distribution of the prepositions *in* and *through* with that of, say, *behind*. A location such as is specified by the prepositional phrase *behind the desk* may function in four different ways – either as the location of a stationary object, *cf* [8a], or as the source, path or goal of a moving object, *cf* [8b–d].

Trevor is behind the desk	[8a]
Trevor appeared from behind the desk	[8b]
Trevor walked behind the desk to the door	[8c]
Trevor walked behind the desk (*ie* to)	[8d]

When we attempt to find a parallel set of examples containing the preposition *in*, we discover that there is a gap in the paradigm, *cf* [9c].

Gwyneth is in the kitchen	[9a]
Gwyneth appeared from in the kitchen	[9b]
*Gwyneth walked in the kitchen to the hall	[9c]
Gwyneth walked into the kitchen	[9d]

(The fact that *from in* is rather rare, and that we say *into* rather than *to in*, will be discussed in **1.2**.) The asterisk in front of [9c] is not intended to suggest that there is no possible circumstance under which this example might be well-formed. It means simply that [9c] is not the way of saying in English that Gwyneth walked via the interior of the kitchen to the hall. Such a message would, in fact, be expressed as

Gwyneth walked through the kitchen to the hall	[10]

Thus the gap in the paradigm of *in* is filled by the preposition *through*. On the basis of the examples [8c] and [8d], in which there is no overt marker of the distinction between a path expression and a goal expression, it might conceivably be claimed that we are dealing with two varieties of a single semantic category rather than with two separate categories. However, the obligatory surface structure distinction between *through* in [10] and *in* in [9d] provides evidence against such an analysis and in support of the path expression versus goal expression analysis.

Very few sentences that are actually attested (as opposed to invented by a linguist) contain three directional prepositional phrases. Many contain two, but probably equally many contain only one. One reason for this is that a directional expression may be realized in other ways than as a prepositional phrase. There is a goal expression in the semantic representation of each of the sentences in [11], but only [11a] contains a directional prepositional phrase.

The bridegroom has gone into the church   [11a]
The bridegroom has entered the church   [11b]

The goal expression in [11b] is realized partly in the transitive verb *enter* and partly in the noun phrase *the church*. Another possibility is illustrated by sentences such as *Trevor appeared from behind the desk* (paraphrasable as *Trevor came into sight from behind the desk*). The semantic representation of this sentence contains a source expression, realized as *from behind the desk*, and a goal expression, realized as the intransitive verb *appear*.

It is not even true that all directional sentences contain three directional expressions in their semantic representation. For one thing, a speaker may regard certain details of a particular change of position as unimportant, and therefore simply not comment on them. For instance, he might say *From York we went to Edinburgh*, specifying the source and goal, but not the path because he considers the route taken to be irrelevant. Or he might say *The procession will pass by our house*, giving information only about the path, and treating the source and goal as irrelevant. A second possibility in the case of this example is that the speaker does not know himself where the procession begins and ends, and so would be unable to specify the source and goal even if he wanted to. Thirdly, certain details of a particular change of position may not need to be specified if they are already clear from the preceding discourse. Consider the following two sentences: *Keith sat at his desk, staring blankly at the letter lying there, for about a quarter of an hour. Then he walked to the window*. The change of position described by the second sentence consists in Keith walking from the desk to the window, but there is no need to specify the source overtly, since it is obvious from the context of the preceding sentence.

Before taking up the point that all directional expressions contain a locative expression, there is a minor terminological matter that needs to be commented on. It was indicated in 0.2 that the same meaning would be ascribed to *from* and *to* in the sentences *We drove from London to Oxford* and *The film lasted from seven o'clock to nine o'clock*. In discussing sentences of the former kind we have used the terms 'source' and 'goal' – thus London is the source and Oxford the goal of the journey described by this particular example. On the other hand, it would sound a little odd, with regard to *The film lasted from seven o'clock to nine o'clock*, to describe seven o'clock as the source of the film and nine o'clock as the goal. We could overcome this problem by substituting the terms 'beginning', 'middle' and 'end' for 'source', 'path' and 'goal'. Thus London represents the beginning of the journey and seven o'clock the beginning of the film. Similarly, Oxford represents the end of the journey and nine o'clock the end of the film. Nevertheless, I shall retain the terms 'source', 'path' and 'goal' throughout this book, since the labels 'source expression', 'path expression' and 'goal expression' are clearly to be preferred to the alternative labels 'beginning expression', 'middle expression' and 'end expression'. It should be remembered throughout, however, that the notions designated here by the terms 'source', 'path' and 'goal' are in fact the general notions of a beginning, middle and end.

The claim that directional expressions contain a locative expression constitutes a particular hypothesis concerning the internal structure of the semantic constructions referred to here as source, path and goal expressions. According to this hypothesis the semantic representation of *Trevor went behind the door* is as in *Fig* 4a rather than, say, *Fig* 4b. In particular, the goal expression (g-ex) underlying the prepositional phrase *behind the door* consists of the case 'goal' in construction with a locative expression, whose internal structure parallels that of *Fig* 3. In *Fig* 4b, on the other hand, the goal expression is attributed an internal structure that is no more complex than that of a locative expression, the difference being simply that 'goal' replaces the 'locative' constituent of a locative expression. Otherwise, *Figs* 4a and 4b are alike. We have a proposition consisting of a subject and a directional predicate (d-pred). The latter consists of the element 'go' and a directional expressions (d-exs) constituent. In the present example the d-exs constituent contains only a goal expression, but in the case of a sentence such as *We went from Waterloo Bridge along the Embankment to Westminster* there would also be a source expression and a path expression.

Three kinds of evidence will now be presented which support *Fig* 4a as the semantic representation of *Trevor went behind the door*, rather than 4b. Consider, first, the set of examples:

Trevor went behind the door   [12a]
Trevor was behind the door   [12b]
Trevor went to behind the door   [12c]
*Trevor was at behind the door   [12d]

The point I am about to make depends on the correctness of the observation that, while [12c] may not be very good stylistically, [12d] is even

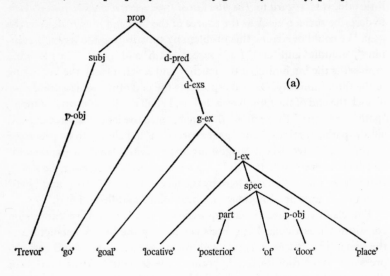

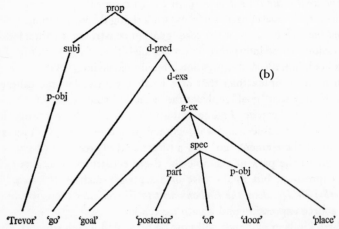

Fig 4 Two candidates for the semantic representation of *Trevor went behind the door*

less acceptable, being in fact ungrammatical. When *behind the door* realizes a goal expression, as in [12a], it is also possible to insert the preposition *to* as an overt marker of the notion 'goal', *cf* [12c]. (After a *from*-phrase, *to* is in fact required – *cf: Trevor went from the desk to behind the door.*) However, when *behind the door* is the realization of a locative expression, as in [12b], it is not possible to insert the preposition *at* as an overt marker of the notion 'locative', *cf* [12d] – despite the fact that elsewhere 'locative' is realized as *at* (*eg* in *Gwyneth is at the supermarket*). Obviously it is relevant to look for some explanation of the ungrammaticality of [12d]. The one that suggests itself most readily is that 'locative' is already present in the original sentence, [12b] – as one component of the meaning of *behind* – so that it is inappropriate to attempt to express it separately as the preposition *at*. According to this view, [12d] would presuppose an ill-formed semantic representation containing two successive occurrences of the element 'locative', one realized as *at* and the other in the preposition *behind*. Now if the meaning of *behind* itself contains the notion 'locative' in [12b], it seems not unreasonable to suggest that it contains the same notion also in [12a and c]. But if 'locative' is present in the semantic representation of [12a and c] – as one component of the meaning of *behind* – then the goal expression in question must have the internal structure shown in *Fig* 4a rather than that shown in 4b.

The above argument depends, of course, on the validity of the assumption that 'locative' is a component of the meaning of *behind* not only in [12b] but also in [12a and c]. Fortunately, there is additional evidence that can be brought to bear on the question. In this connection we need to compare [12a and b] with [13a and b]. (For convenience, [12a and b] are repeated.)

Trevor went behind the door	[12a]
Trevor was behind the door	[12b]
Trevor went out of the office	[13a]
Trevor was out of the office	[13b]

The [a] examples are directional sentences, and may therefore be said to exhibit directional uses of *behind* and *out of*. The [b] examples, on the other hand, are locative sentences and thus may be said to exhibit locative uses of *behind* and *out of*. Fairly early on in the present investigation it seemed that some prepositions have a primarily locative meaning (*eg: at, on, in, under, behind*), whereas others have a primarily directional meaning (*eg: to, from, through, across, out of*). What this means, with regard to the above examples, is that the locative use of *behind* in [12b] seemed more basic than the directional use in [12a]; whereas the directional use of *out of* in [13a] seemed more basic than the locative use in [13b]. To test whether the present writer's intuition was matched by that of other native speakers of English, a simple experiment was carried out. Thirteen subjects were given sheets of paper containing the above four sentences, and also comparable pairs of examples containing *in* and *across*. They were asked to indicate which of the two sentences in each pair contained the 'primary' or 'basic' use of the particular preposition. (No explanation was given of what these terms might mean.) The results are shown in *Table* 3. (An earlier test on *in* and *out of* – reported in Bennett forthcoming – produced comparable results for these two items.)

	locative use	directional use
behind	9	4
out of	1	12
in	12	1
across	1	12

Table 3 Results of asking thirteen subjects which use of four prepositions is 'primary' or 'basic'

Admittedly the test is rather crude, but it served its purpose. There was clearly a good measure of agreement as to which use was primary. Thus even though no indication was given, in administering the test, of what 'primary' might mean, there is undoubtedly some feature of the structure of the sentences to which the subjects responded in a similar way. (Incidentally, in the *out of*, *in* and *across* results it was a different subject who disagreed with the other twelve in each case.) Notice, moreover, that the result cannot be attributed to the effect of the neighbouring verb, since each preposition occurred both with a static verb (*be*) and a dynamic verb (*go*). This result is relevant to the question of the internal structure of directional expressions in the following way. It is desirable that the semantic representations we propose for sentences should reflect the intuitions which native speakers have about them. In the present instance the most obvious way to achieve this is by regarding the primary use of a preposition as having a relatively simpler semantic representation. With regard to [13], sentences such as *The post office is over the hill* and *The ticket office is through the archway* – which will be considered in detail below – force us to recognize the possibility that directional expressions may be embedded inside a locative expression. Invoking this same possibility, we may analyse the locative expression underlying *out of the office* in [13b] as containing inside it the same directional expression which occurs in [13a]. In this way the semantic constituent underlying *out of the office* is shown to be simpler in [13a] than in [13b]. (For the exact details, see **1.2.5**.) With regard now to [12], the semantic constituent underlying *behind the door* will be simpler in [12b] than in [12a] if we analyse all directional expressions as containing an embedded locative expression (as in *Fig* 4a). On the other hand, if we were to adopt the other hypothesis concerning the structure of directional expressions (*cf: Fig* 4b), the semantic constituent underlying *behind the door* would be equally complex in [12a] and [12b], and the semantic representations would therefore not reflect the intuitions of native speakers about these sentences.

The third piece of evidence is of a rather more straightforward kind. The sentence

The bridegroom has arrived at the church [14]

clearly specifies the bridegroom's destination, and it is reasonable therefore to assume that its semantic representation contains a goal expression. In this sentence, however, the element 'goal' is realized as the verb *arrive* rather than as the preposition *to*. Two candidates for the internal structure of the goal expression in question are shown in *Fig* 5. *Fig* 5a is the preferred analysis, the reason being that it provides an obvious explanation for the presence of the preposition *at* in [14]: as in *Gwyneth is at the supermarket*, *at* is the normal prepositional realization of the 'locative' case unaccompanied by any other semantic element. If, on the other hand, *Fig* 5b were taken to be the structure of the goal expression in question, there would be no obvious way to account for the presence of *at* in the surface structure.

It is of interest at this point to comment briefly on the structure of directional expressions in languages other than English. Gross (1967) and Ruwet (1969) propose a similar analysis for French to that proposed here for English. Thus Ruwet writes (1969: 121):

Des faits de ce genre ont amené Maurice Gross (1967) à postuler l'existence d'un *à* sous-jacent après *de* (ou *par*) dans des phrases telles

que: *Cette année, le Tour de France n'est pas passé par la Lorraine* [et]
Il est visible que cet abruti vient de la campagne.

It is suggested, in other words, that *par la Lorraine* and *de la campagne*
derive from an underlying 'par à la Lorraine' and 'de à la campagne'.

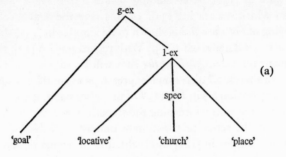

(a)

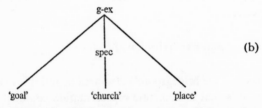

(b)

Fig 5 Two candidates for the internal structure of the goal expression
occurring in the semantic representation of [14]

But there are also languages whose surface structure resembles the underlying structure proposed for English and French. One such language is
Nyanja, a Bantu language spoken in Malawi. *At the door* is translated
into Nyanja as *ku-chitseko*, and *from the door* as *chokera ku-chitseko*
(literally 'from at the door').

I will now refer briefly to other analyses of directional sentences, concentrating in particular on those of Anderson (1971) and Leech (1969),
but commenting also on Fillmore's (1971a) and Stratton's (1971) observations concerning the 'path' case.

Where four cases have been recognized so far in the present analysis
('locative', 'source', 'path' and 'goal'), Anderson (1971) posits only
two: 'locative' and 'ablative'. What I have referred to as 'locative' and
'goal', Anderson regards as two varieties of a single case (which he labels
'locative'). And in place of the path expressions of the present analysis,

Anderson analyses the constituent in question as being simultaneously 'ablative' and 'locative'. My comments on the question of polysemy in 0.2 will have demonstrated that I, too, am in favour of reducing the number of entities in terms of which the description is formulated, wherever this is possible. But it seems to me that Anderson's analysis suffers from defects which can only be remedied by increasing the number of cases recognized, along the lines indicated here.

A relatively minor defect of Anderson's analysis is the fact that he is forced to regard all directional sentences as containing an ablative phrase (*ie* source expression) in their semantic representation, since only in the presence of the 'ablative' case can his 'locative' case be interpreted directionally. In the present analysis source expressions are not obligatory; and it will be recalled that a number of circumstances were discussed above under which a particular directional sentence might contain no source expression in its semantic representation.

It is relevant to consider the evidence that led Anderson to regard 'goal' (or 'allative') simply as the variety of 'locative' that occurs in the presence of 'ablative'. He notes first (1971: 119) that

> There exists a not inconsiderable overlap in the 'prepositional' forms that manifest the allative and the 'static' locative in English . . . and other languages.

Secondly, he refers to the implicational relationship that holds between pairs of sentences such as *He has come here* and *He is here* (*now/already*) (1971: 119–20). However, analysing the allative as a particular variety of the locative is not the only way of accounting for these phenomena. In the present analysis they are accounted for in another way – namely, they follow from the fact that goal expressions are analysed as containing a locative expression. Moreover, the latter analysis has additional advantages, such as the fact that it provides a natural way of explaining the presence of the preposition *at* in [14].

As already indicated, the path expressions of the present analysis are treated by Anderson as being simultaneously ablative and locative (1971: 169–71). Thus he allows ablative and locative to co-occur within a simple sentence in two different ways – either separately, as in *The ball rolled from Jane to Mary*, or simultaneously, as in *He walked along the street* (Anderson 1971: 121, 170). In addition to these two types of sentences, we need to be able to handle examples containing (in the present terms) a source, path and goal expression, *eg*

We walked from Waterloo Bridge along the Embankment to
   Westminster [15a]
We walked from Waterloo Bridge to Westminster along the
   Embankment [15b]
We walked along the Embankment to Westminster from
   Waterloo Bridge [15c]

The differences in emphasis between these sentences involve what
Halliday calls their 'information structure' (1967: 199; 1968: 179). With
regard to their 'experiential' (or 'cognitive') meaning, they are alike.
Now the only example like those in [15] discussed by Anderson (1971:
171) is the following:

John travelled from Edinburgh to Glasgow via Stirling [16]

It is significant that this sentence parallels [15b] rather than [15a or c].
It is analysed as containing two clauses (propositions) in its semantic
representation. In one clause we have a separate ablative and locative
phrase (*from Edinburgh to Glasgow*); in the other we have a simultaneous
ablative and locative (*via Stirling*). To be consistent, if [16] and [15b]
are accorded a two-clause analysis, presumably [15a and c] should be
analysed in a similar way – *ie* as [[*from Waterloo Bridge along the Embankment*] [*to Westminster*]] and [[*along the Embankment to Westminster*]
[*from Waterloo Bridge*]]. Neither analysis is possible according to the
grammar described in Anderson 1971. *From Waterloo Bridge along the
Embankment* would involve two ablatives inside a single clause, one simultaneous with a locative and the other separate. *To Westminster* would
have to be *at Westminster*, since a locative phrase unaccompanied by an
ablative would be interpreted statically. *Along the Embankment to Westminster* would involve two locatives, one simultaneous with an ablative
and the other separate. And finally, *from Waterloo Bridge* could be derived only if the clause in question contained a locative phrase which was
subsequently deleted, since 'ablative' is introduced only in the presence
of 'locative' (Anderson 1971: 120).

We turn now to the analysis of Leech 1969. In the section of his book
devoted to time, and in particular at the point where he discusses the
meaning of *since* and *until*, Leech invokes the notions 'beginning' and
'end' (1969: 132). But there is no mention of these notions in his account of spatial relations, and he recognizes no semantic elements that
would correspond to our 'source', 'path' and 'goal' cases. Sentences of
the kind *a went from b to c* are attributed a semantic structure that can be

characterized informally as 'a came to be not at b but at c'. They are
said to contain two coordinate propositions, 'a was not at b' and 'a was
at c'. Following Gruber (1965: 103), Leech cites the examples [17] and
[18] in support of his analysis (Leech 1969: 276).

The ball rolled out of the house and into the hole	[17a]
The insect crawled off (of) the table and onto my knee	[17b]
*The ball rolled from the house and to the tree	[17c]
The ball rolled from the house to the tree	[18]

Sentence [18] is supposed to fill the gap at [c] in the paradigm represented by [17]. Thus whereas in [17a and b] the 'and' of the semantic representation is expressed as the conjunction *and*, in [17c] it is allegedly
deleted, giving [18]. One unsatisfactory feature of this analysis is that no
explanation is given of the fact that only [17c] undergoes the obligatory
deletion of 'and'. It is relevant to note, therefore, that there is another
way of interpreting the difference between [17a and b], on the one hand,
and [17c], on the other. Namely, one can interpret it as an indication
that the proportion [19] is not a true reflection of the meaning of the
items in question, and that [17] is therefore not a genuine paradigm. In
1.2.5 I shall suggest that [19] is really a conflation of the two proportions
shown in [20].

out of	:	into	::				[19]
off	:	onto	::				
from	:	to					

out of	:	into	::	[20a]	from in	:	into	::	[20b]
off	:	onto	::		from on	:	onto	::	
away from	:	to			from	:	to		

From [20a] we see that [17c] should be replaced by *The ball rolled away
from the house and to the tree* (said with a phonological boundary after
house rather than *away*). The conjunction in this sentence is just as acceptable as in [17a and b]. With regard to path expressions, it would take
us too far afield to indicate how they are represented in Leech's analysis;
but *cf* Leech 1969: 197.

Fillmore (1971a) accepts the need for recognizing a 'path' case, but
suggests that its behaviour is unusual in one respect by comparison with
most other cases:

A particularly interesting property of the Path (or 'Itinerative'?) case
is that a sentence with the path designated can contain an unlimited

number of Path expressions, as long as these are understood as indicating successive stretches of the same path . . .

> Superficially, at least, the Path case requires a qualification of the
> one-instance-per-clause principle. (1971a: 51)

Stratton (1971) lists several respects in which 'path' appears to be exceptional, including the point that it breaks the one-instance-per-clause
rule:

> Perhaps the most serious manner in which Path is pathological lies in
> the fact that Path – alone among all the cases – can be repeated within
> a simple clause. (1971: 226)

My own opinion is that 'path' is not particularly exceptional. In the
following paragraphs I shall attempt a general account of coordination in
relation to locative and directional expressions. Some of what I have to
say will not be directly relevant to the issue mentioned by Fillmore and
Stratton, but in the course of my remarks it will emerge that certain
generalizations can be made which apply not only to 'path' but also to
other cases. We will begin by considering locative expressions.

If we restrict our attention to the most obvious interpretation of the
sentences in [21], they illustrate three different ways in which successive
locative expressions may be related to each other.

The towels are on the shelf in the cupboard near the bathroom	[21a]
The towels are near the bathroom in the cupboard on the shelf	[21b]
The towels are near the bathroom, in the cupboard and on the shelf	[21c]

Only [21b and c] contain coordinate locative expressions; [21a] is included for the sake of comparison. To reflect the fact that the towels of
[21a] are on the shelf WHICH IS in the cupboard WHICH IS near the
bathroom, the semantic representation would need to contain a locative
expression containing an embedded locative expression, in which a further locative expression is embedded. Such an analysis can be ruled out
as far as [21b] is concerned, owing to the unlikelihood of a bathroom
being situated in a cupboard, which itself is on a shelf. What [21a and b]
have in common, however, is that they both specify only one location.
On the other hand, [21c] specifies three separate locations, and we are
therefore led to assume that the towels are not all together. As already
stated, [21b and c] each contain coordinate locative expressions, but they
illustrate two different types of coordination. The locative expressions in

[21b] are in apposition to each other; those in [21c] are conjoined. Successive appositive locative expressions provide additional information about a single location. Successive conjoined locative expressions define additional locations.

With regard to directional sentences, the distinction between appositive and conjoined coordination seems to apply to individual directional expressions – whether source, path or goal. But, more interestingly, it applies also to what I shall call 'journeys'. An example of appositive goal expressions is provided by the sentence *Trevor has gone to Wembley to the Cup Final.* Only one destination is involved here, but it is specified in two different ways. A comparable source expression example is: *All this traffic must be coming from Wembley from the Cup Final.* And the following sentence contains two appositive path expressions: *Rather stupidly, we came here along Oxford Street through all the Saturday morning shoppers.* With regard to conjoined directional expressions, example [22] illustrates conjoined source expressions, and it is an easy matter to construct similar examples containing conjoined path or goal expressions.

> Most of the miners at the meeting had travelled to London from South Wales or from the Midlands   [22]

The need to speak of 'journeys' as well as individual source, path and goal expressions is suggested by examples such as

> We drove over the hill and to the next town   [23]

Over the hill in this sentence realizes a path expression, and *to the next town* a goal expression. To claim that it is possible to conjoin a path expression and a goal expression would entail rejecting Fillmore's (1968: 22) hypothesis that 'Only noun phrases representing the same case may be conjoined.' Yet this hypothesis provides a natural explanation of the unacceptability of sentences such as **John and a hammer broke the window.* Invoking the notion of a 'journey' allows us to account for [23] without abandoning Fillmore's hypothesis. [23] describes two successive journeys, of which the first is specified only by means of a path expression and the second only by means of a goal expression. *And* thus conjoins two journeys, rather than two individual directional expressions. Some support for this analysis comes from comments by native speakers of English on the difference between [23] and

> We drove over the hill to the next town   [24]

It is often suggested that 'the next town' in [24] might be just over the crest of the hill, whereas 'the next town' in [23] might well be several miles further along the road. This observation is consistent with the view that [23] describes two successive journeys rather than a single journey.

It needs to be added, however, that the objective facts of the situation are less important than the way in which the speaker happens to conceive of it; one and the same physical event might be described by one speaker with [23] and by another with [24]. At this point I am invoking a distinction to which a number of writers have assigned prominence, *eg* Close 1962: 33, 141, Allen 1966: 34, 208, Leech 1969: 162–3. Addressing himself to the question of tense and aspect in English, Close writes (1959: 64):

> the ultimate choice of tense or aspect will depend, as choice involving meaning often does, less on objective facts (*eg* whether the action is really in progress or not) than on what the speaker is concerned with, or is primarily concerned with, at the time.

One can think of several ways in which one might attempt to define what a journey is by reference to objective facts, but all of them would necessarily be arbitrary. Suppose, for instance, that something moves from X via Y to Z. One attempt at defining a journey might take account of the distance between X, Y and Z – the closer they are together, the more likely it is that we are dealing with a single journey. It is obvious that it would be impossible to apply such a criterion. Secondly, we might ask: does the moving object stop at Y or not? The assumption underlying this question is that if the object stops at Y, we are dealing with two successive journeys; whereas if it does not stop, we are dealing with a single journey. This criterion is not much better than the first. How do we decide, for instance, in the case of an object that slows down on approaching Y and almost stops but is never in fact quite stationary? A third possible criterion might refer to the extent to which Y is situated on the direct route from X to Z – if Y is more or less on the direct route, we are dealing with a single journey, but if Y is right off the direct route, we are dealing with two journeys (X to Y and Y to Z). Clearly, it would again be quite arbitrary where one drew the line.

All of these aspects of the physical situation are relevant in that they may influence the way in which a speaker conceives of the situation. The reason Stratton's (1971: 228) example *?Sam went from Minneapolis to St Paul via New Orleans* sounds strange is that Y lies so far from the direct route between X and Z that we would be more likely to think of Sam's movement as involving two separate journeys (*cf: Sam went from Minneapolis to New Orleans and then back to St Paul*). Nevertheless, it is the way a speaker conceives of a situation that matters, rather than simply the objective facts.

We have seen, then, that whenever directional prepositional phrases represent different phases of a single journey, as in [24], no conjunction is inserted. On the other hand, if they represent different journeys, as in [23], this fact is marked by the insertion of a conjunction. In terms of tree diagrams such as *Fig* 4a, the semantic representation of [23] would contain two conjoined d-exs constituents, one of which happens to contain only a p-ex, while the other contains only a g-ex.

To claim that two d-exs constituents may be conjoined implies that even a source expression and a goal expression may be conjoined, providing they do not represent the source and goal of a single journey. When presented with the sentence *They sailed from Southampton and to New York*, a number of native speakers of English suggested that it implies that the people in question went somewhere else between leaving Southampton and arriving in New York. Such an interpretation is consistent with the suggestion that the sentence would necessarily involve two separate journeys. Admittedly, though, the sentence sounds rather odd. The reason for this is that no indication whatsoever is given of the route or destination of the first journey. Notice now that if the above sentence cannot be ruled out as totally unacceptable, the same is true of [17c], *The ball rolled from the house and to the tree*, which might conceivably be understood as referring to two separate journeys. Two successive journeys are described also by [17a and b], but these two sentences are fully acceptable because they specify the goal of each of the journeys. Thus, for instance, in *The ball rolled out of the house and into the hole*, *out of the house* means 'to the exterior of the house' rather than 'from the interior of the house'; *cf* 1.2.5.

Having discussed the possibility of conjoined journeys at some length, we need to mention also the possibility of appositive coordination in relation to journeys. The kind of example that would be handled in these terms is illustrated by *Trevor intends to walk from Land's End to John o' Groats, from the south-west of England to the north-east of Scotland.*

At the point where he states that a sentence may contain an unlimited number of path expressions, Fillmore cites the example *He walked down the hill across the bridge through the pasture to the chapel* (1971a: 51). As far as my own idiolect of English is concerned, this sentence sounds a little strange. It can be made fully acceptable by inserting *and* either before *through the pasture* or before *to the chapel*. With the *and* before *through*, the sentence describes three successive journeys, the third of which is specified by means of a path expression and a goal expression. On the other hand, if the *and* precedes *to the chapel*, four successive journeys are involved, since *through the pasture* and *to the chapel* represent different journeys in this case. In either case, the coordination is of the conjoined type. Without the conjunction the sentence looks as if it ought to be an example of appositive coordination, but this would imply that the hill, the bridge and the pasture were coextensive, which is of course extremely unlikely.

Up till now we have said nothing about constituents such as *sit* in *Gwyneth was sitting in the garden*, and *run* in *Trevor ran to the door*. There is a semantic category of 'postures', containing items such as 'sit', 'stand' and 'lie', which may be optionally present in locative sentences (*cf* Leech 1969: 189). Similarly, directional sentences frequently specify not only a change of position but also the means by which the change of position is achieved. Thus we posit a semantic category of 'means (of locomotion)', containing items such as 'run', 'walk', 'hop', 'crawl', 'ride' and 'drive' (*cf* Leech 1969: 189 – where the label 'types of locomotion' is used). In the present book we are not directly concerned with these two semantic categories. However, one rather important point needs to be made concerning the relationship between verbs and adverbials, on the one hand, and (say) the means of locomotion and directional expressions, on the other.

On the basis of sentences such as *Trevor walked to the post office* it might seem that the means of locomotion is necessarily expressed by a verb, and that directional expressions are realized as prepositional phrases. We have already seen, however, that the second half of this statement is false – in the sentence *Trevor appeared from behind the desk* a goal expression is realized as the verb *appear*. The first half of the statement is also false – in sentences such as *Trevor went to the post office on foot* the means of locomotion is expressed as a prepositional phrase. We see, then, that the surface structure distinction between verbs and adverbial elements cuts across the semantic distinction between the means of locomotion and directional expressions. For this reason it is also difficult to determine precisely under what circumstances the verb *go* turns up in the surface structure of directional sentences. On the basis simply of sentences such as *Trevor walked to the post office* and *Trevor went to the post office,* one might suppose that *go* is absent whenever a directional sentence specifies the means of locomotion, and present whenever there is no means of locomotion constituent. Yet in *Trevor appeared from behind the desk* we have neither the verb *go* nor any indication of the means of locomotion; and in *Trevor went to the post office on foot* we have both. There seem to be two kinds of differences in meaning between *Trevor walked to the post office* and *Trevor went to the post office on foot*. First, *on foot* is less specific than *walk*, since (unlike *walk*) it subsumes *run*. This is a difference in experiential (or cognitive) meaning. Secondly, there is a difference in information structure.

I will conclude the present subsection by proposing a preliminary account of sentences such as:

The post office is over the hill   [25]
A car appeared from over the hill   [26]

The first of these sentences is locative – it specifies where the post office is located. The second is directional – it describes a particular change of position involving a car. [25] differs from other locative sentences that we have considered so far by virtue of the fact that its locative expression constituent has a rather more complex internal structure. Similarly, the source expression in the semantic representation of [26] has a more complex internal structure than any directional expression that we have encountered up to the present.

One notes first of all, with respect to [25], that the sentence can be paraphrased as *The post office is on the other side of the hill*. This fact has led the compilers of many dictionaries to assume that there is a sense of the preposition *over* which means 'on the other side of'. I shall argue, however, that such an analysis is unsatisfactory. Evidence in support of an alternative analysis will be presented both here and in **1.2.1**. If it were true that there is a sense of *over* meaning simply 'on the other side of', we would expect to be able to substitute *over* for *on the other side of* wherever the latter phrase occurs. Such a substitution can, of course, be made in the sentence *The post office is on the other side of the hill*, giving [25], but it can hardly be made in [27] – *ie* [28] is not really an acceptable paraphrase of [27].

My car is on the other side of the bus   [27]
?My car is over the bus   [28]

We need to explain, therefore, why the substitution of *over* for *on the other side of* is possible in one instance and not in another. The explanation has to do with the route that one would take in order to arrive at the location in question. If one wants to reach a post office which is on the other side of a hill, one goes OVER the hill. On the other hand, if one wants to reach a car which is on the other side of a bus, one would normally go ROUND (or around) the bus, rather than OVER it. Such considerations lead one to the conclusion that some locative sentences (*eg* [25]) identify a location by indicating the journey one would have to take in order to get there. Other examples are listed in [29]:

The post office is across the road   [29]
The post office is round the corner
The post office is past the cinema

Each of the sentences in [25] and [29] is interpreted 'deictically' – *ie* a reference point is involved, and if the listener does not know which location the speaker is taking as his reference point, he is unable to work out where the post office is. The location identified, for instance, by *past the cinema* is a different location according to which side of the cinema the speaker's reference point is on. When the reference point is the present position of the speaker and listener – which is often the case – it may be overtly indicated by means of the phrase *from here, eg: The post office is past the cinema from here.* Usually, however, the reference point is not overtly indicated in such a case, since it can easily be inferred by the listener. But when the listener cannot reasonably be expected to infer the reference point, the speaker makes it explicit by means of a prepositional phrase containing *from, eg: The post office is over the hill from the station.* It is significant that the preposition *from* is used to specify the reference point, and lends support to the suggestion that sentences such as [25] and [29] define a location by indicating the journey one would have to make to get there. A *from*-phrase used to indicate a reference point is simply marking the starting-point of the journey in question. Thus there is no difference between the meaning of *from* in

The post office is over the hill from here   [30]

and its meaning in, say, *Trevor appeared from behind the desk.* Any apparent difference in meaning – such as the fact that only in [30] can we speak of a reference point – is attributable to the environment in which the source expression occurs.

A first approximation to the semantic representation of [30] is shown in *Fig 6*. (The cases 'locative', 'source' and 'path' are abbreviated there as 'L', 'S' and 'P'.) What interests us in particular is the internal structure of the highest locative expression. It will be seen that the

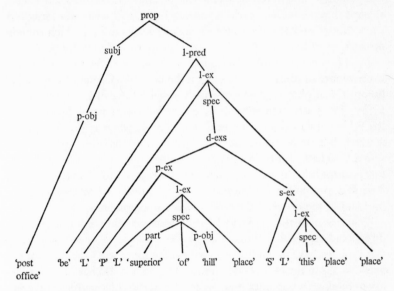

Fig 6 First approximation to a semantic representation of [30]

specifier slot in this locative expression is filled by two directional expressions, a path expression and a source expression. We have already discussed the source expression, but it is necessary to comment on the path expression. The meaning of this constituent can be stated as '[via [at [the superior of the hill] place]]'. The notion 'superior' is another member of the class of 'parts' (*cf* 'interior', 'anterior', 'posterior' and 'surface', which were mentioned above). It designates that part of the space surrounding something which is adjacent to its top. Two kinds of evidence can be given in support of the suggestion that sentences such as [30] do indeed contain a path expression in their semantic representation. Notice, first, that the location of the post office is defined only approximately. Specifically, no indication is given of how far over the hill the post office is situated. It might be just over the hill, or it might be several miles further along the road. Such vagueness is precisely what one would expect if the semantic representation contains a path expression. The sentence says, in effect: if you travel [via] over the hill (from a given starting-point), you will sooner or later reach the post office. The second evidence comes from a consideration of the preposition *through*. We saw earlier that *through* fills the path expression slot in the paradigm illustrated by examples [8] and [9], and in 1.2.8 I shall suggest that the notion 'path' is necessarily present whenever *through* is used. Notice now that there are examples parallel to [30] which contain *through*, eg: *The ticket office is through the archway (from here)*.

Fig 6 is problematical with respect to the order of the two directional expressions. In directional sentences, the unmarked order of directional prepositional phrases is source—path—goal. Other orders are marked, *ie* they focus attention specifically on the source or path. Thus in [15] the [a] example exhibits the unmarked order, whereas [b] and [c] are marked. But in a sentence such as [30] the only possible order for the source and path expressions is: path—source – *ie: The post office is from here over the hill* is not an acceptable paraphrase of [30]. In 1.1.3 we shall discuss two possible modifications to *Fig* 6, designed to overcome the problem of the order of the two directional expressions.

There is a further type of locative sentence containing embedded directional expressions, illustrated by *The caretaker lives to the right*. In this type we have an embedded goal expression, rather than a path expression. As in the other (more frequent) type, we also have the possibility of marking a reference point overtly by means of a source expression – *cf: The caretaker lives to the right from the main entrance*. In addition, since the notions expressed by *right* and *left* are comparable to 'anterior' and 'posterior', it is to be expected that we may mention the physical object whose right (or left) is referred to – *cf: The caretaker lives to the right of the main entrance*. A further possibility is to have both an *of*-phrase and a *from*-phrase: *The caretaker lives to the right of the main entrance from here*, in which the *from*-phrase specifies a 'point of observation' (*cf* 1.2.7 and also Leech 1969: 180–2).

Finally, we need to propose a preliminary semantic representation for [26], *A car appeared from over the hill*. This is a directional sentence, containing a goal expression – realized as the verb *appear* – and a source expression – realized as *from over the hill*. The location 'over the hill' is like that in [25], *ie* it is a location that is identified with reference to a path which leads to it from a given starting-point. But in [26] the locative expression in question is embedded inside a further directional expression (specifically, a source expression). Thus there are two separate journeys involved in [26]: the actual journey that the car made, and the hypothetical journey by means of which the location 'over the hill' is defined. These facts are reflected in the phrase marker shown in *Fig* 7. With regard to the constituent labelled 'visible', it is obvious that we are dealing with a complex notion which could be

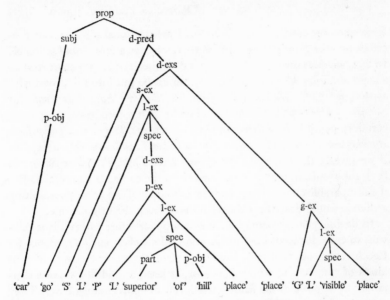

Fig 7 First approximation to a semantic representation of [26]

analysed into more elementary notions. However, I have not attempted such an analysis, since it does not directly concern us here. The source and goal expressions in *Fig* 7 are treated as occurring in the order: source —goal; *ie* I am assuming that the underlying order of directional expressions is: source—path—goal. Thus there is a discrepancy between the underlying order of the source and goal expressions of [26] and their realization in surface structure. We may attribute this discrepancy to the fact that the goal expression is realized, in this instance, as a verb. Of course, this statement merely raises the further question: why is the goal expression realized as a verb in this sentence? More generally – if we make the not unreasonable assumption that sentences have a (prelexical) semantic structure and that part of the process of expressing this structure consists in selecting appropriate lexical items, then what are the factors that determine which bits of the semantic structure are expressed in the verb? At the present time I am unable to provide a very satisfactory answer to this question beyond what was said above on the subject of *walk* and *go on foot*.

1.1.2 Extent sentences

We shall turn our attention now to sentences such as

The Mall goes from Buckingham Palace to Trafalgar Square   [31]

This sentence contains two directional prepositional phrases, but describes no change of position and is therefore not a directional sentence.
In fact, whereas directional sentences describe events, [31] characterizes
a state of affairs. Consequently, [31] cannot be put into the progressive
aspect; *ie: *The Mall is going from Buckingham Palace to Trafalgar
Square* is unacceptable. On the other hand, the progressive aspect is
certainly possible in a directional sentence, *eg: Trevor was going from
Buckingham Palace to Trafalgar Square (when I saw him)*. Notice also that
if we reverse the order of *Buckingham Palace* and *Trafalgar Square* in
[31], the resulting sentence still describes the same state of affairs. But
if a comparable change were made in a directional sentence, the resulting
sentence would describe a different event from the original one.

In deciding how to analyse the semantic structure of [31], it is relevant to consider what kind of question might elicit such a sentence (*cf*
Leech 1969: 102, 126, 129). We find, in fact, that there are two different
kinds of question to which [31] – or, at least, a modified version containing *it* in place of *the Mall* – would be an appropriate answer. They
are:

How long is the Mall?   [32a]
Where is the Mall?   [32b]

In each case there is more than one possible answer to the question. For
instance, we may answer [32a] by saying *It's approximately 1,000 yards
long*. But under certain circumstances (stated below) it would be appropriate to specify the length of the Mall as in [31] – *ie* by indicating the
location of the two extremities, using for this purpose a source expression
and a goal expression (each of which contains a locative expression). One
possible answer to [32b] would be: *It's in S.W.1.* (*ie* the South-West 1
postal district of London). But if one assumed that the person asking the
question knew the location of Buckingham Palace and Trafalgar Square,
then it would be appropriate to specify where the Mall is by saying *It
goes from Buckingham Palace to Trafalgar Square*.

The question [32a] asks for information about the extent of the Mall
(in one particular dimension). It thus represents a type of sentence that is
distinct both from directional sentences and from locative sentences, for
which I propose to use the label 'extent sentence'. [32b], on the other

hand, is a locative sentence. If we make the reasonable assumption that a well-formed answer to a question exemplifies the same type of sentence as the question itself, then it follows that [31] is either an extent sentence or a locative sentence, and needs, accordingly, to be ascribed two alternative semantic representations. The extent sentence interpretation will be discussed in the present subsection, and the locative sentence interpretation in 1.1.3.

Before presenting a general discussion of extent sentences, it is appropriate to mention the kind of circumstances under which [32a] might be answered with *It goes from Buckingham Palace to Trafalgar Square*. In indicating the length of the Mall by specifying the location of its two extremities, the speaker is, as it were, inviting the questioner to figure out for himself how long it is. It is quite possible, therefore, that the speaker does not know the length of the Mall himself, and is not prepared to hazard a guess. At the same time, he clearly assumes that the questioner knows the location of Buckingham Palace and Trafalgar Square (otherwise the reply would be of no help). Yet he must assume also that the questioner was unaware of the exact location of the Mall. (If the speaker thought the questioner knew perfectly well where the Mall was located, the set of appropriate answers would include: *It's approximately 1,000 yards long*, *I don't know* and *Your guess is as good as mine*; but not *It goes from Buckingham Palace to Trafalgar Square*, which would merely repeat already known information.) All of this adds up to a fairly complex set of assumptions which would need to be satisfied before it would be appropriate to answer [32a] with the pronominalized version of [31]. However, this does not affect the claim that [31] can be interpreted as an extent sentence.

From the preceding discussion it would seem that an extent sentence such as [31] necessarily indicates the location of the thing whose extent is specified. In fact, however, this is not the case – as can be demonstrated by considering a further question-and-answer pair of the same type:

How long is your new tent? [33a]
It goes from the back of our garage to the apple tree in the
   middle of the lawn [33b]

[33b] is a perfectly acceptable answer even if at the time of speaking the tent is rolled up and lying in a box in the garage. Thus although [31], in its extent sentence interpretation, appears necessarily to indicate the location of the Mall, it is apparently our knowledge of the world that

forces us to understand the sentence in this way (in particular, the knowledge that roads tend to remain in one place), rather than the semantic structure of the sentence.

Within the set of extent sentences two subtypes need to be distinguished, each of which has already been exemplified. Sentence [31] illustrates one type, and

The Mall is approximately 1,000 yards long   [34]

is an example of the other type. It is convenient to label the two types. I shall refer to the [34] type as 'measured extent sentences', in view of the fact that they contain a measurement phrase. The [31] type will be referred to as 'directional extent sentences', since their semantic structure contains embedded directional expressions. The following are additional examples of measured extent sentences:

This pencil is five inches long
Our car is five feet wide
The door is two inches thick
The trench is three feet deep

It is clear from these examples that an extent sentence frequently indicates not only the extent of something but also the particular dimension in which it has that extent. Such matters have been discussed in detail by Bierwisch (1967). In the present context, measured extent sentences are of only marginal interest, since they are not related to locative or directional sentences in any way. On the other hand, directional extent sentences do concern us. The slot in the semantic structure of an extent sentence which is filled by a measurement phrase in examples such as [34] is occupied by embedded directional expressions in examples like [31]. The directional expressions may include a path expression, as we see from: *The A379 goes from Exeter round the coast to Plymouth.* However, a sentence such as *The A379 goes round the coast*, which contains only a path expression, is unlikely to occur as an extent sentence, since on its own it gives no indication of the length of the road in question.

The predicate of an extent sentence contains a constituent for which the label 'extent expression' suggests itself (by analogy with 'locative expression', 'source expression', etc). In deciding what structure to attribute to extent expressions, it is relevant to consider examples such as:

We walked along the road for three miles   [35a]
We walked along the road for three hours   [35b]
We walked along the road for a long time   [35c]

Each of these sentences indicates the extent of 'our walking along the road'. The distinction between [35a], on the one hand, and [35b and c], on the other, draws attention to the need for recognizing spatial and temporal extent expressions; and the appearance of the word *time* in [35c] suggests that spatial and temporal extent expressions should be differentiated in the same way that spatial and temporal locative expressions were differentiated. Thus we posit a position in the structure of an extent expression which may be filled by one or other of the elements 'place' and 'time'. It should be noted that in the context of an extent expression, as opposed to a locative expression, the notion designated here as 'place' would be expressed as *space* rather than *place* – whereas things are located at a particular *place*, they occupy a certain amount of *space* rather than *place*. In the present analysis, then, *place* and *space* are treated as alternative realizations of a single more abstract notion (arbitrarily labelled 'place'). Such a treatment is suggested by the fact that the distribution of the word *time* is equivalent to the combined distribution of *place* and *space* – *ie* things occur or exist at a particular *time*, and occupy a certain amount of *time*. It should be added, however, that another possibility (not adopted here) may in fact be preferable. *Place* could be taken

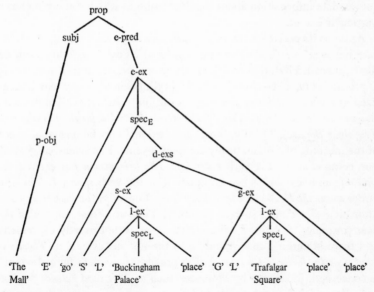

Fig 8 Semantic representation of [31] in its extent sentence interpretation

to mean 'point in space'. Similarly, $time_L$ (the locative use of *time*) could be taken to mean 'point in $time_E$'. A further slot in the structure of an extent expression is filled by the specifier of the place or time in question. Since the set of things that can function as the specifier of an extent is different from the set of things that specify locations, we shall distinguish from now on between a 'specifier$_E$' and a 'specifier$_L$'. A third constituent of an extent expression is the element 'extent' ('E'), which – like 'locative', 'source', 'path' and 'goal' – is a case (see below). An extent expression conforming to this description occurs in *Fig* 8, the semantic representation of [31]. The fact that the 'spec$_E$' contains the element 'go' in addition to a source expression and a goal expression will be commented on in 3.2.2. Two further things should be noted with regard to *Fig* 8. First, it may not be necessary to distinguish between 'e-pred' and 'e-ex' constituents. Specifically, if all extent predicates were analysed as consisting simply of an extent expression, one of the two labels would clearly be redundant. For the moment I will retain both labels, under the influence of locative and directional sentences, where a comparable distinction (*eg* between 'l-pred' and 'l-ex') is justified. Secondly, the extent expression constituent of a measured extent sentence such as [34] would need to be more complex than that of *Fig* 8, in order to accommodate information about the dimension in which something has a particular extent.

As far as its possible syntactic realizations are concerned, the 'extent' case behaves in a similar way to, say, 'goal'. Four possibilities can be distinguished. First, they may be realized as a preposition – 'goal' being expressed as *to*, and 'extent' as *for* (*cf* [35]). Secondly, they may be realized as a verb – *arrive* expressing the notion 'goal' (*cf* [14]) and *extend* the notion 'extent' (*cf: The Mall extends from Buckingham Palace to Trafalgar Square*). Thirdly, 'goal' and 'extent' may be one component of the meaning of a semantically complex lexeme. For instance, 'goal' is one component of the verb *enter* (*cf: The bridegroom has entered the church*); and 'extent' is one component of the verb *span* (*cf: The new bridge spans the river and the railway line*). Fourthly, the case may have no overt realization in surface structure. Thus in *Trevor ran behind the door* (meaning 'to behind') the notion 'goal' is not overtly expressed; and there is nothing corresponding to the notion 'extent' in *There's a road from the house to the lake*. A fifth possibility exists as far as 'extent' is concerned, illustrated by sentences such as *This road extends for five miles*, in which both the verb and the preposition express the notion 'extent'.

I.I.3 Locative and directional sentences revisited

In this subsection we shall first of all propose a semantic structure corresponding to the locative interpretation of sentences such as [31], *The Mall goes from Buckingham Palace to Trafalgar Square*. Then we shall continue the discussion, begun in **I.I.I**, of sentences such as [25], *The post office is over the hill*, and [26], *A car appeared from over the hill*.

When [31] specifies where the Mall is located, the source and goal expressions underlying *from Buckingham Palace* and *to Trafalgar Square* are embedded inside a locative expression. Since no change of position is involved, I shall treat the two directional expressions as being first embedded inside an extent expression, which in turn is embedded inside the locative expression – *cf: Fig* 9. It was pointed out in **I.I.2** that a direc-

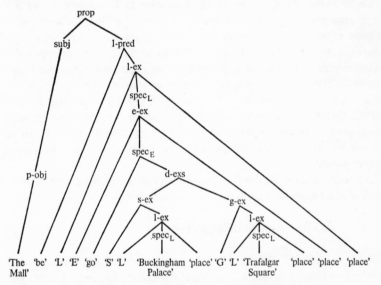

Fig 9 Tentative semantic representation of [31] in its locative sentence interpretation

tional extent expression does not necessarily specify the location of the thing whose extent is specified (*cf* [33b]). On the other hand, the semantic structure shown in *Fig* 9 does imply that this type of locative sentence necessarily indicates the extent of the thing whose location is specified. This seems to be correct. At the same time, it should be noted that the semantic structures of *Figs* 8 and 9 imply that [31] is more complex semantically when it occurs as a locative sentence than when it occurs as an extent sentence. I am aware of no evidence in support of this particular suggestion. *Fig* 9 should therefore be regarded as tentative. Fortunately, the exact details of the semantic structure of sentences such as [31] will in no way affect the analysis of the meaning of English prepositions presented in **1.2**.

We return now to the question of how to represent the semantic structure of [25], *The post office is over the hill*, and [30] (the same sentence except for the addition of *from here*, indicating the location that the speaker is using as his reference point). It will be recalled that there is a problem with regard to the order of *over the hill* and *from here* in [30]. The unmarked order of directional prepositional phrases is source—path—goal. This is true of directional sentences, such as *We walked from Waterloo Bridge along the Embankment to Westminster*; and it is true also when directional expressions are embedded inside a higher extent expression in examples such as *The A379 goes from Exeter round the coast to Plymouth* (*cf* **1.1.2**) – whether or not the extent expression itself is embedded inside a higher locative expression (*cf* present subsection). But in [30], not only is the order source—path (*ie: from here over the hill*) not the unmarked order, but it is not even a possible order at all. Two ways will now be discussed in which *Fig* 6, the first approximation to a semantic representation of [30], might be revised in an attempt to overcome the problem of the order of the two directional expressions.

In connection with the first possible revision, we need first of all to consider an example of a type not yet discussed:

The post office is three miles from here   [36]

Like [25] and [30], this is a locative sentence specifying the location of the post office. It contains a locative expression, inside which are embedded an extent expression (*three miles*) and a source expression (*from here*). Now it will be recalled that there are two types of extent expressions, measured and directional (*cf* **1.1.2**). *Three miles* obviously realizes a measured extent expression. The question thus arises whether we need to recognize a kind of locative sentence similar to [36] but containing a directional extent expression in place of a measured extent expression. The answer to this question would be affirmative if the path expression in the semantic structure of [25] and [30] were analysed as being embedded inside an extent expression, which in turn is embedded inside a locative expression. The resulting semantic representation of

[30] would look like *Fig* 10. One is led to consider this possible modification of *Fig* 6 in the first place on grounds of simplicity. Admittedly, *Fig* 10 is no simpler than *Fig* 6; but the grammar for generating our semantic representations will be simpler if it incorporates the statement

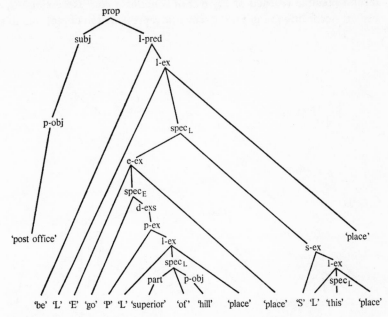

Fig 10 Further possible semantic representation of [30]

that extent expressions in general may be embedded (along with a source expression) inside a locative expression, rather than merely measured extent expressions. But the main advantage of *Fig* 10 relates to the question of the order of the two directional expressions. In *Fig* 10 (as opposed to *Fig* 6) the path and source expressions are not treated as belonging to a single directional expressions constituent. The path expression is inside an extent expression, but the source expression is outside it. Thus according to *Fig* 10, [30] is no longer an exception to the rule that the unmarked order of directional expressions is source—path —goal, which concerns only source, path and goal expressions that are dominated by a single directional expressions node.

There is, however, another respect in which neither *Fig* 6 nor *Fig* 10 is satisfactory – which leads us to consider other ways in which *Fig* 6 might be modified. The post office of [25] and [30] may be said to be at

the end of a path leading over the hill. Alternatively, it is at a place at
which a path over the hill ends. The use of the word *end* in these two
formulations suggests that the semantic representation should contain
not only a source and path expression but also a goal expression. The
second possible revision of *Fig* 6 thus contains a goal expression – *cf:*
Fig 11. According to *Fig* 11, the semantic representation of [30] contains

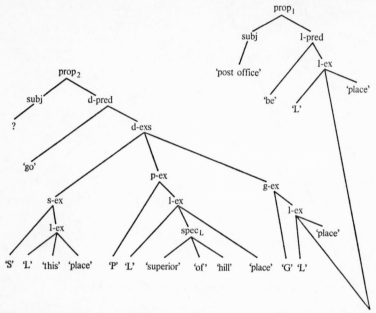

Fig 11 Further approximation to the semantic representation of [30]

two propositions. The higher of the two is a locative proposition, which
specifies that the post office is located at a particular place (let us call it
P). The embedded proposition is directional and defines a journey which
leads from the speaker's location over the hill to the place P. Thus the
same location – 'at P' – features in each of the propositions. We therefore know two things about P – first, that it is where the post office is
located; and secondly, that it is where a journey leading over the hill
from the speaker's position would end. This second fact enables one to
calculate the approximate position of P, whereupon one is aware also of
the location of the post office.

With regard to the question of the constituent functioning as subject
in the directional proposition, there would seem to be two possibilities.

If we say that the post office is at a place at which a path leading over the hill ends, this implies that 'path' is the subject of the proposition in question. It will be realized, however, that this use of the word *path* conflicts with its use as a label for the 'path' case. This becomes quite apparent when we consider the phrase 'a path leading via . . .', in which *via* expresses the meaning of the 'path' case. To avoid confusion it would be desirable to substitute a different term for one or other of these two uses of the word *path*. It may be preferable, however, to regard the subject as being equivalent to *anyone* – in which case the sentence means 'the post office is at a place that you (*ie* anyone) could reach by going over the hill', or if we passivize *reach* 'the post office is at a place that can be reached by going over the hill'. Such a maximally general subject could be represented by means of Chomsky's (1965: 122) dummy symbol or Leech's (1969: 40–1) null symbol.

The mechanism for linking the two propositions of *Fig* 11 in the way indicated will be discussed in 3.2.3. At this point I will simply comment on the way in which *Fig* 11 may provide a solution to the problem of the order of *over the hill* and *from here*. In converting *Fig* 11 into a surface structure, we enter $prop_2$ from $prop_1$ by way of the locative expression constituent of the goal expression. Conceivably, then, the source, path and goal expression constituents are realized in this instance in the reverse order – simply because we enter the structure from what, on paper, is the right-hand side. (There is, of course, no overt realization of the goal expression.)

We shall see, however, that (as in the case of sentence [31]) the account of the meaning of English prepositions given in 1.2 is in no way affected by the precise details of the final solution to examples such as [30]. Whatever semantic structure is eventually ascribed to *over the hill* in [30], the same structure will need to be embedded inside a higher source expression in the semantic representation of [26], *A car appeared from over the hill*, the resulting structure replacing *Fig* 7.

1.2 Componential analysis of the prepositions investigated

In this section I shall present a componential analysis of the meaning of the prepositions that were investigated. They will be discussed in small groups, membership of the groups being determined by relatedness of meaning. The only significance of the order in which the groups occur is convenience of presentation. After all the groups of prepositions have been discussed, the analysis will be summarized in 1.2.11.

1.2.1 *Over* and *under*

We can identify many distinct uses of the preposition *over*. I shall consider first of all a selection of uses that are directly related to the account of locative and directional sentences given in 1.1.1:

My hand is over the table	[37a]
I removed the lamp from over the counter	[37b]
Please put the lamp over the counter (*ie* via)	[37c]
Please put the lamp over the counter (*ie* to)	[37d]
The post office is over the hill	[37e]
A car appeared from over the hill	[37f]

The semantic representation of [37a] contains a simple locative expression; [37b, c and d] contain directional expressions (source, path and goal respectively); [37e] contains a locative expression of the more complex, deictically interpreted kind; and in [37f] the locative expression of [37e] is embedded inside a source expression. The semantic constituents in question are shown in [38] as bracketed strings. (The labels of the various constituents are not included, since they do not concern us at the present moment, but it is clear from *Figs* 1–7 what the labels would be.)

[L [superior of table] place]	[38a]
[S [L [superior of counter] place]]	[38b]
[P [L [superior of counter] place]]	[38c]
[G [L [superior of counter] place]]	[38d]
[L [P [L [superior of hill] place]] place]	[38e]
[S [L [P [L [superior of hill] place]] place]]	[38f]

In proposing a componential definition of the meaning of *over*, one has to decide how much of these semantic representations is realized as the preposition *over*. Saying the same thing in slightly different terms, one has to decide what particular string, or strings, of semantic elements *over* gets mapped onto. My first observation is so obvious as to sound trivial. It is that the element 'table' in [38a] is not part of the meaning of the preposition *over*. Nor is 'counter' part of the meaning of *over* in the [b, c and d] examples, or 'hill' in [e and f]. We are confident that this is so, because of the presence of the lexemes *table*, *counter* and *hill* in [37] – *ie* the notions 'table', 'counter' and 'hill' are expressed by means of the lexemes *table*, *counter* and *hill*. Slightly less trivially, one may observe that the semantic element 'source' is not part of the meaning of *over* in the [b and f] examples. Again, we are confident that this is so, because of the presence of a separate lexeme expressing the notion 'source' – namely, the preposition *from*. Consider now the [c and d] examples. There is no overt marker in [37c] of the notion 'path', nor is there an overt marker of the notion 'goal' in [37d]. Yet when we encounter the sentence *Please put the lamp over the counter* and understand it in one or other of its two interpretations, either 'path' or 'goal' is present in the total meaning that we derive from the sentence. Now it seems to be a fundamental assumption of most lexicographers that any meaning we derive from a sentence must be contained, as it were, in one of the words of the sentence (unless it is contributed by a particular construction or intonation pattern). In accordance with this assumption, the notions 'path' and 'goal' are frequently ascribed to the meaning of *over*, as it is represented in dictionaries. Thus we might read that *over* may mean, among other things, 'passing directly above' and also 'to a position directly above'. With regard to [38], this amounts to saying that *over* may be mapped onto either

path locative superior of   [39]

(in [c]), or

goal locative superior of   [40]

(in [d]). Each of these two senses of *over* would be directional. In addition, dictionaries list locative senses of *over*, two of which might be glossed as 'directly above' and 'on the other side of'. Recognizing these two senses would be equivalent to saying that *over* is mapped onto

locative superior of   [41]

in [38a and b], and

locative path locative superior of   [42]

in [38e and f]. Thus if we were to suggest that *over* may be mapped onto any of the strings [39]–[42], this would entail accepting the analysis of many dictionaries, according to which four different senses of *over* are represented by the examples in [37]. However, there is evidence to suggest that this is not the best analysis.

Consider in this connection the examples:

The dog is under the table   [43a]
The dog emerged from under the table   [43b]
The dog ran under the table to the door   [43c]
The dog ran under the table (*ie* to)   [43d]
The cathedral is under the bridge   [43e]
A rabbit appeared from under the hedge   [43f]

(The location in [43e] is intended to be interpreted deictically, as in *under the bridge from here*. Similarly, *under the hedge* in [43f] is taken to mean 'on the other side of the hedge, via a path leading under it' rather than simply 'beneath the hedge'. The [e and f] use of *under* is less common than the corresponding use of *over*, but nevertheless needs to be recognized; *cf* Leech 1969: 186.) The *under* examples in [43] are exactly parallel, then, to the *over* examples in [37]. Thus if we identify four senses of *over* in [37], we shall presumably have to recognize four exactly parallel senses of *under* in [43]. Such an analysis would involve a certain amount of repetition. It is worth considering, therefore, whether there is any other way of showing that *over* and *under* behave in an exactly comparable manner. The possibility of finding an alternative analysis becomes more pressing as soon as we consider other prepositions and realize that the repetition referred to above would, in fact, be quite considerable. For instance, the [a–d] examples in [37] and [43] can be matched by similar examples containing *in front of*, *behind* and *by*. Thus the three senses of *over* that were glossed as 'directly above', 'passing directly above' and 'to a position directly above' – *ie* the locative, path and goal senses – would be matched by locative, path and goal senses not only of *under*, but also of *in front of*, *behind* and *by*.

A more general account of these facts can be provided in the following way. We allow the possibility that the element 'path' of a path expression and the element 'goal' of a goal expression may be realized as zero, *ie* may have no overt manifestation in surface structure. *Over* is then regarded as being mapped onto simply 'locative superior' in [38a, c and d]; and, of course, also in [38b], where there was never any question of the element 'source' being part of the meaning of *over*. (I will comment below on why the element 'of' is not ascribed to the meaning of *over*.) *Over* thus has a single sense in the [a–d] examples of [37] and [38]. By analogy with the component 'superior' of *over*, we recognize a component 'inferior' – defined loosely as the space adjacent to the bottom (or underside) of something – and analyse *under* as being mapped onto 'locative inferior' in [43a–d]. Similarly, only one sense of *in front of*, *behind* and *by* would be recognized in comparable sets of examples containing these prepositions. We see, then, that by stating that 'path' and 'goal' may be realized as zero, we are able to give a general account of the fact that *over*, *under*, *in front of*, *behind* and *by* all exhibit locative, path and goal uses.

With regard to the [e and f] examples in [37], [38] and [43], I shall adopt a similar policy. Rather than treating *over* as being mapped onto 'locative path locative superior' in [38e and f] – which would entail recognizing a different sense of *over* in these two examples from the sense that occurs in the [a–d] examples – I shall regard the initial 'locative path' as having no overt realization in surface structure. Thus *over* is mapped onto the same two components – 'locative superior' – in each of the examples of [38]. Evidence in support of the suggested analysis of the [e and f] examples comes from ambiguous sentences such as

The helicopter is over the hill   [44a]
The ticket office is under the archway   [44b]

The helicopter of [44a] is either above the hill or at the end of a path leading over the hill. Similarly, the ticket office in [44b] is either below the archway or at the end of a path leading under the archway. In other words, the two sentences are ambiguous in an exactly parallel way. Thus it is desirable to give a single, general account of the two cases of ambiguity. We achieve such a treatment if we state that the initial 'locative path' of the kind of locative expression shown in [38e] can have zero realization in surface structure. On the other hand, to handle the [44a] ambiguity by setting up two locative senses of *over*, and the [44b] ambiguity by setting up two locative senses of *under*, would amount to treating the two examples as isolated and unrelated instances of ambiguity.

The semantic element 'of' which occurs in each of the examples in [38] is present in the semantic representation of a locative expression whenever the specifier slot contains both a part and a physical object – *eg* in [locative [interior of supermarket] place], realized as *in the supermarket*. However, there is no 'of' if the specifier contains only a physical object – *eg* [locative [supermarket] place], realized as *at the supermarket*. Nor is 'of' present if the specifier contains only a part – *eg* [locative [interior] place], realized as the adverb *in*, as in the sentence *He's not in*. Now many of the prepositions discussed in this book function also as adverbs. This means that when such an item (*eg: in*) appears in surface structure, in some instances the semantic structure will contain 'of' whereas in others it will not. If we treat 'of' as being a component of the meaning of the items in question, they will necessarily have a different componential definition depending on whether they occur as prepositions or as adverbs ('of' being absent in the latter case). Yet it seems preferable to say that the meaning is the same, and only the syntactic function different. (*On* would be an exception to this statement – *eg* in *We drove on until it became dark*, in which the meaning of *on* seems quite different from its meaning as a preposition.) I shall therefore not ascribe 'of' to the meaning of specific prepositions, treating it instead as having no realization in surface structure. There is, however, an instance of 'of' in the componential definitions of *inside* and *outside* (1.2.6); and, of course, 'of' may also be realized as the preposition *of*.

In regarding the meaning of *over* to be 'locative superior' in each of the examples of [37] and [38], as well as in sentences such as *I have to drive over to the post office*, we have in fact ascribed to its componential definition only such components as are always present in the semantic representation. Elements such as 'path' and 'goal' are present in the semantic representation of some sentences containing *over*, but are by no means necessarily present. In the following subsections I shall adopt the policy of determining what components of meaning are necessarily present whenever a given preposition is used.

It should now be clear why the precise details of the semantic structures discussed in 1.1.3 would have no effect on the componential definitions proposed in the present section. With regard to the semantic representation of [30], for instance, the element 'extent' of *Fig* 10 or the element 'goal' of *Fig* 11 would not be taken to be part of the meaning of the preposition *over*. Thus whether the semantic representation of [30] contains an extent expression, or a goal expression, or indeed both, the componential definition of *over* would remain as before.

In 0.2, at the point where I mentioned Jakobson's analysis of the Russian case system, I used the phrase 'bundle of distinctive semantic features'. It should therefore be pointed out that in componential definitions such as 'locative superior' (*over*) and 'locative inferior' (*under*), the meaning of the particular items is being stated not simply as an unstructured bundle of components. Rather, it is significant which order the components occur in. This will become especially apparent during the discussion of *beyond*, to which it is necessary to ascribe two separate instances of the component 'locative'.

We will now consider a number of additional examples containing *over*. Among the fifteen senses of *over* listed in Wood 1967 (67–9) are two that bear the glosses 'downwards from the edge of' – *eg: Jeremy fell over the cliff* – and 'as the result of collision with' – *eg: Jeremy fell over the kerb*. These two senses are supposed to be distinct from Wood's directional sense 'above, and on to the other side of'. According to the present analysis, the semantic representation of each of the above sentences contains a path expression – the 'superior' of the cliff and the 'superior' of the kerb are on the path that Jeremy follows in falling. As in [37c] and [38c], 'path' has no overt realization in the surface structure, and *over* realizes simply 'locative superior'. But how is it, then, that the one sentence is understood as describing a fall downwards from the edge of something, and the other the result of colliding with something? The answer is that all of this is inferred; it is not contained in any of the words of the two sentences. Two things are relevant in this connection. First, in the absence of any counter-evidence a listener will naturally assume that the Jeremy referred to is a male human being. Secondly, the listener makes unconscious use of his knowledge of human beings and cliffs, on the one hand, and human beings and kerbs, on the other. Cliffs are considerably larger than human beings; kerbs are considerably smaller. The fact that we imagine Jeremy to be rather smaller than the cliff forces us to picture him falling from the top of the cliff – it would be a physical impossibility for him to fall over the cliff from the bottom to the top. On the other hand, since we imagine Jeremy to be rather larger than the kerb, it is quite natural for us to picture him falling over the kerb from the lower to the higher level. Moreover, in the absence of any indication of the reason for his falling, we infer that he must have collided with the kerb. It is of interest to see how our understanding of the two sentences is affected by changing the original assumption that Jeremy is a male human being. Suppose, on the one hand, that Jeremy is a giant in a fairy tale. Then the sentence *Jeremy fell over the cliff* might well conjure up the picture of a giant tripping over a cliff in the same way in which a normal-sized man might trip over a kerb. Alternatively, if we have previously been informed that Jeremy is somebody's pet flea, the sentence *Jeremy fell over the kerb* might well evoke the picture of a flea falling downwards from the edge of a kerb. I hope to have demonstrated that the meanings which Wood ascribes to the preposition *over* in these two sentences have, in fact, a quite different origin.

Among the many senses of *over* to be found in any large dictionary, one usually encounters a sense that is said to mean 'covering'. A typical example would be: *There's a cloth over the table*. It seems not unreasonable to treat *over the table* here as the realization of a path expression which is embedded inside an extent expression (*cf* 1.1.2). A similar analysis would apply also in the case of a sentence such as *Gwyneth spread a cloth over the table* (paraphrasable as *Gwyneth caused a cloth to extend over the table*), in which *Gwyneth* derives from an ergative expression (*cf* Anderson 1971: 40 *ff*). Given such an account of the semantic structure of these two sentences, it would be unnecessary to set up a 'covering' sense of *over*. The notion 'covering' would follow automatically from the fact that the extent of the cloth takes in the 'superior' of the table.

Over and *under* are antonyms. Specifically, the one is the 'converse' of the other (*cf* Lyons 1968: 467 *ff*). This aspect of the meaning of *over* and *under* is not reflected in the present analysis, as a result of the fact that the notions 'superior' and 'inferior' have not been decomposed into still more elementary components. Nevertheless, it is relevant to comment on one respect in which the range of situations covered by *over* appears not to parallel that of *under*. The sentence *My hand is under the table* can be appropriately applied to either of two distinct situations; namely, the hand either may or may not be in contact with the table. This observation is quite compatible with our definition of the meaning of *under* as 'locative inferior'. 'Inferior' designates a part of the space surrounding an object which begins at – or alternatively, extends right up to – the object itself. *My hand is under the table* is simply vague on the subject of whether or not there is contact between the hand and the table. Consider now the parallel example containing *over*: *My hand is over the table*. When one tries to picture the kind of situations that are appropriately described by means of this sentence, one is inclined to rule out the possibility that the hand may be in contact with the table. It seems, namely, that such a situation would be more appropriately described with the sentence *My hand is on the table*. This observation raises the question whether our definition of *over* as 'locative superior' is adequate, in view of the fact that the 'superior' of a physical object – like the 'inferior' – extends all the way to the object itself. One's first reaction is that one should perhaps invoke a component 'detached', and analyse *over* as meaning 'at the detached superior' (of something). For two reasons, however, such a revised analysis is not to be recommended. First, it is relevant to note that directional and extent uses of *over* frequently involve contact. Thus in *We drove over the hill* there is contact between, say, our car and the hill; and in *There's a cloth over the table* there is contact between the cloth and the table. Each of these examples supports the view that 'superior' rather than 'detached superior' is part of the meaning of *over*. Secondly, to ascribe a component 'detached' to *over* but not to *under* would conflict with the fact that *over* and *under* are felt to be antonyms.

Fortunately, there is another way of accounting for the apparent asymmetry of *over* and *under*. If a hand is in contact with the upper surface of a table-top, it is related to the table-top in two ways. It is 'superior to' the table and at the same time 'in contact with' it. Now it would appear to be true that under normal circumstances the relationship of contact somehow takes precedence over superiority in commanding the speaker's attention, with the result that he comments on the former rather than the latter (using *on* rather than *over*). On the other hand, when a situation involves contact and inferiority, the latter relation seems under normal circumstances to command the speaker's attention more than the contact. If this explanation of the facts is correct, one would expect that under certain circumstances the normal priority might be reversed. This seems, in fact, to be the case. For instance, if the issue is simply whether the hand is over the table or under it – *ie* if the superiority of *over* is being directly contrasted with the inferiority of *under* – then the fact that the hand happens also to be in contact with the table would not rule out the possibility of using the sentence *My hand is over the table*.

1.2.2 *Above* and *below*

Locative, source and goal uses of *above* are frequently encountered, *eg*:

John's picture is above the shelf
I've removed John's picture from above the shelf
I've put John's picture above the fireplace

Path expression uses, on the other hand, seem rare, if indeed they occur at all. Thus while we can certainly say *The bird flew over the hill to its nest*, the corresponding sentence containing *above* strikes one as being a little odd:

?The bird flew above the hill to its nest

Below exhibits a parallel behaviour – *ie* locative, source and goal uses are quite normal, but path uses seem a little strange (*?The dog ran below the table to the door*). There is another respect in which *above* and *below* have a more restricted distribution than *over* and *under*. It will be recalled that *The helicopter is over the hill* may mean 'the helicopter is at the end of a path leading over the hill'. On the other hand, the sentence *The helicopter is above the hill* cannot mean 'the helicopter is at the end of a path leading above the hill'. If it is true that path expression uses of *above* do not occur, then this fact in itself would explain the absence of a deictically interpreted locative use (which would involve a path expression embedded inside a locative expression).

Usually when a physical object X is above some other physical object Y, X is at the 'superior' of Y, *ie* in the space adjacent to the top of Y. However, this is not necessarily the case. For instance, one can hold one's hands above one's head without them being over one's head (Wood 1967: 67). Accordingly, the notion 'superior' will not be ascribed to the meaning of *above*. The essential meaning of X *is above* Y seems to be simply that X is higher than Y. *Above* will therefore be defined as 'locative higher'. Similarly, *below* will be defined as 'locative lower'. The notions 'higher' and 'lower' are clearly complex. Moreover, it would seem that the semantic representation must contain extent expressions (comparatives in general involve the notion 'extent'). However, I shall not attempt to reduce 'higher' and 'lower' to more elementary components of meaning. (They will be invoked again, though, in defining the meaning of *up* and *down, cf* 1.2.9.)

Referring once more to the apparent absence of path expression uses of *above* and *below*, the componential definitions proposed for *over*, *under*, *above* and *below* suggest a possible explanation. If the route followed by some moving object takes in the 'superior' or 'inferior' of another object, *over* and *under* are the obvious prepositions to use, since their meaning includes these notions. Presumably it would be appropriate to use *above* and *below* if one wanted to indicate that something went via a higher or lower place than something else without necessarily going over or under it. But the chances of anyone wanting to convey such a message are rather remote. This explanation is not entirely satisfactory, in that it is difficult to reconcile with the fact that *above* and *below* do occur in source and goal uses.

1.2.3 *By*, *past* and *beyond*

According to the present analysis, *past* and *beyond* have only one sense each (even though several different uses can be identified). However, the uses of *by* are more varied and cannot be explained in terms of a single sense. For instance, the two spatial uses illustrated by *My car is by the post office* and *The carpet measures 12 feet by 10 feet* would seem to necessitate recognizing distinct senses. I shall consider only the former sense. As with all prepositions, we need to determine what kinds of locative and/or directional expressions may be present in the semantic representation when *by*, *past* or *beyond* occurs. In addition, we need to determine whether the meaning of these three prepositions contains any member of the category of parts (comparable to the 'superior' of *over*).

Locative, source, path and goal uses of *by* are illustrated by the following examples:

My car is by the post office	[45a]
I took this chair from by the window	[45b]
We drove by the post office	[45c]
I've put the book by the telephone	[45d]

In at least one variety of English – that spoken in Leicester – sentence [45a] can also mean 'my car is at the end of a path leading by the post office' (providing *by* is stressed). However, the normal way of conveying this information involves using the preposition *past – My car is past the post office –* and it would seem that the existence of *past* makes it unnecessary to use *by* in this type of sentence.

For the purposes of contrasting the various uses of *by* with those of *past* and *beyond* it is convenient to employ tables. *Table* 4 summarizes the four uses of *by* illustrated by [45]. The [45a] use involves a simple locative expression, at level 1 of the table. Examples [45b–d] involve directional expressions, at level 2.

A set of examples containing *past* is given in [46], and *Table* 5 indicates how these examples are analysed. In particular, it is claimed that the locative expression occurring in the semantic representation of [46b]

	S	P	G
level 4, directional	–	–	–
level 3, locative		–	
level 2, directional	S by	P by	G by
level 1, locative		by	

Table 4 Summary of the various uses of *by*

	S	P	G
level 4, directional	past	?	past
level 3, locative		past	
level 2, directional	S –	P past	G –
level 1, locative		–	

Table 5 Summary of the various uses of *past*

is a level 3 rather than a level 1 locative expression, and that there is in fact no level 1 use of *past*.

We drove past the post office	[46a]
The theatre is past the post office	[46b]
The sound of gunfire came from past the post office	[46c]
The passenger fell asleep and went past his station	[46d]

Notice in this connection that it is impossible to find examples containing *past* that are ambiguous as between a level 1 and a level 3 locative use (*cf: The helicopter is over the hill*); and furthermore that the theatre of [46b] is 'past the post office' not in any absolute sense, but only relative to a particular reference point – *ie* it is at the end of a path leading past the post office from a given starting-point. In [46c] the same level 3 locative expression that occurs in [46b] is embedded inside a source expression. This source expression is, therefore, a level 4 rather than a level 2 directional expression. A further example of a level 4 directional expression is provided by [46d] (taken from Wood 1967: 70), in which *past his station* seems to mean 'to a place at the end of a path leading past his station'. This example therefore involves a goal expression. I am uncertain whether there are also level 4 path expression uses of *past*. The path expression underlying *past the post office* in [46a] is a level 2 path expression, meaning 'via the proximity of the post office' rather than 'via a place at the end of a path leading past the post office'.

With regard to the question of whether or not *by* and *past* need to be attributed a component comparable to the 'superior' of *over*, it is relevant to consider also *at* and *via*. The sentence *Trevor is at the post office* does not specify whether Trevor is inside or outside the post office. We are told simply that the post office, *ie* the post office as a whole, is where Trevor is located. On the other hand, *Trevor is by the post office* rules out the possibility of Trevor being inside the post office. Thus it is necessary to ascribe a 'part' component to the meaning of *by* in order to reflect the fact that it is more specific in meaning than *at*. Similarly, whereas *Trevor went via the library to the post office* leaves unspecified the question of whether or not Trevor entered the library on his way to the post office, the sentence *Trevor went past the library to the post office* states specifically that he did not enter the library. *Past* must therefore be ascribed a 'part' component in order to reflect the fact that it is more specific than *via*. The component I shall ascribe to *by* and *past* will be designated 'proximity'. It may be loosely defined as the space adjacent to some side of a thing. Like 'superior' and other members of our category of parts, 'proximity' could in fact be decomposed into more elementary components of meaning, one of which would be the notion 'side'. It is pointed out by Leech (1969: 175) that the word *side* has three distinct uses, as when we speak of the six sides of a dice, the four sides of a box (excluding top and bottom), and the two sides of a car (excluding top and bottom, and front and back). Accordingly, Leech suggests (1969: 170) that the preposition *by* can express either a general notion of proximity or (more specifically) horizontal proximity, as in *I placed my hat by his*, or (still more specifically) lateral proximity, as in *His car was by mine*. Whether or not we recognize three distinct senses of *by* here depends, of course, on whether or not we recognize three distinct senses of *side*. I am inclined to regard *side* as having only one sense, definable as 'any smooth facet of an object which has not been designated as a top or bottom extremity or as a front or back extremity' (Fillmore 1971b). In fact, however, the present analysis leaves open the question of whether it is necessary at this point to recognize three senses of *by*, since the disjunction in question would involve one component of the notion 'proximity', which we are treating as though it were unanalysable.

We are now able to supply semantic representations for the relevant sections of [45] and [46]. The semantic representations of the *by* examples, [45], are:

[L [proximity of post-office] place]	[47a]
[S [L [proximity of window] place]]	[47b]
[P [L [proximity of post-office] place]]	[47c]
[G [L [proximity of telephone] place]]	[47d]

The string 'locative proximity of' occurs in each of these semantic representations. On the other hand, 'of' would be absent from the semantic representation of *The 113 has just gone by*. Accordingly, I shall regard *by* as being mapped onto the string 'locative proximity'. The semantic representations of the *past* examples, [46], are given in [48].

[P [L [proximity of post-office] place]]	[48a]
[L [P [L [proximity of post-office] place]] place]	[48b]
[S [L [P [L [proximity of post-office] place]] place]]	[48c]
[G [L [P [L [proximity of station] place]] place]]	[48d]

On the basis of these examples *past* is defined componentially as 'path locative proximity'. Of particular interest is the fact that the component 'path' is necessarily present whenever it is appropriate to use *past*, ie the semantic representation necessarily contains a path expression. Thus whereas *over, under, above, below* and *by* may be said to have a locative meaning, *past* has a directional meaning.

It will be observed that the path expression shown as [47c] is identical with the one given as [48a]. The suggestion is, then, that one and the same path expression may be realized either as *by the post office* (*cf* [45c]) or as *past the post office* (*cf* [46a]). When it is realized in the former way, *by* expresses 'locative proximity' and 'path' has no overt realization. When the path expression is realized as *past the post office*, 'path' does have an overt realization in the surface structure, since it is one component of the meaning of *past*.

Notice now also that the gaps in the distribution of *past* (see *Table* 5) are filled by the preposition *by*. Similarly, the gaps in the distribution of *by* (see *Table* 4) are filled by *past*. As is clear from [47] and [48], a single semantic paradigm underlies both the *by* examples, [45], and the *past* examples, [46]. It is appropriate, therefore, to collapse *Tables* 4 and 5 into a single table – see *Table* 6.

In 1.1.1 we spoke at one point of the primary, or basic, use of prepositions such as *behind* and *out of*, and suggested that the semantic representation is relatively simpler in the case of a primary use (compared with a secondary, or derived, use). Let us consider in this connection examples [49] and [50]:

My car is by the post office   [49a]
We drove by the post office   [49b]
My car is past the post office   [50a]
We drove past the post office   [50b]

	S	P	G
level 4, directional	past	?	past
level 3, locative		past	
level 2, directional	S by	P by/past	G by
level 1, locative		by	

Table 6 Summary of the various uses of *by* and *past*

According to the analysis proposed above, the locative expression underlying *by the post office* in [49a] is simpler than the path expression occurring in the semantic representation of [49b]. On the other hand, the locative expression underlying *past the post office* in [50a] is more complex than the path expression occurring in the semantic representation of [50b]. On the question of which use of the two prepositions is primary, it is generally agreed that the locative use of *by* is primary – *cf* [49a] – whereas the directional use of *past* is primary – *cf* [50b]. Thus our semantic representations reflect the intuitions that native speakers of English have about these sentences. With regard to tables such as *Table* 6, the primary use of a preposition corresponds to the lowest of the levels at which the particular preposition occurs (level 1 in the case of *by*, level 2 in the case of *past*). We might also refer to this use as the 'unmarked' use. It would seem likely that the unmarked (or primary, or basic) use of any preposition is more frequent than any of the marked uses.

We turn now to *beyond*. The following examples illustrate the ways in which this preposition can be used:

The theatre is beyond the post office	[51a]
The sound of gunfire came from beyond the post office	[51b]
Trevor walked beyond the post office to his car	[51c]
The passenger fell asleep and went beyond his station	[51d]

As in the case of *past*, there is no simple locative use (*ie* level 1 use) of *beyond*. The locative expression underlying *beyond the post office* in [51a] is a level 3 locative expression. In support of the claim that there is no simple locative use of *beyond*, it should be noted first of all that it is impossible to find sentences containing *beyond* that are ambiguous in the same way as *The helicopter is over the hill*, and secondly that prepositional phrases containing *beyond* are always interpreted deictically. Thus, for instance, the theatre of [51a] is beyond the post office relative to a particular reference point. In the semantic representation of [51b] the level 3 locative expression of [51a] is embedded inside a source expression. The latter is, therefore, a level 4 directional expression. The semantic representation of [51d] contains a level 4 goal expression (*beyond his station* here means 'to a place beyond his station'). And I will assume that *beyond the post office* in [51c] realizes a level 4 path expression. (An alternative analysis would treat it, like [51d], as involving a level 4 goal expression, in which case *beyond the post office* and *to his car* would be in apposition.) The various uses of *beyond* are summarized in *Table* 7. As is clear from this table, we are claiming not only that there is no simple locative use of *beyond* but also that there is no simple directional use (*ie* level 2 use). Two kinds of evidence confirm that this is correct. First, whereas *Trevor walked past the post office to his car* (which contains a level 2 path expression) can be paraphrased as 'Trevor walked via the proximity of the post office to his car', the only way in which [51c] can be paraphrased is by saying 'Trevor walked via a place beyond the post office to his car'. Thus there are two separate journeys involved in [51c]:

	S	P	G
level 4, directional	beyond	beyond	beyond
level 3, locative		beyond	
	S	P	G
level 2, directional	–	–	–
level 1, locative		–	

Table 7 Summary of the various uses of *beyond*

the actual journey that Trevor made in order to get to his car, and the hypothetical journey with reference to which the location 'beyond the post office' is defined. Secondly, the locative use of *beyond*, as in [51a], is felt to be the unmarked use, rather than any directional use, *eg* in *We drove beyond the post office*. The suggestion made earlier that the semantic representation is simpler in the case of the unmarked use implies that the semantic constituent underlying *beyond the post office* should be simpler in *The theatre is beyond the post office* than in *We drove beyond the post office*. This will be true if directional uses of *beyond* are analysed as involving level 4 directional expressions.

Whereas *by* and *past* were attributed a component 'proximity', *beyond* will be attributed no such component. Let us consider in this connection the sentence *The household goods department is beyond children's clothing*. The layout of a particular department store might be such that one would have to go PAST the children's clothing department in order to get to household goods (from a given starting-point). On the other hand, it is equally possible that one would need to go THROUGH children's clothing. The sentence covers either of these two possibilities. This is because *beyond children's clothing* means 'at the end of a path leading VIA children's clothing'. *Via children's clothing* is neutral between *past children's clothing* and *through children's clothing*, in the same way that *at the post office* is neutral between *by the post office* and *in the post office*.

We are now able to give the semantic representations of the relevant sections of [51]:

[L [P [L post-office place]] place]	[52a]
[S [L [P [L post-office place]] place]]	[52b]
[P [L [P [L post-office place]] place]]	[52c]
[G [L [P [L station place]] place]]	[52d]

It will be observed that each of these semantic representations contains the string 'locative path locative'. We therefore propose this as our componential definition of *beyond*.

In conclusion, it should be noted that [52] represents a partial semantic paradigm. It may be augmented by adding the semantic representations listed in [53] ([a] is a level 1 locative expression, and [b–d] are level 2 directional expressions).

[L post-office place]	[53a]
[S [L post-office place]]	[53b]
[P [L post-office place]]	[53c]
[G [L post-office place]]	[53d]

Notice now that the gaps at levels 1 and 2 in *Table 7* by no means imply that the semantic representations of [53] do not occur. They imply simply that it is not appropriate to use *beyond* in realizing [53]. The prepositions that would be used are *at, from, via* and *to*. Before it is appropriate to use *beyond*, the semantic representation must be at least as complex as a level 3 locative expression. Like *over, under, above, below* and *by* (and unlike *past*), *beyond* has a locative meaning. (In the componential definition of all locative prepositions, the leftmost component is the element 'locative'.) However, since *beyond* also contains the directional component 'path', it would be appropriate to say that *beyond* has a directional-locative meaning.

1.2.4 *At, on, in, onto* and *into*

In a study of the spatial uses of four English prepositions Lindkvist (1950) recognizes five senses of *at* and seven senses each of *on* and *in*. According to that analysis, *at* is supposed to have a different meaning in each of the following: *at the door, at the station, at Oxford Street, at the Old Bailey*. From the point of view of the present analysis, the differences reside in the context of the preposition rather than in *at* itself. I shall discuss only one sense of *at, on* and *in*. I leave open the question of whether or not all spatial uses of each preposition can be accounted for in terms of a single sense. At the present time there are a number of uses that are not fully explained. Consider, for instance, the use of *at* exemplified by the sentence *Someone's just thrown a stone at me*. One's first reaction is that this must involve a different sense of *at* from the one occurring in *Gwyneth is at the supermarket*. However, there is a certain similarity between *throw at* and *arrive at*, and it will be recalled that the *at* of *arrive at* is treated here as a realization of the element 'locative' (just like the *at* of *Gwyneth is at the supermarket*). It is conceivable, therefore, that it might ultimately be possible to treat the *at* of *throw at* as yet another realization of the element 'locative'.

I will mention one more problematic example. The sentence *The men were standing in a circle* is ambiguous: either the circle exists separately (*eg* as a white line on the floor) and the men are enclosed by it; or the men are standing in such a way as to form a circle. The most obvious way of handling this ambiguity would be by setting up two distinct senses of the preposition *in*. The trouble with the obvious solution is that, as soon as one has postulated two senses of *in* and characterized them with some appropriate gloss, one is apt to think that all has been said that needs to be said. Specifically, if the ambiguity is treated as residing in the preposition segment of the sentence, there is a danger of assuming that the remainder of the sentence is constant for each interpretation. In fact, however, the underlying structure of the two versions of *The men were standing in a circle* must be very different. Notice in this connection that *The man was standing in a circle* can only have the first kind of interpretation. The same is true of *The men were standing in the circle*. Similarly, it is only when the circle has its own separate existence that one may say *The circle had men in it*. It is, above all, facts of this kind that need to be explained. It is possible that an adequate explanation of these facts might at the same time provide a satisfactory account of the ambiguity of the original sentence, in which case one might no longer need to posit two distinct senses of *in*.

At the opposite extreme from analyses that set up many senses of *at*, *on* and *in* is the kind of analysis that implies that they have the same meaning and that the choice of one rather than another is determined by the nature of the referent of the noun with which it occurs. For instance, in textbooks on English for non-native speakers it is sometimes claimed that large towns require *in*, small islands *on*, and villages *at*. It is true that the physical characteristics of an object may play an important role; however, they do not entirely determine the speaker's usage. What matters is the way an object is thought of on a particular occasion. A town such as Coventry may be thought of as the area enclosed by the city boundary (*eg: The Hollands live in Coventry*), or as a point on an itinerary (*eg: You'll have to change trains at Coventry*), or as a surface (*eg: More bombs were dropped on Coventry than on Nottingham*).

At, on and *in* have a rather restricted distribution, compared with (say) *over. At* may occur in the realization of a goal expression only if the element 'goal' is itself not realized as the preposition *to, eg* in *We've arrived at the station.* When 'goal' is realized as *to*, 'locative' has no realization in the surface structure (which consequently contains no instance of *at*). Thus we say *We went to the station*, rather than **We went to at the station.* I know of no examples in which 'locative' of a source or path expression is realized as *at.* In the majority of cases, then, where a surface structure contains the preposition *at*, the underlying semantic constituent is a simple locative expression. *On* and *in* have a somewhat wider distribution from this point of view. Besides occurring in the realization of simple locative expressions, as in *The book is on the table* and *Gwyneth is in the supermarket*, they also feature in the realization of source and goal expressions: *from on the shelf, from in the kitchen, onto the table, into the kitchen. Onto* and *into* will be discussed below, and *from on* and *from in* will be discussed in 1.2.5, where they will be contrasted with *off* and *out of.* Neither *at*, nor *on*, nor *in* occurs in the realization of a path expression. The path expression preposition corresponding to *at* is *via* (*cf* 1.2.10), and corresponding to *in* we have *through* (*cf* 1.1.1 and again, below, 1.2.8). I shall suggest in 1.2.8 that there is really no path expression counterpart of *on*, but *across* and *along* (jointly) come closest to filling the bill. The fact that *at, on* and *in* do not occur in the realization of path expressions explains also why they have no level 3 locative use of the kind illustrated by *The post office is over the hill* (in which a path expression is embedded inside a locative expression). However, a sentence such as *The lamp stood well into the corner* contains a goal expression embedded inside a locative expression and is therefore similar to *The caretaker lives to the right*, which was briefly mentioned in 1.1.1.

Since *at, on* and *in* occur in the realization of simple locative expressions, it is clear that they have a locative meaning (like *over* and *under*, and unlike *past*). The proposed componential definitions are

> *at:* 'locative'
> *on:* 'locative surface'
> *in:* 'locative interior'

Whereas *on* and *in* are ascribed a 'part' component ('surface' and 'interior', respectively), no such component is attributed to the meaning of *at*. It has been suggested to me on a number of occasions that the meaning of *at* is more specific than is implied by the componential definition given here. It has been pointed out, for instance, that it would be inappropriate to use the sentence *Trevor is at the sofa* to describe a situation in which Trevor is sitting on the floor with his back resting against a sofa. The conclusion drawn from this observation was that an utterance of the form *A is at B* must mean that A is in a specific locative relation to B incompatible with that of the situation just described. It seems to me, however, that we need to draw a distinction at this point between utterances that give an INACCURATE account of a situation and utterances that give an INCOMPLETE account of a situation. If I use the sentence *The dog is under the table* to describe a situation in which a dog is sitting on top of a table, I have given an inaccurate account of the situation. But the sentence *Trevor is at the sofa*, said in response to the situation described above, is not so much an inaccurate account as an incomplete account of the situation. Of course, no account of a situation can be complete. However, it would seem that there are certain features in any situation which command the attention of the majority of observers, with the result that we would expect a speaker to refer to them. (A similar point was made in 1.2.1, when it was suggested that the existence of contact between a hand and a table would normally take precedence over the fact that the hand was in a 'superiority' relation to the table, so that the preposition *on* would be used rather than *over*.) With regard to the situation in which Trevor is sitting on the floor with his back against a sofa, if we describe the situation by means of the sentence *Trevor is at the sofa*, we have simply failed to refer to certain prominent aspects of the situation. Some support for this interpretation of the facts is provided by the following observation. Faced with a situation in which Trevor is sitting on the floor with his back against a sofa, Gwyneth is sitting on the floor with her back against a chair, and several other people occupy an identical position relative to other objects, it would be perfectly appropriate to respond with the sentence *Trevor is at the sofa*. In this instance the exact nature of Trevor's position is of less interest, in view of the fact that it is the generally adopted position.

The relationship between the notion 'contact', which was mentioned in the preceding paragraph and, earlier, in 1.2.1, and the notion 'surface' is exactly parallel to the relationship between 'superiority' and 'superior'. We may say that an object A is in the superiority relationship

to another object B, or that A is at the superior of B. The second formulation comes closer to the kind of semantic representations proposed
here. Similarly, we may say that A is in contact with B, or alternatively
that A is at the surface of B.

The meaning of *on* is considered to be 'locative surface' not only in

There's a picture on the wall [54]

but also in

There's a book on the table [55]

In other words, we recognize no separate sense of *on* that means specifically 'on top of'. The desirability of this policy can be demonstrated by
considering, in addition, a sentence such as

There's a fly on the table [56]

If we were to postulate two distinct senses of *on* in [54] and [55], then
presumably one or other of these two senses would occur in [56] – depending on whether the fly was on top of the table or, say, walking up
one of the legs. But which of the two putative senses occurs if the fly is
standing at the edge of the table with three of its feet on top and the
other three on the side?! The only satisfactory way to handle [56] is to
regard it as indicating simply that the fly is in contact with the table. The
uncertainty that exists as to the exact location of the fly on the table is a
matter of referential vagueness rather than genuine linguistic ambiguity.
Now the only difference between [56] and [55], semantically as well as
syntactically, is that [55] contains *book* where [56] contains *fly*. There is
no difference as far as the meaning of *on* is concerned. A possible objection to this claim might run as follows. Admittedly *on* in [56] means
simply 'at the surface (of)'. In [55], however, it must have a more specific meaning; namely, it must mean 'on top of'. Otherwise we would expect [55] to be capable of describing also a situation in which a book is
attached to some vertical part of a table. Yet to describe such a situation
one would have to say *There's a book attached to the side/leg of the table*;
[55] itself would never convey the appropriate message. The objection
can be answered. The four physically distinct situations implicit in the
above discussion are stated explicitly in [57].

Fly	at	upward horizontal	surface of table	[57a]
Fly	at	vertical	surface of table	[57b]
Book	at	upward horizontal	surface of table	[57c]
Book	at	vertical	surface of table	[57d]

The physical situations of [57a and b] may be said to be different in degree, but are not different in kind. Owing to certain characteristic properties of a fly's feet, there is nothing special about a fly being located on a vertical surface as opposed to an upward-facing horizontal surface. As a result, [56] may describe either situation. The [57c and d] situations, on the other hand, are different in kind. Whereas the force of gravity is sufficient to maintain the state of affairs represented by [c], [d] requires the book to be attached to the table by some means. Thus [d] constitutes a special state of affairs, compared with [c]. Sentence [55] gives an incomplete account of [57d] precisely because it makes no mention of this important feature of the situation. The correctness of the above explanation seems to be confirmed by the observation that there is, after all, a circumstance under which [57d] could be described by [55] – namely, if it was already known that several objects were attached to various items of furniture. In this case it would not be necessary to mention the fact that the book was ATTACHED to the table.

To conclude the discussion of *at*, *on* and *in*, I will briefly contrast my own approach with that of Leech 1969 (65, 161–3). In the course of these remarks I shall refer to the schema for sentences containing the three prepositions given in [58].

A at B	[58a]
A on B	[58b]
A in B	[58c]

The discussion of such sentences in Leech 1969 implies that they do two distinct things: (i) they all specify that B is where A is located, and (ii) they 'ascribe' to B a particular 'dimensionality'. As far as (ii) is concerned, *at* is said to indicate that the dimensions of B are irrelevant; *on* that B is perceived as a line or an area (or surface) – *ie* as one or two dimensional; and *in* that B is seen as an area or volume – *ie* as two or three dimensional. The present approach differs from that of Leech in two respects.

First, I have avoided disjunctions of the kind 'one or two dimensions', 'two or three dimensions'. That is, I do not distinguish between [a] and [b] in [59] and [60].

on the road to London, on the touch-line	[59a]
on the floor, on the grass	[59b]
in Russia, in the garden	[60a]
in the house, in the oven	[60b]

From a mathematical point of view, the touch-line running the length of a football field is no doubt one-dimensional, but no one has ever seen a one-dimensional touch-line. To be visible a touchline needs to have width as well as length. Thus from the point of view of the everyday use of the English language, all the examples in [59] seem to involve surfaces. Similarly, all the examples in [60] involve enclosures, and it would appear that there is little to be gained from drawing a distinction between 'enclosure within an area' (*eg: in Russia*) and 'enclosure within a volume' (*eg: in the house*).

Secondly, in accounting for the difference in meaning between *at, on* and *in,* I have not needed to postulate what Leech refers to as 'ascription features' of dimensionality. (Leech defines 'ascription feature' (1969: 249) as: 'a feature which belongs to a medial cluster, and which does not form part of its componential content, but rather is matched against the content of an adjacent terminal cluster, such that co-occurrence with a systemically contrasting component is marked as a violation'.) In stating the meaning of sentences containing *at, on* and *in,* I refer not so much to the schema of [58] as to that of [61].

A [locative B]	[61a]
A [locative [surface of B]]	[61b]
A [locative [interior of B]]	[61c]

(These formulae may be read as:

B is the location of A
The surface of B is the location of A
The interior of B is the location of A)

Contrasting the two approaches with reference to an actual example, Leech – if I understand him correctly – would say that the sentence *The key is in the drawer* does two things: (i) conveys the message that the drawer is where the key is located, and (ii) ascribes to the drawer the property of being three-dimensional. According to the present analysis, this sentence simply conveys the message that the interior of the drawer is where the key is located.

It has frequently been observed (see, for instance, Gruber 1965: 85 and Leech 1969: 193) that *onto* and *into* can be said to result from the permutation of a more abstract order 'to on' and 'to in'. *Onto* and *into* are regarded in the present analysis as being mapped onto the strings 'goal locative surface' and 'goal locative interior', respectively. Since 'goal' occurs at the left of these strings but *to* occurs at the right of *onto* and *into*, it will be necessary here also to provide some mechanism for delaying the realization of the element 'goal'. The details will be given in 3.5.3.

It will have been noticed that I write *onto* as one word despite the fact that elsewhere the spelling *on to* is rather more common. In general I have no particular desire to tamper with the English orthography, but it seems reasonable to let it reflect the parallelism that exists between *into* and *onto*. Notice that both *into* and *in to* occur and that this orthographic difference is used to represent a difference in meaning. Consider, for instance:

The student went into the library	[62a]
The student went in to the library	[62b]

In [62a] there is only one goal, the interior of the library. In [62b], on the other hand, there are two goals. One of these, expressed simply as *in*, conveys the message: 'to the interior (of some unspecified object)'. The other goal is the library. Thus the sentence says, in effect, 'the student went into the building, to the library'. Notice now that a similar distinction applies also to (what I write as) *onto* and *on to* – see, for instance:

The child ran onto the grass	[63a]
The child ran on to the grass	[63b]

The second of these sentences means 'the child ran further, to the grass'. [63] differs from [62] in so far as the adverb *on* seems to be different in meaning from the first part of *onto*. Nevertheless the two examples have sufficient in common – including especially their rhythmic and intonational patterns – to justify making an orthographic distinction between *onto* and *on to*, parallel to the *into* versus *in to* distinction.

1.2.5 *Away from, off* and *out of*

Wherever the relationship between the meaning of a set of items can be stated in the form of a proportion – *eg: bring: take:: come: go* – it would seem that there ought to be a rather direct connection between the proportion and the componential definition of the items in question. A problem arises in the case of *away from, off* and *out of* in that one can set up different proportions depending on whether locative or directional uses are considered. On the basis of locative uses such as

Trevor is away from home	[64a]
The ball is off the grass	[64b]
Gwyneth is out of the room	[64c]

one can set up the proportion

away from	:	at	::	[65]
off	:	on	::	
out of	:	in		

But [67] is the proportion one would set up on the basis of directional uses such as

John is going away from London	[66a]
The ball has rolled off the table	[66b]
Janet has gone out of the office	[66c]

away from	:	to	::	[67]
off	:	onto	::	
out of	:	into		

Proportion [65] might lead one to propose a componential definition of *away from*, *off* and *out of* like that of [68], which incorporates the earlier definitions of *at*, *on* and *in*, together with an additional component 'negative' (see, for instance, Leech 1969: 163).

away from:	'negative locative'	[68]
off:	'negative locative surface'	
out of:	'negative locative interior'	

However, for two reasons I intend to base the present componential definitions on proportion [67] rather than [65]. We shall see that the resulting definitions will bear little resemblance to [68].

First, it should be noted that the directional uses of *away from*, *off* and *out of* in [66] represent the unmarked, or basic, use of these items, whereas the locative uses in [64] are felt to be marked, or derived. This observation suggests that the semantic representations of [64] should contain level 3 locative expressions, *ie* locative expressions which incorporate directional expressions. However, the definitions given in [68] would be incompatible with such an analysis.

Secondly, there is evidence in support of treating *away from* not as a complex preposition but as a sequence of the adverb *away* followed by the preposition *from*, in which case the meaning of the whole should be derivable from the meaning of *away* and the meaning of *from*. There is no problem in this respect if we base our componential definition on proportion [67] (see below), but the definition of *away from* on the basis of [65] as 'negative locative' (*cf* [68]) treats it as though it were a single unit. The evidence in support of the *away+from* analysis comes from

sentences such as *Trevor is away* and *John is going away*. If we identify
the same item *away* in these two sentences as in [64a] and [66a] – and it
would be uneconomical, to say the least, to do otherwise – then the *away
from* of [64a] and [66a] must be segmentable syntactically into *away+
from*.

We have decided, then, that *away from*, *off* and *out of* are to be attributed a directional meaning, and also that the meaning of *away from* is
to be stated in terms of the meaning of the individual constituents, *away*
and *from*. We need to decide still on the precise details of the analysis,
and in particular we need to determine what directional cases are present. In discussing directional uses of *off* and *out of* a number of writers
have assumed that the proportion

from	: to	::
off	: onto	::
out of	: into	

[69]

is a correct reflection of the meanings of the items in question, *eg* Close
1962: 141 *ff*, Gruber 1965: 86 *ff*, Leech 1969: 194. Now it is quite certain that *from* expresses the notion 'source'. If [69] is correct, then, one
is forced to conclude that phrases such as *off the table* and *out of the office*
realize source expressions. Gruber in fact derives *off* and *out of* from an
underlying 'from on' and 'from in', by means of the same mechanism
that converts 'to on' and 'to in' into *onto* and *into* (1965: 86). However,
as was pointed out in **1.1.1**, it seems to me that [69] is really a conflation
of two separate proportions:

away from	: to	::	[70a]	from	: to	::	[70b]
off	: onto	::		from on	: onto	::	
out of	: into			from in	: into		

One reason for preferring [70] (=[20]) to [69] (=[19]) was indicated in
1.1.1. It has to do with the possibility of conjoining particular phrases.
The pairs of items in the three rows of [69] do not behave alike with regard to conjunction. Thus while *out of the house and into the hole* (see
[17a]) and *off the table and onto my knee* (see [17b]) are perfectly acceptable, *from the house and to the tree* sounds rather less acceptable. In [70],
on the other hand, the pairs of items in the three rows of each proportion behave alike with regard to conjunction. Specifically, conjunction is
quite possible in the case of [70a] but considerably less likely in the case
of [70b].

A second reason for preferring [70] to [69] is that it gives recognition not only to *off* and *out of* but also to *from on* and *from in*. According to Gruber's analysis, *from on* and *from in* do not occur in surface structures, their place being taken by *off* and *out of* (just as 'to on' and 'to in' are converted into *onto* and *into*). It seems to me, however, that the status of *from on* and *from in* is quite different from that of *to on* and *to in*. The latter are simply ungrammatical (**Trevor stepped to on the grass*, **Gwyneth went to in the kitchen*), and it is quite correct to suggest that 'to on' and 'to in' – or in our terms 'goal locative surface' and 'goal locative interior' – are converted into the surface structure forms *onto* and *into*. *From on* and *from in*, on the other hand, while admittedly rare (for reasons that will be explained below), cannot be ruled out as ungrammatical – cf: *A book fell down from on the shelf, Gwyneth appeared from in the kitchen*.

Once we accept the correctness of the two proportions in [70], it becomes necessary to characterize the difference between the left-hand column of [70a] and the left-hand column of [70b], *eg* between *out of* and *from in*. *Out of* involves an underlying goal expression, meaning 'to the exterior (of something)', whereas *from in* involves a source expression, meaning 'from the interior (of something)'. In general, the items in the left-hand column of [70a] involve goal expressions (in the case of *away from* there is also a source expression present); and the left-hand column of [70b] involves source expressions. We see now why it is quite normal to conjoin, say, *out of the house* and *into the hole* – we are dealing with two goal expressions, representing different journeys. On the other hand, *from the house and to the tree* sounds strange because a source expression and a goal expression are normally not conjoined.

We are now in a position to suggest why prepositional phrases containing *from in* and *from on* are rare. The first point that needs to be made can be stated most easily with reference to a diagram – cf: *Fig* 12. The two arrows in this diagram represent the route taken by two people, Trevor and Gwyneth. I will assume, further, that they achieved their respective changes of position by running. Before moving, Trevor was located behind the car shown in *Fig* 12, and Gwyneth was in the post office; *ie* Trevor was 'at the posterior of the car' and Gwyneth was 'at the interior of the post office'. They both ended up at the bus. Notice now that

Trevor ran from behind the car to the bus   [71]

is a perfectly acceptable sentence, but the exactly parallel sentence

Gwyneth ran from in the post office to the bus   [72]

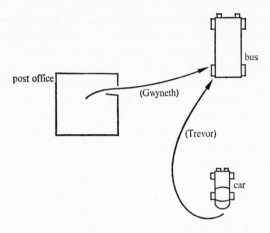

Fig 12 Diagrammatic representation of the journeys described by [71] and [72]

sounds somewhat unusual. We need to account for this difference. On the way from the 'interior' of the post office to the bus, Gwyneth passes from the 'interior' to the 'exterior' of the post office. Similarly, Trevor passes from being at the 'posterior' of the car to being at a place which is not at the 'posterior' of the car. However, the transition from 'interior' to 'exterior' seems to involve a more clearly defined boundary than the transition from 'posterior' to 'non-posterior' – so much so, in fact, that reaching the 'exterior' of something is normally perceived as constituting a journey in itself. I base this statement on the observation that

Gwyneth ran out of the post office and to the bus   [73]

– which describes two successive journeys – gives a more acceptable account of Gwyneth's change of position than [72]. (The sentence *Gwyneth ran from the post office to the bus* describes only one journey, but avoids the present issue by treating the post office in general as the source, rather than specifically the 'interior' of the post office.)

A journey from the interior of some object X necessarily involves going to the exterior of X. Similarly, a journey to the exterior of X necessitates moving from the interior of X. For this reason it would be redundant for a directional sentence to contain both *out of X* and *from in X*. Thus a choice will always be made between these alternative ways of specifying the change of position in question. Now if we refer to the location which features in a goal or path expression as the 'later location' and the location that features in a source expression as the 'earlier location', then it seems to be true that the later location is usually treated by a speaker as more important than the earlier location (presumably because it is frequently the location of some subsequent event). Often the earlier location is treated as being recoverable from the preceding discourse, and therefore not overtly indicated. In other words, source expressions are marked, vis-à-vis path and goal expressions. With regard to the choice between *out of X* and *from in X*, this explains why *out of X* is more frequently chosen (it specifies the later location). *From in X* typically occurs in sentences in which the later location is specified in some other way, *eg: Gwyneth suddenly appeared from in the post office* (in which *appear* realizes a goal expression).

(Besides [73], it is possible also to say

Gwyneth ran out of the post office to the bus   [74]

in which the two goal expressions are in apposition. This sentence describes a single journey rather than two successive journeys, but defines the journey in two different ways: the movement that takes Gwyneth to the exterior of the post office takes her at the same time to where the bus is located.)

The facts concerning *from on* are quite similar. The sentence *?The book fell from on the shelf onto the table* is just as odd as [72]. Far more acceptable is *The book fell off the shelf and onto the table*, in which the movement of the book is broken down into two successive journeys. It would seem, then, that the transition from the 'surface' of some object to a position not in contact with the object is normally perceived as constituting a journey in itself. *The book fell from the shelf onto the table* describes only one journey, but treats the shelf in general as the source, rather than specifically the 'surface' of the shelf. In *The book fell down from on the shelf*, *down* specifies the later location and *from on the shelf* the earlier location.

The semantic representation of *Gwyneth went out of the kitchen* is:

[Gwyneth [go [G [L [exterior of kitchen] place]]]]

and that of *Gwyneth went out* is:

[Gwyneth [go [G [L exterior place]]]]

In the locative sentence *Gwyneth is out of the room* the goal expression underlying *out of the room* is embedded inside a higher locative expression:

[Gwyneth [be [L [G [L [exterior of room] place]] place]]]

Each of these semantic representations contains the string 'goal locative exterior', which is therefore proposed as the componential definition of *out*. (The relationship between *out* and *out of* will be discussed after componential definitions have been proposed for *off* and *away from*.)

Semantic representations of sentences containing *off* are quite parallel to those containing *out of* and will therefore not be given here. A minor labelling problem arises, however, owing to the fact that there is no obvious term for X in the following proportion

interior : exterior ::
surface :   X

– *ie* while 'exterior' is the converse of 'interior', 'surface' has no obvious converse term. I shall therefore use 'off' for the component of the meaning of *off* which is analogous to the component 'exterior' of *out*. (The fact that it is enclosed by quotation marks rather than italicized will remind us that 'off' is not the lexeme *off* but merely one component of its meaning.) *Off* may now be defined componentially as 'goal locative off'.

The semantic representation of the sentence *Trevor went away from London* is:

[Trevor [go [[S [L London place]] [G [L some place]]]]]

From London realizes the source expression '[source [locative London place]]'; and *away* realizes the goal expression '[goal [locative some place]]', *ie* the suggestion is that *away* means 'to some place'. The two directional expressions are regarded as occurring in the order: source— goal in the semantic representation. The fact that they appear in the opposite order in the surface structure is attributable to the fact that the goal expression is realized in this instance as an adverb and that adverbs apparently have to precede prepositional phrases irrespective of the cases that they represent – *cf*

The bird flew in through the window
*The bird flew through the window in
Trevor walked across to the post office
*Trevor walked to the post office across

(For further discussion, see 3.4.2.) In *Trevor is away from home* the source and goal expressions underlying *away from home* are embedded inside a locative expression. The componential definition of *away* is 'goal locative some place'; *from* realizes 'source' (as elsewhere).

Finally, it should be noted that the policy adopted in this book on the subject of the semantic element 'of' and the preposition *of* was determined to a large extent by the behaviour of *out* and *out of*. Of particular interest in this connection is a dialect difference between the writer's dialect, standard British English, and certain other varieties of English including most varieties of American English. Corresponding to standard British English

The bird flew out of the window [75]

American English has

The bird flew out the window [76]

either instead of or at least in addition to [75]. Now it is not the case that all prepositional phrases consisting of *out of* followed by a noun phrase in standard British English correspond to prepositional phrases in American English consisting of *out* followed by a noun phrase. For instance, [77] is said in each of the dialects; moreover, [78] – from which *of* is omitted – is ungrammatical not only in standard British English but also in American English.

The bird flew out of the house [77]
*The bird flew out the house [78]

It is clear that the surface structure distinction in American English between *out* in [76] and *out of* in [77] is determined by the semantic structure of the two sentences. *Out of the house* means 'to the exterior of the house'. On the other hand, *out (of) the window* does not mean 'to the exterior of the window'; rather, it means 'to the exterior (*eg* of the house) via the window'. Thus *out of the house* realizes the goal expression

[G [L [exterior of house] place]] [79]

but *out (of) the window* realizes a path expression and a goal expression:

[P [L window place]] [G [L exterior place]] [80]

We see from [79] and [80] that the preposition *of* may be said to be semantically justified in *out of the house* – it marks the fact that the 'exterior' referred to is the exterior of the house, *cf* [79]. On the other hand, the *of* of standard British English *out of the window* is not semantically justified, *cf* [80]. Thus American English and all other dialects that say [76] and [77] (rather than [75] and [77]) reflect the semantic structure more directly than standard British English. As far as the latter dialect is concerned, it is desirable to recognize two different *ofs* in *out of the house* and *out of the window*. We need to show that the first *of* is the realization in surface structure of the semantic element 'of', whereas the second *of* is an empty preposition which is inserted in the absence of any other preposition (*out* itself functions only as an adverb in standard British English). Further discussion of 'of' and *of* is postponed until Part III.

1.2.6 *Inside* and *outside*

Whereas *out* has a directional meaning, *inside* and *outside* have a locative meaning. The examples in [81] and [82] exhibit locative, source, path and goal uses of each preposition.

The dog was inside the house	[81a]
There's a noise coming from inside your car	[81b]
The dog ran from the front door inside the house to the back door	[81c]
The dog ran inside the house (*ie* to)	[81d]
The dog was outside the house	[82a]
I fetched this chair from outside the dining room	[82b]
The dog ran from the front door outside the house to the back door	[82c]
The dog ran outside the house (*ie* to)	[82d]

[81a] and [82a] represent the unmarked use of *inside* and *outside*, rather than (say) [81d] and [82d]. This provides evidence that [81a] and [82a] involve level 1 locative expressions, the internal structure of which is simpler than that of the goal expressions in [81d] and [82d]. *Out of* can be substituted for the goal use of *outside* in [82d], giving *The dog ran out of the house*. This is to be expected in view of the fact that the notion 'goal' is part of the meaning of *out of*. It is likewise to be expected that *out of* cannot replace *outside* in [82b]. In what is usually regarded as sub-standard English one can encounter sentences such as *I fetched this chair from out of the dining room*, but the meaning would be different from that of [82b] since this sentence would indicate that the chair was originally inside the dining room rather than outside (as in the case of [82b]). With regard to the path use of *outside*, *cf* [82c], again we would predict that *out of* cannot be substituted for *outside*. There is a sentence *The dog ran from the front door out of the house to the back door*, but it is not a paraphrase of [82c]. Finally, *out of* can be substituted for *outside* in [82a], but the resulting sentence would be analysed as containing a level 3 rather than a level 1 locative expression (*cf* **1.2.5**).

When we compare the prepositions *in* and *inside*, we see that *inside* may be substituted for *in* in some contexts but not in others. Besides *Trevor is in the house* we may also say *Trevor is inside the house*. However, corresponding to *Trevor is in the water* there is no sentence **Trevor is inside the water*; nor is there a sentence **I found this spoon inside the sand* corresponding to *I found this spoon in the sand*. It would seem, then, that the morphological structure of *inside* – specifically, the fact that it contains the morpheme *side* – reflects its semantic structure. Before it is appropriate to say X *is inside* Y it must be the case that Y has sides. A house does have sides, but water and sand do not. Accordingly, sentences of the form X *is inside* Y will be attributed the semantic structure:

[X [be [L [interior of [side of Y]] place]]]

Similarly, sentences of the form X *is outside* Y will be attributed the semantic structure:

[X [be [L [exterior of [side of Y]] place]]]

Inside and *outside* are then defined as 'locative interior of side' and 'locative exterior of side', respectively. In 1.2.3 it was pointed out that the notion 'proximity', which was ascribed to the meaning of *by* and *past*, is in fact complex and contains the notion 'side'. Since many of the 'part' components of the present analysis are semantically complex, no attempt was made to reduce 'proximity' to a set of components that are not further analysable. It is a little arbitrary, therefore, to invoke the notion 'side' in defining the meaning of *inside* and *outside*. However, it was necessary to assign *inside* a different componential definition from *in*.

1.2.7 *In front of* and *behind*
A typical set of examples containing *in front of* and *behind* is given in [83] and [84].

Your car is in front of the bus	[83a]
You must move your car from in front of the bus	[83b]
Trevor ran in front of the bus to his car	[83c]
Trevor ran in front of the bus (*ie* to)	[83d]
Your car is behind the bus	[84a]
You must move your car from behind the bus	[84b]
Trevor ran behind the bus to his car	[84c]
Trevor ran behind the bus (*ie* to)	[84d]

The [a] examples involve simple locative expressions; the [b, c and d] examples involve source, path and goal expressions. There is no level 3 locative use of *in front of* or *behind*. Thus *behind the station* could never mean 'at the end of a path leading behind the station'. To express this meaning in English one would have to say something like *past the back of the station*.

The existence of level 1 locative uses makes it clear that *in front of* and *behind* have a locative meaning, *ie* 'locative' is their leftmost component. In addition, *in front of* is ascribed a component 'anterior', loosely definable as the space adjacent to the front of something, and *behind* is attributed a component 'posterior', definable as the space adjacent to the back of something. These two components are ascribed also to *before* and *after* (*cf* 2.2.2). In order to reflect the fact that *in front of* and *behind* have a specifically spatial meaning, the element 'place' is also regarded as part of their meaning. In this way we ensure that *in front of* and *behind* are used only in the realization of spatial locative expressions. The two componential definitions are, therefore:

in front of: 'locative anterior place'
behind: 'locative posterior place'

It is appropriate that 'place' should be regarded as one of the components of *in front of* and *behind* but not of, say, *in*. *In* is, namely, less specific in meaning, in so far as it has both spatial and temporal uses. The question now arises whether all prepositions that have only spatial uses should be ascribed the component 'place'. For instance, should *under* be defined as 'locative inferior place' rather than simply 'locative inferior'? It is, in fact, unnecessary to ascribe the component 'place' to *under*, since there is another way of blocking the generation of prepositional phrases such as *under September*. Speakers of English are aware of what things have, say, an 'interior' or an 'inferior'. They know that both physical objects and periods of time (but not points in time) have an 'interior' – *cf: in the house, in August*, but not **in 10 o'clock*. And they know that while physical objects have an 'inferior', periods of time and points in time do not – *cf: under the table*, but not **under September*, **under 10 o'clock*. If we were to characterize this knowledge and make it available to the parts of the grammar that we are more directly concerned with here, then *under September* would be blocked by virtue of the fact that 'September' has no 'inferior'. (I should perhaps add that it is not difficult to imagine certain contexts in which it would be appropriate to say *under September*. For instance, the following is a perfectly acceptable discourse: *The October page is missing from this calendar. It should be under September, but it's not there.* However, *September* here designates a physical object, namely a sheet of paper, rather than a period of time.) With regard to *in front of* and *behind*, it is necessary to employ a different method of showing that they are specifically spatial in meaning (than that used in the case of *under*), since not only physical objects but also periods of time, points in time and events and states have an 'anterior' and a 'posterior'.

Buses and stations both belong to the class of objects that have an inherent front and back. The front of a bus is the side which normally leads when it moves. And the front of a station is the side which is most frequently seen (*cf* Leech 1969: 167). Objects such as trees and wastepaper baskets have no inherent front and back. Nevertheless, we can still describe something as being *behind the tree* or *in front of the wastepaper basket.* This is because front and back may be deictically defined: the front of an object, according to this usage, is the side nearest to the place which the speaker treats as a reference point, and the back is the side furthest away from the reference point. Frequently the speaker's own position is his reference point, but in a sentence such as *I was hiding behind a tree* the location 'behind a tree' is defined from someone else's point of view. Even in the case of an object that has an inherent front and back, a speaker may nevertheless refer to a deictically defined front and back. This is why sentences such as *Trevor is behind the bus* are often ambiguous.

The location specified in a sentence such as *The post office is over the hill* was also said to be deictically interpreted. There is a difference, however, between this kind of sentence and, say, *The ball is behind the tree.* In the former example the reference point is the starting-point of a journey that would take one to the location in question. In *The ball is behind the tree*, on the other hand, the speaker's reference point is a 'point of observation' (Leech 1969: 180–2). What the two examples have in common, however, is that they use the same means of indicating the speaker's reference point whenever it is overtly specified: namely, a prepositional phrase introduced by *from.* Thus we say *The post office is over the hill from here* and *The ball is behind the tree from here.*

In American English *behind* has a synonym *in back of* (not used in British English). *In back of* may be assigned the same componential definition as *behind.* It seems, however, that *in back of* has only a non-deictic interpretation. This poses a particular problem as regards the formalization of the analysis which I have not attempted to solve.

1.2.8 *Through, across, along* and *(a)round*

Through occurs in sentences such as

The train went through the tunnel	[85a]
The station is through the tunnel	[85b]
A faint cry was heard coming from through the tunnel	[85c]

Admittedly the last example sounds a little far-fetched. Nevertheless, native speakers are able to understand what it is supposed to mean, and the mechanism for generating the directional expression in question is already available. There is no level 1 locative use of *through*, *in* being the preposition that would occur in the realization of such a structure (*cf* 1.1.1, 1.2.4). [85a] contains a path expression in its semantic representation; [85b] contains a level 3 locative expression; and in [85c] the locative expression of the preceding example is embedded inside a level 4 source expression. The various locative and directional uses of *in* and *through* are summarized in *Table* 8. This table is similar to *Table* 6, which summarizes the locative and directional uses of *by* and *past*. The most important difference between the two involves level 2 path expressions. Both *by* and *past* may occur in the realization of such a structure – *cf: The bus drove by/past the station* – but only *through* of the pair *through/in* has a comparable use.

When we consider sentences such as

There's a wire through the tube	[86]

it becomes clear that it is necessary to recognize an additional locative use of *through*. The sentence is ambiguous. On one interpretation it is

	S	P	G
level 4, directional	through	?	?
level 3, locative		through	
	S	P	G
level 2, directional	in	through	in
level 1, locative		in	

Table 8 Summary of the locative and directional uses of *in* and *through*

like [85b] and involves a level 3 locative expression. On the other interpretation, the wire extends through the tube from one end to the
other. In this case the sentence is like *It goes from Buckingham Palace to
Trafalgar Square*, said in answer to the question *Where is the Mall?* (*cf*
1.1.2, 1.1.3). The relevant section of the semantic representation of this
version of [86] is given as [87d] (*cf: Fig* 9, 1.1.3). Semantic representations corresponding to [85a–c] are given as [87a–c].

[P [L [interior of tunnel] place]]	[87a]
[L [P [L [interior of tunnel] place]] place]	[87b]
[S [L [P [L [interior of tunnel] place]] place]]	[87c]
[L [E [go [P [L [interior of tube] place]]] place] place]	[87d]

According to the proposals made in 1.1.3 concerning level 3 locative
expressions, [87b and c] would need to be elaborated somewhat. Nevertheless, it is clear that *through* needs to be defined as 'path locative interior'. (The 'of' that occurs in [87a–d] is, of course, absent whenever
we are dealing with an adverbial use of *through*.)

The various uses of *through* are paralleled by uses of *across*, *along* and
(*a*)*round*. Path expression uses of these three prepositions occur in

She walked across the road to the bank
She walked along the road to the bank
She walked round the corner to the bank

The path expressions in question are:

[P [L [transverse of road] place]]	[88a]
[P [L [length of road] place]]	[88b]
[P [L [surround of corner] place]]	[88c]

'Transverse', 'length' and 'surround' – like 'interior' – are members of
the semantic category of 'parts'. It has been pointed out above, with
regard to other members of this category, that they are semantically
complex. The same is certainly true of 'transverse', 'length' and 'surround', but as in the case of other members of the category I shall not
attempt here to reduce them to more elementary components of meaning.
The following loose definitions of 'transverse', 'length' and 'surround'
should be regarded as having no more than a purely practical value.
'Length' will be defined first. The 'length' of an object (in the present
sense) is a part of the space surrounding it which runs in the same direction as its major horizontal axis. Now when one walks along a road, one
is in contact with the road. This might suggest that [88b] should contain
the notion 'surface', which was ascribed in 1.2.4 to the meaning of *on*.

However, like 'superior', 'posterior', etc, the 'length' of an object should be understood as extending right up to the object itself – which means that the possibility of contact is already catered for. In any case, one can argue that in many instances there is no contact – *cf: There are trees all along the road*, in which the trees might well be at the side of the road rather than actually on it. The 'transverse' of an object is a part of the space surrounding it which runs roughly at right angles to the direction of its major horizontal axis. (Leech points out that *across* is also used, rather than *along*, when an object has no major horizontal axis (1969: 185).) As in the case of *along*, it is both unnecessary and, indeed, undesirable to attribute the notion 'surface' to the meaning of *across* – unnecessary because the 'transverse' of an object extends right up to the object itself, and undesirable in view of examples such as *Trevor jumped across the stream*, in which there is presumably no contact between Trevor and the stream.

Expanding somewhat on the above remarks concerning the notion 'surface', it seems to me that there is no English preposition which fills the space occupied by X in the following proportion:

at : on : in   ::
via : X : through

The best candidates are (jointly) *along* and *across*. However, whereas *through* – like *in* – necessarily involves the notion 'interior', the notion 'surface' is not necessarily present when *along* and *across* are used. In other words, there is no preposition which necessarily implies 'via the surface of'.

The 'surround' of an object may be loosely defined as the space surrounding it. The difference between this and 'proximity' (*cf* 1.2.3) can be made clear by comparing the two sentences *We drove past the church* and *We drove round the church*. 'Proximity' involves some side of an object; the 'surround' of an object involves all, or at least, most of its sides.

So far we have considered only the path expression use of *across*, *along* and *(a)round*. Level 3 locative expressions occur in the semantic representations of the following examples, which are therefore parallel to the [85b] *through* example:

The post office is across the road   [89]
The post office is along the road
The post office is round the corner

Level 4 directional uses are illustrated by:

The sound of hammering was heard coming from across the road/
along the road/round the corner

(cf [85c]). Parallel to the ambiguous *through* example *There's a wire
through the tube* we have:

There's a tree across the road	[90a]
There are some trees along the road	[90b]
There's a white line round the corner	[90c]

On one interpretation these sentences simply provide further examples
of the type illustrated by [89]. On the other interpretation, the tree of
[90a] is lying across the road, the trees of [90b] are lining the road, and
the white line of [90c] extends round the corner. Semantic representations for each of the above examples need not be given explicitly, since
they can easily be derived from [87] and [88].

At this point we are almost in a position to propose componential
definitions for *across*, *along* and *(a)round*. There is just one further use of
(a)round that needs to be taken into consideration. The sentence

People were thronging the streets around St Paul's Cathedral

involves a locative use of *around*. However, the streets referred to are not
at the end of a path leading around St Paul's Cathedral from a given
starting-point – *ie* we are not dealing with a level 3 locative expression.
Nor do they extend around St Paul's Cathedral. What we have, rather,
is a simple locative use, comparable to the use of *in* in the sentence *There's
a wire in the tube*. The locative expression in question is:

[L [surround of St-Paul's-Cathedral] place]

There is no comparable level 1 locative use of *across* and *along*; and
there is certainly no level 1 locative use of *through*, since *in* is its corresponding simple locative preposition. Here, then, is a difference between
(a)round, on the one hand, and *through*, *across* and *along*, on the other,
which is important as far as our componential definitions are concerned.
Through, *across* and *along* have a directional meaning; *(a)round* is locative. The meaning of *through* was defined above. The other three componential definitions are:

across:	'path locative transverse'
along:	'path locative length'
(a)round:	'locative surround'

A brief word may be added, in conclusion, on the relative frequency of *around* and *round*. In American English *around* is rather more common than *round*, and the shorter form is sometimes written with an initial apostrophe (*'round*), indicating that it is felt to be an abbreviation of *around*. In British English, on the other hand, *round* is far more common. In a book aimed primarily at foreign students of (British) English, Wood writes (1967: 72):

> Since there is a great deal of confusion over these two words, the best advice that can be given is to restrict *around* to the expression of the idea of vicinity . . ., and in all other cases to use *round*.

Examples such as *the streets around St Paul's Cathedral* are what Wood has in mind in speaking of 'the idea of vicinity'; but, as is seen from Wood's own examples of this use, *round* is also possible here. It is unclear to me whether any correlation can be made between the semantic structure in a given instance and the likelihood that one or other of the two forms will occur.

1.2.9 *Up* and *down*

Up and *down* occur in sentences such as

Trevor walks up the hill every day	[91a]
Gwyneth lives up the hill	[91b]
The dog has just run down the stairs	[92a]
The dog is downstairs	[92b]

The [a] examples are directional and the [b] examples locative. Two facts indicate that the locative expressions occurring in the semantic representation of the [b] examples are level 3 locative expressions. First, the directional examples seem to represent the unmarked use of *up* and *down*, which suggests that the locative expressions have a more complex internal structure. Secondly, locative prepositional phrases containing *up* and *down* are always interpreted deictically – a location which is 'up the hill' from, say, the bottom of the hill may at the same time be 'down the hill' with reference to some other point. Other types of sentences in which *up* and *down* occur are illustrated by *This ball must have come from up the hill* and *There's a road up the hill*. The former involves a level 4 source expression. The latter example is ambiguous in the same way as [86], *There's a wire through the tube*. Thus the road is either located up the hill from some reference point, or it extends up the hill.

From our remarks concerning [91] and [92] it is clear that *up* and *down* are directional in meaning, but we have still to determine what directional case is present in their meaning. At first sight the evidence is somewhat conflicting. The similarity between *We walked up the hill to the church* and *We walked through the park to the church* implies that *up the hill* – like *through the park* – realizes a path expression. Such an analysis is supported also by the observation that the hill must have been on the route to the church. Evidence of a different kind is provided by the fact that *up* and *down* belong to the set of items that can take the suffix *-wards*, *cf*: *towards, outwards, inwards, backwards, forwards, upwards, downwards*. All of these words seem to contain the notion 'goal' rather than 'path' (see further 1.2.10). Our account of the semantic structure of [75] and [76], *The bird flew out (of) the window*, suggests a way of resolving the conflict. It will be recalled that *out (of) the window* was considered to realize not one but two directional expressions, a goal expression meaning 'to the exterior' and a path expression meaning 'via the window'. I propose, therefore, to analyse *up the hill* in a parallel way. *Up* derives from a goal expression meaning 'to a higher place', and *the hill* derives from a path expression meaning 'via the hill'. (Gruber's (1965: 36, 98) analysis is similar.)

Up and *down* may now be defined as 'goal locative higher' and 'goal locative lower'. (It seems unnecessary to ascribe the notion 'place' to them, in view of the fact that 'higher' and 'lower' could not apply to times.) As was pointed out in 1.2.2, the notions 'higher' and 'lower' are obviously complex and probably involve extent expressions. In reducing them to more elementary components of meaning, it would be necessary also to pay adequate attention to the implied *than*-phrase, explaining how it is that the higher place involved in *John's picture is above the shelf* is higher than the shelf, whereas the higher place involved in *Trevor walked up the hill* is higher than Trevor's starting-point rather than higher than the hill. The explanation will presumably have to refer to the fact that *above the shelf* derives from a single locative expression, whereas *up the hill* derives from two separate directional expressions, but the exact details are not clear to me.

1.2.10 *From, via, to, towards* and *for*

From, via, to and *for* realize the notions 'source', 'path', 'goal' and 'extent'. ('Path' may also be realized as *by way of*.) 'Source' is apparently the only one of these four notions which is always overtly expressed in the surface structure – either as one component of a verb such as *leave* or as the preposition *from*. In *Trevor walked behind the desk to the door* there is no overt realization of the element 'path'. In *Trevor walked behind the door*, meaning 'to behind the door', 'goal' has zero realization;

and the same is true of 'extent' in *There's a railway line from Darlington to Stockton*. Specifying the conditions under which 'path', 'goal' and 'extent' (and also 'locative') may be realized as zero is a difficult task. I will do no more than mention a few of the facts concerning the notion 'goal' that need to be taken into account, and at the same time refer to one proposal – that of Gruber 1965 – for handling some of these facts.

Consider first of all the sentences in [93] and the accompanying semantic representations of the relevant sections:

The ball has rolled behind the tree   [93a]
    [G [L [posterior of tree] place]]
The ball has rolled to the tree   [93b]
    [G [L tree place]]
The ball is to the right of the tree   [93c]
    [L [G [L [right of tree] place]] place]

In [93a] 'locative posterior of tree place' is realized as *behind the tree*, and 'goal' has zero realization. If [93b] were to parallel [93a], presumably 'locative tree place' would have to be realized as *at the tree* and 'goal' would again have zero realization. In fact, however, 'goal' is expressed as *to*, and there is no overt realization of the notion 'locative'. The goal expression of [93c] is embedded inside a higher locative expression and the sentence as a whole specifies the location of the ball. Nevertheless, the initial 'locative' element has no overt realization, only 'goal' being expressed (as *to*). [93b and c] seem to indicate that *to* takes precedence over *at*, irrespective of whether the semantic representation contains a level 2 goal expression or a level 3 locative expression. On the other hand, in the presence of the more specific locative preposition *behind*, *to* itself is omitted (*cf* [93a]).

In sentences containing the locative prepositions *on* and *in*, the presence or absence of *to* in the realization of a goal expression depends on the meaning of the neighbouring verb. Thus while *The ball has rolled into the hole*, containing *to*, is undoubtedly more acceptable than *The ball has rolled in the hole*, there is no need to insert *to* in a sentence such as *Trevor has jumped in the river*. Gruber notes that *drop* may be followed either by *on* or by *onto*, but that *sink* requires *onto* rather than *on*:

The ball dropped on the table   [94a]
The ball dropped onto the table   [94b]
The rocks sank onto the floor of the tub   [94c]
*The rocks sank on the floor of the tub   [94d]

He suggests (1965: 154) that whenever the underlying representation of a sentence contains a succession of 'Motional' (*ie* directional) prepositions, the second one may become 'nonMotional'. *Onto* in [94b] is affected by this rule, since *drop* is said to incorporate *down*, which means that *onto* is the second of two Motional prepositions; hence the possibility also of [94a]. But the *onto* that occurs in [94c] is unaffected by the rule, since *sink* is analysed as incorporating not only *down* but also a *from*-phrase, which means that *onto* is not the second but the third Motional preposition in this sentence. One would like to see more evidence in support of the claim that *sink* incorporates a *from*-phrase. But in any case it is difficult to reconcile Gruber's rule with sentences of the kind *The dog went from under the table to behind the door*, in which it is not possible to delete the *to*. (Gruber suggests that in such sentences the tendency for the deletion of *to* is not so strong, 1965: 87.)

Towards (American English *toward*) is usually glossed in dictionaries as 'in the direction of'. Accordingly, one might perhaps suppose that a prepositional phrase introduced by *towards* realizes a path expression rather than a goal expression. However, when we examine relevant examples, we are forced to conclude that, like *to*, *towards* occurs in the realization of goal expressions. Specifically, the pair of sentences in [95] parallel each other semantically, but not those in [96].

We walked through the park to the river   [95]
We walked through the park towards the river
We drove past the post office to the station   [96]
We drove towards the post office to the station

Thus we assign the notion 'goal' to the meaning of *towards*, together with an additional component that can conveniently be labelled 'wards'. This second component seems to have an aspectual meaning of incompletion, *ie* it indicates that the goal in question is not actually reached. We may note in this connection that *towards* frequently co-occurs with the progressive aspect, *eg: John was walking towards the bus station when I saw him*.

Both *to* and *towards* occur also in locative sentences, in the realization of level 3 locative expressions. [93c] illustrates such a use of *to*. The corresponding use of *towards* occurs in *The post office is towards the station* (*from here*). There is no comparable use of the preposition *via* – presumably as a result of the existence of *beyond*, which means 'at the end of a path leading via'.

The only sense of the preposition *for* with which we have been directly concerned is the one that occurs in sentences such as *We walked along the road for three miles*, in which *for* expresses the notion 'extent'. Another important spatial use of this preposition is illustrated by sentences such as *When are you leaving for South America?* Here *for* seems to indicate a destination. Conceivably, then, we should treat *for*, as well as *to*, as a possible realization of the element 'goal'. However, it would be necessary to specify the conditions under which 'goal' is realized as *for* rather than *to*. It is relevant here to note that the various verbs with which *for* occurs – *eg: leave, set sail, take off, depart, set out* – all seem to contain the notion 'goal' as part of their meaning. Thus if *for* does express the notion 'goal' – and this is by no means certain – it would appear that we are dealing with a subsequent goal rather than a single goal (as in *Trevor walked to the window*).

1.2.11 Summary of the componential analysis

The componential analysis of the meaning of the prepositions discussed in the foregoing subsections is now summarized in two tables. *Table* 9 contains the prepositions which were analysed as having a locative meaning. *Table* 10 contains the directional prepositions and *for*. In each table the prepositions occur in alphabetical order. They will be arranged rather differently in 3.3.1.

above:	'locative higher'
(a)round:	'locative surround'
at:	'locative'
behind:	'locative posterior place'
below:	'locative lower'
beyond:	'locative path locative'
by:	'locative proximity'
in:	'locative interior'
in back of:	'locative posterior place'
in front of:	'locative anterior place'
inside:	'locative interior of side'
on:	'locative surface'
outside:	'locative exterior of side'
over:	'locative superior'
under:	'locative inferior'

Table 9 Summary of the componential analysis of the locative prepositions

across:	'path locative transverse'
along:	'path locative length'
away (from):	'goal locative some place'
down:	'goal locative lower'
for:	'extent'
from:	'source'
into:	'goal locative interior'
off:	'goal locative off'
onto:	'goal locative surface'
out (of):	'goal locative exterior'
past:	'path locative proximity'
through:	'path locative interior'
to:	'goal'
towards:	'goal wards'
up:	'goal locative higher'
via:	'path'

Table 10 Summary of the componential analysis of the non-locative prepositions

Part Two

Temporal uses of English prepositions

2.1 Overall structure of the analysis

2.1.1 Location, direction and extent in relation to time

In the course of Part I five cases were recognized: 'locative', 'source', 'path', 'goal' and 'extent'. I shall begin the discussion of temporal uses of English prepositions by determining whether all five of these cases are again relevant. In introducing the 'locative' and 'extent' cases in 1.1.1 and 1.1.2, it was pointed out that it would be necessary to postulate temporal locative expressions and extent expressions in addition to spatial ones. For instance, the sentence *I saw Gwyneth at 10 o'clock* locates the event of 'my seeing Gwyneth' at a particular point in time; and *We were walking through the forest for two hours* indicates the temporal extent of 'our walking through the forest'. Clearly, then, it is necessary to invoke these two cases in relation to time. Similarly, 'source' and 'goal' – the labels we chose to apply to the general notions 'beginning' and 'end' (*cf* 0.2 and 1.1.1) – apply both to space and time. Temporal instances of 'source' and 'goal' occur in the sentence *The film lasted from seven o'clock to nine o'clock*. With regard to 'path', it would seem that there must be a fixed route between any pair of points in time, owing to the unidimensional nature of time (see below). For instance, when it is a question of getting from seven o'clock to nine o'clock, there is hardly any choice of which way to go. Consequently, one might suppose that it would be unnecessary to posit path expressions as far as time is concerned. However, prepositional phrases such as *throughout the evening* in the sentence *I was writing letters throughout the evening until one o'clock in the morning* force us to recognize temporal path expressions after all.

We see, then, that all five cases which featured in Part I will again be invoked in Part II. Nevertheless, there are a number of respects in which the temporal analysis will not parallel the spatial analysis. To a large extent this asymmetry is the result of two well-known properties of time, its unidimensionality and its unidirectionality.

The consequences of the unidimensionality of time are rather straightforward. Besides the fact (already noted) that there is only one possible route between any two points in time, there are simply fewer ways in which two things may be related to each other in time than in space. Since space is three-dimensional, the various possible ways in which two objects may be related to each other include not only *at, on, in, in front of* and *behind* but also *over* and *under*, and *at/to the right of* and *at/to the left of*. As far as time is concerned, the last four possibilities have no equivalent. (A rather marginal possible exception to this statement is provided by examples such as *We were in Brighton over the weekend*, in which it might conceivably be claimed that the use of *over* implies that the weekend is something to which one can be related in a vertical dimension – as though it were a kind of hill or chasm.)

With regard to the unidirectional nature of time, whereas space is regarded from the point of view of the English language as motionless, time is regarded as perpetually moving, and moving always in the same direction. To say, however, that time is perpetually moving is not sufficiently precise. Fillmore points out (1971b) that English uses two quite distinct metaphors in talking about time. One and the same period of time may be referred to as *the coming months* or *the months ahead*. Only in the case of the first phrase is time itself treated as moving. Here it is as though time were a kind of conveyor-belt travelling past a stationary observer. *The coming months* designates a particular stretch of the conveyor-belt which has not yet reached the observer. On the other hand, when we say *the months ahead*, we seem to be picturing time as stationary and ourselves as moving through it. *The months ahead* designates a particular stretch of time that the observer has not yet reached. According to either metaphor the past and the future are anchored to the observer, extending on either side of him. The statement that time is unidirectional may be interpreted in accordance with either one of these two metaphors.

Having mentioned the unidirectionality of time, it is now appropriate to ask whether the three-way distinction between location, direction and extent applies to time in the same way that it applies to space. It will be recalled that three kinds of sentences were recognized in Part I: locative sentences (*eg* [97a]), directional sentences (*eg* [97b]) and extent sentences (*eg* [97c]).

The book is on the table   [97a]

Trevor walked from Buckingham Palace to Trafalgar Square   [97b]

The Mall goes from Buckingham Palace to Trafalgar Square   [97c]

The three kinds are quite distinct. In particular, directional and extent sentences are quite distinct. On the one hand, something moves through a particular stretch of space, starting out at one point and ending up at another. On the other hand, the whole of a particular stretch of space is occupied at the same time. We need to ask, therefore, whether

The film lasted from seven o'clock to nine o'clock   [98]

is like [97b] or [97c]; *ie* does the film move through time from one point to another, or does it simply occupy a particular stretch of time? Whereas a comparable question in relation to space would be quite in order, it seems somehow inappropriate to ask this question about [98]. Specifically, [98] appears to resemble both [97b] and [97c]; the film moves through time from one point to another, but it may also be thought of as occupying a particular stretch of time. One's first reaction, then, is that the distinction between direction and extent is neutralized in relation to time. It is necessary, however, to decide how to represent the semantic structure of *lasted from seven o'clock to nine o'clock* in [98]. If it is modelled on [97b], we are dealing simply with a source expression and a goal expression. But if [97c] is the model, the source and goal expressions must be embedded inside a higher extent expression.

The way out of the present dilemma entails subjecting the spatial examples to a further scrutiny and realizing that it makes sense to distinguish not just three but four types of sentences. Example [97b] can be interpreted in two different ways and therefore represents two separate types of sentences. On the one hand, it presupposes a question such as *Where did Trevor go?* (or less specifically *What did Trevor do?*). On the other hand, it may be said to supply information answering the question *How far did Trevor walk?* In this case the questioner is interested not so much in the locations at the beginning and end of the journey as in the distance covered (on foot). One way of answering such a question is to specify the distance by means of a measurement phrase, as in *He walked just over half a mile, but then caught a bus because his foot was hurting.* The alternative is to specify the actual change of position involved, since the distance covered is derivable from the location of the beginning and end of the journey. The questions *Where did Trevor go?* and *How far did*

Trevor walk? are examples of directional and extent sentences, respectively. Accordingly, [97b] has to be regarded either as a directional sentence or as an extent sentence. The sentences in [97] thus provide two examples of extent sentences – [97b] in its extent interpretation and [97c]. The similarity between the two examples is seen in the fact that they both presuppose *how?* questions – *how far?* in the one case and *how long?* in the other. The difference between them depends on the fact that [97c] specifies the extent of something static whereas [97b] specifies the extent of something dynamic. In 1.1.2 it was noted that we may reverse the order of *Buckingham Palace* and *Trafalgar Square* in [97c] (=[31]) without affecting the state of affairs described by the sentence. All extent sentences that specify the extent of something static behave alike in this respect. Dynamic extent sentences behave differently, however. Thus in [97b] it is not possible to reverse *Buckingham Palace* and *Trafalgar Square* without changing the meaning of the original sentence, since it indicates the extent of a particular journey in which Buckingham Palace was the source and Trafalgar Square the goal.

We are now in a position to return to a consideration of temporal examples. Corresponding to the four types of spatial examples, it would appear that there are only two possibilities as regards time. On the one hand, we have examples such as *I saw Gwyneth at 10 o'clock*. This sentence, which locates an event ('my seeing Gwyneth') at a particular point in time, is comparable to [97a]. On the other hand, we have examples such as [98], which I regard as specifying the extent of something dynamic. Two things support the suggestion that [98] specifies the extent of something. First, there is an obvious similarity between [98] and *The film lasted for two hours*, and the presence in the latter example of a measurement phrase makes it clear that the semantic representation must contain an extent expression. Secondly, the question *How long did the film last?* – to which [98] is an acceptable answer – parallels such spatial extent sentences as *How long is that ruler?* In support of the suggestion that it is something dynamic whose extent is specified in [98], we may note that the noun phrases *seven o'clock* and *nine o'clock* cannot be reversed without changing the meaning of the original sentence. With regard to the semantic representation of *lasted from seven o'clock to nine o'clock* in [98], the preceding discussion has demonstrated that the source and goal expressions underlying the two prepositional phrases must be embedded inside an extent expression.

It follows also from the preceding discussion that the notion 'duration' is neither simply 'direction' applied to time nor simply 'extent' applied to time, but rather the extent of something directional. This suggestion will be further supported if we can provide some explanation for the fact that two of the spatial examples have no parallel as far as time is concerned ([97b], considered simply as a directional sentence, and [97c]). This is where the unidirectionality of time becomes relevant. The reason there is no counterpart of [97c] is presumably that, owing to the unidirectionality of time, it is impossible to occupy an extent of time without moving through it from the beginning to the end. The following explanation of the fact that directional sentences have no counterpart is rather more tentative. It was suggested above that [97b] either characterizes a particular change of position or else specifies a particular distance covered. Frequently one is interested in the details of a change of position because the location attained is then maintained for some time and constitutes the location of other events. For instance, [97b] might be followed in a narrative by an account of what happened at Trafalgar Square. Since time is perpetually moving (or alternatively, since an observer is perpetually moving in relation to time), the possibility of moving through time to a certain point and then remaining there does not exist. Consequently, it may be that the only aspect of movement through time that can be of interest is the distance covered.

The overall structure of the analysis presented in Part I was characterized by the recognition of a hierarchy of semantic constituents – see, for instance, [38] in **1.2.1** and *Tables* 4 to 8 later in **1.2**. The same hierarchy is again relevant in relation to temporal uses of English prepositions. Directional expressions such as the source expression underlying *from before the First World War* and the goal expression underlying *until after the Second World War* will be analysed as containing locative expressions. Part of the evidence given in **1.1.1** in support of the claim that directional expressions contain a locative expression was provided by the occurrence of the preposition *at* (expressing the notion 'locative') in sentences such as *The bridegroom has arrived at the church* (in which *arrive* expresses the notion 'goal'). It is of interest to observe that this sentence is paralleled, as far as temporal relations are concerned, by examples such as *The film ended at nine o'clock*. In fact, we can set up the proportion [99a] : [99b] : : [100a] : [100b].

(Then) the bridegroom went to the church	[99a]
(Then) the bridegroom arrived at the church	[99b]
The film lasted until nine o'clock	[100a]
The film ended at nine o'clock	[100b]

Even though [99a] contains nothing which could be said to realize a source expression or path expression, the sentence nevertheless describes a complete journey. On the other hand, [99b] focuses on the end-point of a journey. Similarly, [100a] describes the duration of the film, even though no source or path expression is present; whereas [100b] simply specifies the end-point.

A more complex semantic constituent – specifically, a level 4 directional expression – is illustrated by the sentence

Books may not be kept out beyond the end of the third term [101]

The prepositional phrase in this sentence means 'until a point in time which is beyond the end of the third term'. As in its spatial uses, *beyond* means 'at the end of a path leading via'. Also, the beginning of the path constitutes a reference point. However, since all paths through time necessarily proceed in the same direction, the reference point is always an earlier time than the time mentioned overtly ('the end of the third term' in [101]) and therefore does not need to be specified. *Beyond* seems to differ in its temporal uses from its spatial uses in so far as level 3 locative uses seem not to occur, or at least are rather less common than the level 4 directional use exemplified by [101]. Thus [102] seems less acceptable than [101]. The meaning that [102] would convey is more likely to be expressed as [103].

Books may not be borrowed beyond the end of the third term [102]
Books may not be borrowed after the end of the third term [103]

The fact that *beyond* sounds more normal in [101] than in [102] is obviously related to the fact that 'keeping a book out' involves causing a state to persist, whereas 'borrowing a book' is an event. The state referred to in [101] extends on either side of 'the end of the third term'. Thus three points in time are relevant – the end of the third term, an earlier time and a later time. In the 'borrowing' example, on the other hand, it seems that only two points in time are relevant – the end of the third term and the time of the (prohibited) borrowing. Conceivably, then, *beyond* is less appropriate than *after* in this instance because it implies that some earlier time is also relevant – which is not the case.

2.1.2 The English verb

It is well known that temporal adverbials are intimately related to the verb of a sentence. This is seen, for instance, in the fact that a sentence may be ungrammatical because of an incompatibility between the verb and a temporal adverbial. Thus while [104a and b] are perfectly grammatical, [105a and b] are deviant.

Trevor waited at the corner for three hours	[104a]
Harry went to Cambridge two days ago	[104b]
*Trevor recognized Gwyneth for three hours	[105a]
*Harry will go to Cambridge two days ago	[105b]

Using the terms 'lexical' and 'grammatical' in familiar ways, we may add that *for three hours* in [105a] is incompatible with the lexical meaning of the verb, *ie* with the meaning of *recognize*, whereas *two days ago* in [105b] is incompatible with the grammatical meaning of the verb, specifically the future tense. Somewhat less dramatically but equally interestingly, the meaning of a temporal adverbial may appear to vary depending on the nature of the verb with which it co-occurs. Sandhagen (1956) sets up several temporal senses of the preposition *for*, two of which may be glossed as 'duration', *cf* [106a], and 'intended duration', *cf* [106b].

Gwyneth stayed in Cardiff for a week	[106a]
Gwyneth went to Cardiff for a week	[106b]

In accordance with the general approach adopted in this book, I shall not distinguish separate senses of *for* in these examples. The apparent difference in meaning is more satisfactorily explained in terms of the context in which *for* occurs in each case. Specifically, it is the lexical context – the difference between 'staying in Cardiff' and 'going to Cardiff' – that is relevant here, rather than the grammatical context. In [107] *on Friday* appears to have a different meaning in the two examples. In the [a] example it is equivalent to *last Friday*; whereas in [b] it seems to mean 'on some Friday/Fridays in the past' (*of a Friday* would be a possible alternative in some dialects of English).

I ate meat on Friday	[107a]
I've eaten meat on Friday	[107b]

[107] differs from [106] in that it is the grammatical context rather than the lexical context – *ie* the difference between past tense and present perfect – which determines the apparent difference in the meaning of *on Friday*.

The aim of the present subsection is to provide a brief discussion of those features of the lexical and grammatical meaning of the English verb which are crucial for an understanding of temporal adverbials. I shall begin by considering the question of a classification of verbs according to their lexical meaning. The account that I shall adopt is that of Vendler 1957 (*cf* also Bauer 1970: 191–2).

Vendler presents a four-way classification of verbs, labelling the classes 'activity', 'accomplishment', 'achievement' and 'state'. *Running* or *pushing a cart* involve activities; *running a mile* or *writing a letter* illustrate the accomplishment class; *finding something* and *recognizing someone* are achievements; and *loving someone* and *owning a house* are states. From the examples given it is clear that the classification is really a classification of predications, or propositions, rather than a classification of verbs alone. For instance, *run a mile* belongs to a different class from *run* on its own. Similarly, while *write a letter* and *write the letter(s)* belong to the accomplishment class, *write letters* – as in *She was writing letters all evening* – belongs to the activity class.

Activity and accomplishment predications, on the one hand, are distinguished from achievement and state predications, on the other, by the 'formal' criterion that the former pair may be used in the progressive aspect, whereas the latter pair are not. The difference between the first two classes is that the accomplishment class involves the notion of a goal, which is absent in the case of the activity class. Using Garey's (1957: 106) terms, accomplishment predications are 'telic', whereas activity predications are 'atelic'. In *run a mile* the goal that is implied is a point in space one mile distant from the point at which the running begins. In *write the letter* the goal is the end of a specific letter. The third class – achievement predications – is similar to the accomplishment class in so far as it involves the notion of a goal. It differs from accomplishment predications in that the notion of activity is absent. *Writing a letter*, an accomplishment predication, describes an activity which leads to a goal. *Recognizing someone* and *finding something* – achievement predications – describe the attainment of a goal without referring to any prior activity (and since the attainment of a goal takes place at a point in time, *recognize* and *find* may be said to be punctual in meaning). The moment of finding something may, of course, be preceded by the activity of looking for it. However, it is also possible to find something without having looked for it. On the other hand, it is impossible to write a letter without engaging in the activity of writing. Stative predications (I will use this term henceforth, rather than state predications) involve neither activity nor the attainment of a goal. Besides *love* and *own* (given above), other verbs which typically occur in stative predications are: *know*, *understand*, *believe* and *contain*. Just as some verbs – *eg: run* and *write* –

may occur in either activity or accomplishment predications, so also there are verbs which occur both in stative predications and in some other type(s) of predications. For instance, *think* occurs in a stative predication in *I think it's going to rain*, but in an activity predication in *Don't bother me; I'm thinking*. Similarly, *see* occurs in a stative predication in *I could see him until he turned the corner*, but in an achievement predication in *I saw him as soon as he entered the gate*.

In the course of the above discussion we have spoken of activity, the attainment of goals, and states. In *Fig* 13a I suggest a way of representing these three notions graphically, and in *Fig* 13b Vendler's four classes are represented according to the same diagramming conventions. It will be recalled that the first two classes differ from the last two with regard to the possibility of being used in the progressive aspect. *Fig* 13b suggests that the reason for this is that classes 1 and 2 (the classes which may take the progressive) are the only ones that involve activity. Apparently only activity may be thought of as being in progress. This last statement receives some support from the fact that when an accomplishment predication is put in the progressive aspect, no indication is given of

activity	———————
goal	>
state	··········

Fig 13a A graphic representation of the notions 'activity', 'goal' and 'state'

1	activity	(*pushing a cart*)	———————
2	accomplishment	(*writing a letter*)	——————→
3	achievement	(*recognizing someone*)	>
4	state	(*owning something*)	··········

Fig 13b A graphic representation of the four types of predication

whether the goal in question is attained. For instance, while *She wrote a letter* implies that the letter was completed, *She was writing a letter* leaves open the question of whether the letter was ever completed. The progressive aspect marker, *be* + *-ing*, indicates that the speaker is focusing his attention on the progression of the activity (the shaft of the arrow in line 2 of *Fig* 13b). The attainment of the goal (the arrowhead) remains outside the speaker's remarks. It is conceivable that the speaker does not know whether the goal was attained. It is just as likely, however, that he is simply not interested in commenting upon it, being more interested in the preceding activity. The progressive aspect does not occur with achievement predications. The reason for this lies in the punctual nature of their meaning – by definition a punctual event cannot progress. (The term 'event' is conveniently applied to predications of the first three classes.) Stative predications, too, do not occur in the progressive aspect. States either exist or do not exist. They do not progress (see below).

Writing letters was mentioned above as an example of an activity predication. The activity involved may be described, in this instance, as iterative activity. It consists of a series of events of writing individual letters. Each such event in isolation would be an example of an accomplishment predication, but the series constitutes activity. Similarly, a series of achievement events also counts as activity. Thus it is quite normal to encounter *recognize* in the progressive aspect when it refers to a series of acts of recognition, *eg: I've been recognizing people I know all morning.* Moreover, the same is true also of states, *ie* a series of states constitutes iterative activity. The sentence *For the last two hours I've been thinking we should leave* illustrates the same use of *think* as *I think it's going to rain* rather than *Don't bother me; I'm thinking.* Thus the speaker seems to be referring to a series of times during the past two hours at which he was aware of being of the opinion that it was appropriate to leave.

While only activity (including iterative activity) may be viewed as progressing, both activity and states have duration. Thus predications of types 1 and 4 are frequently accompanied by a temporal adverbial of the kind *for a few hours, for several years.* For instance, one may *dig the garden* (activity) *for a few hours* and *own a house* (state) *for several years.* Achievement predications, being punctual, are by definition not capable of being durative. An accomplishment predication, on the other hand, may be durative, since it contains an activity component. In fact, when a phrase such as *for two hours* is used with an accomplishment predication, the effect is similar to that produced by selecting the progressive aspect with such a predication. That is to say, attention is focused on the activity component of the predication, with the result that the question of whether or not the goal was attained is left open (*cf* Garey 1957: 106, 108 for discussion of a similar point). Consider, for instance:

Trevor painted the ceiling for two hours   [108]

which is equivalent to (although less likely than) *Trevor was painting the ceiling for two hours*. Neither sentence tells us whether the ceiling was completed. On the other hand,

Trevor painted the ceiling [109]

would be understood as indicating that the ceiling was completed. Thus the presence of a durational adverbial, as in [108], is sufficient to force an activity alone interpretation rather than the activity + goal interpretation that would otherwise be placed on the predication, *cf* [109].

Before proceeding to a consideration of grammatical (as opposed to lexical) features of the English verb, it is appropriate to indicate how the types of sentences discussed in Part I fit into the framework of Vendler's four classes of predications. Locative and extent sentences both involve stative predications, class 4. Directional sentences provide examples of class 2 and class 3 predications. *We walked along the Mall to Trafalgar Square* is an accomplishment predication, class 2. It describes activity which results in the attainment of a goal. *They've just reached Trafalgar Square* is an achievement predication, class 3. It describes the attainment of a goal without referring to prior activity. The same is true of (*Then*) *the bridegroom arrived at the church*, example [99b]. At this point it might seem not only that the notion of a 'goal' that was invoked in discussing Vendler's four classes is identical to the notion 'goal' which featured in Part I, but also that 'activity' and 'path expressions' are similarly equivalent. According to this view, class 3 predications would contain a goal expression but no path expression, class 2 predications would involve a path expression and a goal expression, and class I predications would contain a path expression but no goal expression (and directional sentences would, therefore, illustrate class I as well as 2 and 3). Unfortunately, the situation is not so simple. (*Then*) *the bridegroom went to the church*, [99a], contains no path expression, and is in this respect like [99b]; but whereas [99b] is an example of an achievement predication, [99a] has to be considered as illustrating the accomplishment class. For one thing, *go to the church* can take the progressive aspect – *eg: The bridegroom must have been going to the church when we saw him*. Also, as was pointed out in 2.1.1, while [99b] focuses on the endpoint of a journey, [99a] describes a complete journey and therefore refers not only to the attainment of a goal but also to prior activity. Furthermore, it is not even the case that the notion 'goal' which featured in the discussion of Vendler's four classes is identical with 'goal' as used in Part I. *Trevor walked across the road* contains a path expression but no goal expression in its semantic representation. Nevertheless, it implies

that Trevor reached the other side of the road and therefore describes
activity which results in the attainment of a goal (class 2). Since directional sentences by definition describe a change of position, it would
seem that they necessarily involve a goal in the more general sense that
was ascribed to this term in connection with Vendler's classification of
predications. If this is so, then none of the sentences discussed in Part 1
illustrates class 1, activity predications. Admittedly, a predication such as
'walking across the road' seems to involve only activity if it is accompanied by the progressive aspect (*eg: Trevor was walking across the road*).
However, in this respect it is no different from 'writing a letter', which
would still be an accomplishment predication even if accompanied by
the progressive aspect.

We turn now to a consideration of such constituents of the verb as the
italicized elements in:

Harry play*ed* tennis yesterday
The newspapers *have* be*en* here for over an hour
Keith may *be* wait*ing* for us downstairs

Considerable attention has been devoted in the past to describing the
meaning of such elements; among recent contributions see, for instance,
Close 1962, Ota 1963, Joos 1964, Palmer 1965, Allen 1966, Halliday
1966, Huddleston 1969, Leech 1969, Bauer 1970, McCawley 1971,
Hudson 1971. In the necessarily brief and somewhat sketchy account
presented here, I shall draw on the work of the above scholars. In the
course of my remarks a certain amount of prominence will be given to
two questions. First, do the elements *-ed*, *have*+*-en* and *be*+*-ing* represent the separate semantic categories of tense, tempus (*cf* Garey 1955:
13) and aspect, or do they represent a single semantic category? Secondly, to what extent can the meaning of *-ed*, *have*+*-en* and *be*+*-ing* be
stated in the same terms as that of temporal adverbials?

In using the past, present or future tense, a speaker indicates that he is
focusing his attention on a time prior to the moment of speaking, on a
time simultaneous with (or including) the moment of speaking, or on a
time that will follow the moment of speaking. To suggest that *-ed*,
have+*-en* and *be*+*-ing* represent a single semantic category would entail claiming that the meaning of *have*+*-en* and *be*+*-ing* is also to be
stated in terms of the notions anteriority, simultaneity and posteriority.
Such a claim is made with respect to *have*+*-en* by McCawley, who regards all occurrences of the auxiliary *have* as underlying past tenses
(1971: 99) which expresses the meaning 'prior to' relative to the

context in which they are embedded (1971:110). A rather more extensive single-category analysis is proposed by Halliday (1966). According to this analysis, 'past', 'present' and 'future' each have two realizations. In the first (or finite) position in the verb they are realized as *-ed*, zero and *will* (or *shall*). In subsequent positions they are realized as *have*+ *-en*, *be*+*-ing* and *be going to* (respectively). Thus *be*+*-ing* is an embedded present tense according to this analysis, and there is no category of aspect as far as the finite verb is concerned. Example [110] shows the underlying representation, an intermediate representation and the surface structure of a rather complex verb-form according to Halliday 1966:

past	past	future	past	present	(take)	[110]
ed	have+en	be+going+to	have+en	be+ing	(take)	
had	been	going to	have	been	taking	

The top line in [110], the underlying representation, is generated by making repeated selections from what is essentially a recursive three-term system. In practice, the length of such strings is limited to five elements, and the number of distinct verb-forms to thirty-six, as a result of three conditions that are said to apply. These are:

(1) 'Present' may be chosen either first, or last, or both.
(2) The same choice may not be made twice in succession, except as choices 1 and 2.
(3) 'Future' may occur only once after the first slot.

From condition (1) we see that in the single-category analysis 'present' has a rather different distribution from 'past' and 'future', in that it never occurs in the middle of a string such as the top line of [110] (*take* is, of course, not part of the string generated by the tense system). This condition does not exist if a separate-category analysis is adopted, since in this case 'past', 'present' and 'future' occur only in the first position, representing the category of tense in the narrow sense (as opposed to tempus and aspect). The last position is then the aspect slot, in which a choice is made between 'progressive' and zero; and in between is the tempus system, whose terms are: *have*+*-en* and *be going to*. (Not only Halliday but also Joos has observed that the meaning of *be going to* is the exact reversal of that of *have*+*-en*, cf Joos 1964: 141.) It is now specifically the tempus system that comes closest to being recursive, and it is the tempus system to which conditions (2) and (3) – appropriately modified – apply. Condition (2) ensures that *have*+*-en* and *be going to* alternate, whenever more than one selection is made; and condition (3) prevents the system from being truly recursive, by allowing only one occurrence of *be going to* per verb-form. The most complex string that can be generated by the tempus system is, therefore, *have+en be+going+to have+en*, as in [110]. The least complex is zero – *ie* tempus is an optional category.

We see, then, that Halliday's three conditions are considerably simplified if a separate-category analysis is adopted, rather than a single-category analysis. In particular, condition (1) is absorbed into the analysis proper. Such considerations thus provide a certain amount of support for the separate-category analysis. The really crucial question, however, is whether or not the meaning of the perfect (*have+-en*) and the progressive (*be+-ing*) can be adequately stated in terms of the notions anteriority, simultaneity and posteriority. I shall suggest that it is necessary, in fact, to invoke other notions – which amounts to adopting a separate-category analysis.

Before looking in more detail at the perfect and the progressive, let us consider how to represent the notions anteriority, simultaneity and posteriority themselves. Temporal adverbials such as *before 10 o'clock*, *at 10 o'clock* and *after 10 o'clock* parallel the spatial prepositional phrases *in front of the church*, *at the church* and *behind the church*, and are therefore ascribed a parallel semantic representation:

[locative [anterior of 10-o'clock] time]
[locative 10-o'clock time]
[locative [posterior of 10-o'clock] time]

As was stated above, the past, present and future tenses express anteriority, simultaneity and posteriority relative to the moment of speaking. Accordingly, they may be represented as:

[locative [anterior of this] time]
[locative this time]
[locative [posterior of this] time]

(see also Leech 1969: 134 *ff*). Some writers have noted similarities between tenses, on the one hand, and definite articles (*eg* Allen 1966: 155) or pronouns (*eg* McCawley 1971: 110–12), on the other. These similarities are clearly important. At the same time, they pose certain questions as regards formalization, to which I am unable to provide answers.

Turning now to *have+-en*, the first thing to note is the need for recognizing two distinct meanings (*cf* Huddleston 1969: 786, 792; and Hudson 1971), exemplified in [111] and [112].

John may have arrived yesterday	[111]
John has lost his watch	[112a]
John has lived in Canada	[112b]
John has lived in Canada for two years	[112c]

With regard to sentences such as [111], Huddleston writes (1969: 792): '*Have* is thus a reserve marker, as it were, of past . . ., used when the usual marker, the -*ed* morpheme, is not available.' The evidence in support of treating *have*+-*en* as expressing anteriority in this instance is partly the similarity in meaning between [111] and *Maybe John arrived yesterday* (which contains a simple past tense), and partly the presence in [111] of a temporal adverbial referring to a definite time in the past, which would be incompatible with the meaning of *have*+-*en* in [112] – **John has lost his watch yesterday*, **John has lived in Canada last year*. The *have*+-*en* of [112] may be called the perfect proper. I shall adopt the account of its meaning presented in Ota 1963 and Bauer 1970, which are essentially similar even if in disagreement on certain details (*cf* Bauer 1970: 193). In discussing previous writings on the meaning of the perfect, Ota claims (1963: 41–58) that notions such as continuation, completeness, result and current relevance are not its essential meaning but are determined by the context in which it occurs in a given instance. Context here covers both the grammatical environment (in particular, whether or not the verb-form is progressive) and especially the lexical environment, *ie* the class to which the predication in question belongs on the basis of its lexical meaning. The essential meaning of *have*+-*en*, according to Ota, is that it locates an event or state of affairs in a period of time leading up to some reference point. For instance, the event referred to in [112a] is located in a period of time which ends at the moment of speaking. This formulation suggests that, in terms of semantic representations such as those of Part I, we need to posit a locative expression containing a goal expression. Such a structure is shown in *Fig* 14. In invoking the notion 'goal' – *ie* 'end' – in representing the meaning of the perfect, we are, of course, simply making further use of a notion which is needed in any case to represent the meaning of such items as *to*, *out*, *arrive*, *enter* and *until*. Leech also invokes the notion 'end' in discussing the perfect (1969: 152 *ff*). The main respect in which Leech's treatment differs from that of Ota 1963 and Bauer 1970 (and also Allen 1966 – *cf* 0.2 above) is that he sets up as allegedly separate senses of the perfect what they would regard as combinatory variants of a single meaning (*cf* Bauer 1970: 194). Leech objects to unitary definitions of the perfect on

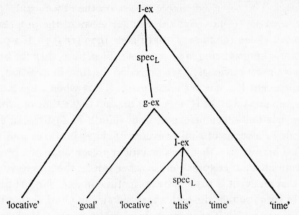

Fig 14 Semantic representation of the present perfect

the grounds that they are 'too vague to explain the complex factors which determine [its] use and interpretation in various contexts' (1969: 152–3). But Leech's position can be criticized on the grounds that the 'complex factors' to which he refers are properties of the context of the perfect rather than of the perfect itself.

The label 'tempus' (Garey 1955: 13) seems as good a label as any for the category represented by the perfect, since it draws attention to the fact that the meaning of the perfect has to do with locating events and states in time (*cf* also Bauer 1970: 197).

In suggesting how the meaning of tense and tempus may be represented, I have adopted the view that the same framework should be used as in stating the meaning of temporal adverbials, which in turn receive a similar analysis to the spatial analysis of Part 1 (see further **2.2**). Leech adopts a similar standpoint (*cf* 1969: 134). I shall now attempt to show that the meaning of the progressive aspect can also be stated within the same framework.

In a discussion of *be+-ing* which parallels his discussion of *have+-en*, Ota claims (1963: 63) that attempts to characterize its meaning as 'durative', 'continuous', 'incomplete', 'non-habitual', 'temporary' or 'simultaneous' have concentrated on

> 'redundant features' which sometimes reveal themselves rather conspicuously depending on the particular context or the particular lexical meanings of the verbs employed.

According to Ota, the essential meaning of *be+-ing* is that it marks an action as being in the process of taking place. 'Progressive' is therefore an apt label. The so-called simple tenses, on the other hand, 'grasp an action as a whole' (Ota 1963: 59). Similar views of the progressive are contained in Close 1962 (70 *ff*) and Bauer 1970 (194–7). If a particular event is thought of as being in progress at a given time, then the beginning of the event must obviously have preceded the time in question, and the end of the event has not yet taken place. Thus when a speaker uses a progressive verb-form, he is signalling the fact that a time on which he is focusing his attention coincides with the middle of a particular event (or the middle of a series of similar events or states in the case of iterative activity). This suggests that the semantic representation of a progressive should contain a path expression; in other words, the progressive marks the fact that an event is passing by at the time in question. At first sight, one might suppose that the path expression is temporal, *ie* that the locative expression which it contains defines a point in time. However, there is evidence suggesting that this is not the case. Not only activity but also states may pass by a point in time, since (as was pointed out above) both activity and states have duration. Thus if we posit a temporal path expression underlying *be+-ing*, we have no explanation of the fact that stative predications cannot be put in the progressive. We may shed light on the present issue by referring to the three diagrams in *Fig* 15, which

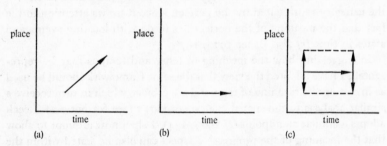

Fig 15 The essential spatial and temporal information conveyed by (a) directional, (b) locative and (c) extent sentences

represent directional, locative and extent sentences, showing the relevant spatial and temporal information. Directional sentences – diagram (a) – are seen to involve movement through both time and space. There is movement through time from T_1 to T_n and movement through space from P_1 to P_n. In the case of a locative sentence also, *eg: The book was on the table*, there is movement through time, *ie* the book remained on the table for a certain amount of time. However, there is no movement through space. Instead of $P_1 \rightarrow P_n$, we have simply P_1, which is maintained throughout the time in question (*cf: Fig* 15b). Diagram (c) represents an extent sentence, *eg: The original Watling Street went from London to Wroxeter*. Again there is movement through time, *ie* the road in question had the indicated extent for a particular period of time; but as in the case of the locative sentence, there is no movement through space. Rather, the stretch $P_1 \leftrightarrow P_n$ is occupied throughout the time in question. The directional sentence is the only one in which there is movement through space, $P_1 \rightarrow P_n$, and it is the only one which permits the progressive. Generalizing to other types of sentences, one is led to conclude that there must be some sort of development other than simply movement through time, before it is appropriate to use the progressive. A predication such as *Harry read the newspaper* qualifies: as one reads a newspaper, or indeed any text, one proceeds through it, gradually reading more and more. In the case of stative predications, on the other hand, there is no development other than movement through time. Thus while a state undoubtedly has a temporal beginning, middle and end, it has no beginning, middle and end in any other respect; rather, it is the same throughout. Consequently it is impossible to focus attention on the middle of a state (in the relevant sense of the word middle). It will be realized that an explanation along these lines of the fact that stative predications do not occur in the progressive treats progression as being incompatible with the notion of a state. An alternative, but to my mind less satisfactory, account has been proposed by some writers (*eg* Lyons 1968: 315–16, Leech 1969: 149). According to this account, the progressive is supposed to be redundant with stative predications, since it expresses the notion of duration, which is in any case necessarily implied by a stative predication.

We are now in a position to propose a semantic representation for a sentence containing a progressive verb-form. *Fig* 16 is the semantic representation of

I was driving to Wales   [113]

A number of features of *Fig* 16 are irrelevant to the present discussion – such as whether or not prop$_1$ and prop$_2$ should be collapsed into a single proposition containing both a spatial and a temporal locative expression. To the extent that they are important, such issues will be taken up in Part III. Among the things that interest us at the moment are, in particular, the content of $prop_2$, the path expression in $prop_3$ and its relationship both to $prop_2$ and to $prop_4$.

The locative expression in $prop_1$ represents the past tense. With regard to the lower part of *Fig* 16, a path expression is predicated of the event 'I drive to Wales' – *ie* we represent the progressive by indicating that the event in question was passing by a particular point. It was decided that it is specifically the non-temporal side of an event that is important in the progressive, *ie* the movement $P_1 \rightarrow P_n$ rather than $T_1 \rightarrow T_n$. This means that the point which 'I drive to Wales' passes by is a point in space rather than a point in time; hence the locative expression constituent of the path expression is spatial. The point in space which it defines is somewhere in the middle of a journey to Wales (from an unspecified source). The place thus defined features also in $prop_2$, being in fact the place at which the subject of the sentence was located at the time in question (*cf Fig* 11 for a similar use of merging lines). In support of the decision to include a locative proposition in the semantic representation of [113], notice that the sentence could be said in answer to a question such as *Where were you this time last week?* (and notice also that *I drove to Wales* would not be an acceptable answer to this question). The *be* of *be + -ing* may now be regarded as the same verb that occurs in a sentence such as *Gwyneth is at the supermarket* or *Trelleborg is in Sweden* – *ie* it is derived from the locative proposition in *Fig* 16 ($prop_2$). The morpheme *-ing*, on the other hand, expresses the meaning 'path' (*ie* 'middle'), which is a constituent of $prop_3$. It should be added, however, that in some instances *-ing* does not express the meaning 'path'. Allen points out (1966: 241) that *washing* is not progressive in *After washing his hands, he sat down at the table*. This is evident from the fact that **After he was washing his hands, he sat down at the table* is unacceptable (owing to the incompatibility of the progressive, which suggests incompletion in this context, and *after*, which implies completion).

The possibility of collapsing $prop_3$ and $prop_4$ and incorporating the path expression of $prop_3$ into the directional proposition $prop_4$ is not feasible. $Prop_4$ may, in fact, contain a path expression in any case – *eg* in the semantic representation of *I was driving through Somerset*. The somewhat odd nature of *?I was driving through Somerset to Wales* might lead one to conclude that a directional sentence in the progressive aspect contains either a path expression or a goal expression, but not both. Such a conclusion would, however, be incorrect. A path expression and a goal expression may both be present. What is special in this instance is the way in which the semantic structure would be realized –

not as *I was driving through Somerset to Wales*, but as *I was driving through Somerset on the way to Wales.* This last sentence is of particular

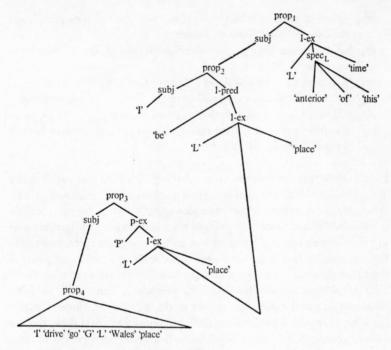

Fig 16 Semantic representation of [113]

interest in that the locative phrase *on the way* lends further support to our decision to posit a locative proposition in the underlying representation of [113].

2.2 Componential analysis of the prepositions investigated

As in 1.2, the prepositions investigated will be discussed in small groups, membership of the groups being determined by relatedness of meaning. After each group has been discussed, the componential analysis will be summarized in 2.2.7.

2.2.1 *At, on* and *in*

According to Sandhagen 1956 (86–150) there are five distinct temporal senses of the preposition *in*. The five meanings are characterized and illustrated as follows:

> in_1: 'space of time in which something is done or takes place', *eg: They bought their house in January;*
>
> in_2: 'units of time only part of which is occupied', *eg: ten minutes in every hour;*
>
> in_3: 'length of time occupied', *eg: It can be learned in six weeks;*
>
> in_4: 'a space of time immediately after the lapse of which something will occur', *eg: I shall be home in half an hour;*
>
> in_5: 'the function of *in* is the same as that of *for*', *eg: Nature has not changed in thousands of years.*

I shall argue that the differences in meaning identified here reside really in the context of *in* rather than in the preposition *in* itself. In characterizing the context of *in* in the various examples, the distinction between 'calendrical' and 'non-calendrical' units of time is important (*cf* Leech 1969: 113 *ff*, Fillmore 1971b). A calendrical unit of time is one which not only has a particular length but also begins and ends at a particular point in time (Leech 1969: 113–14). *Thursday* and *August* are examples. Non-calendrical time expressions designate periods of time with no fixed starting-point and end-point, *eg: six weeks, a fortnight*. Some words – *eg: hour, year* – have both calendrical and non-calendrical uses. For instance, *year* is being used calendrically if it refers to a period of time which begins on January 1 and ends on December 31, but non-calendrically if it designates any 12-month period.

We will consider first of all in_1 and in_3. The unit of time with which *in* occurs in the in_1 example (*January*) is calendrical. On the other hand, *six weeks* in the in_3 example is non-calendrical. *In January* in the first example indicates WHEN the house was bought. *In six weeks* in the other example indicates HOW LONG it takes to learn whatever *it* refers to. On the basis of these two examples, then, we may set up the tentative hypothesis that when *in* occurs with a calendrical period of time it seems to answer the question *when?* and when it occurs with a non-calendrical period it seems to answer the question *how long?* Let us look now at in_4. *Half an hour*, like *six weeks*, is typically non-calendrical. Notice, however, that *I shall be home in half an hour* is equivalent to *I shall be home in half an hour from now*. Thus the period of time in question has a fixed beginning and end, since the beginning coincides with the moment of speaking. For this reason it seems justified to regard *half an hour* as designating a calendrical period in this instance. Alternatively, one might perhaps claim that the period in question is both calendrical and non-calendrical. Notice now that the example certainly provides information of the *when?* kind, *ie* it specifies when the speaker will arrive home. In addition, one might claim that it also provides information of the *how long?* kind, in that it indicates how long the journey home will take. Thus our hypothesis appears to be supported. When there is a case for saying that the immediate environment of *in* is both calendrical and non-calendrical, it is also true that *in* seems to have both a locative and a durational meaning. Furthermore, the correlation that we have established between the apparent meaning of *in* and the nature of its context in specific examples lends support to the view that the alleged differences in meaning between in_1, in_3 and in_4 are really differences in the context of the preposition rather than the preposition itself.

With regard to in_5, we need to decide whether Sandhagen is correct in suggesting that this use of *in* is equivalent to *for*. It is revealing to attempt to insert the word *once* both in the original in_5 example and also in the modified example containing *for* in place of *in*. The insertion is possible in the original example, giving *Nature has not changed once in thousands of years*. On the other hand, *Nature has not changed once for thousands of years* is rather less acceptable. The crucial facts concerning these examples would appear to be as follows. The verb *change* designates an event rather than a state. However, when it is negated, it may be interpreted as referring either to an event or to a state. That is, a sentence of the form *X has not changed* means either 'there has been no occurrence of an event of X changing' or 'the state of affairs constituted by no change in X has persisted'. Inserting the word *once* seems to exclude the stative interpretation, with the result that the durational preposition *for* is no longer appropriate. On the other hand, the locative preposition *in* is quite acceptable. Moreover, it would seem that the use of *in* itself involves placing an event interpretation on *Nature has not changed*, whereas the use of *for* requires the stative interpretation. It should be clear from the above that it would be a mistake to set up a sense of *in* which is synonymous with *for*. In_5 represents the same sense of *in* as in_1, in_3 and in_4. In_2, which we have not yet mentioned, is regarded as a further instance of the same sense. One may draw attention, in this connection, to a correlation between the context of in_1 and in_2 and their alleged meanings. Both *January* in the in_1 example and *every hour* in the in_2 example refer to calendrical periods (the hours involved in the second example are hours that begin at x o'clock and end at $x+1$ o'clock). The *in*₂ gloss specifically notes that only part of the period is occupied, but the same is true also of the *in*₁ example – *ie* the buying of the house presumably occupied only part of January. Calendrical units typically occur in the realization of locative expressions, and when the location of events and states is specified – as opposed to their duration – it is frequently the case that they occupy only part of the period in question.

In short, it is unnecessary to invoke more than one sense of *in* in accounting for its various temporal uses. Its meaning is locative in all the examples we have considered, including *It can be learned in six weeks*. When a durational preposition, such as *for*, occurs with an accomplishment predication, attention is focused on its activity component, and the question of whether or not the goal was attained is left open. Thus *I learned French for six weeks* by no means implies that I completely learned French. On the other hand, *I learned French in six weeks* implies that I completely learned the language. The whole event of my learning French is contained in the period in question, including not only the activity but also the goal.

Statements of the form *X* (*is*) *in Y* indicate that X is at the interior of Y, and are neutral as between time and space (*cf* our remarks on *in Sussex* and *in the evening* in **0.2**). Thus the componential definition of *in* as 'locative interior' given in **1.2.4** covers not only its spatial uses but also its temporal uses.

Contrasts between *at* and *in* are not difficult to find. The situation here is quite comparable to the situation with regard to their spatial uses. What matters is how one views a particular period of time – whether as a period or as a point – rather than its actual physical size. Certainly one more frequently encounters *at* occurring with small units of time, such as *instant, moment, minute*, which are obviously more easily conceived as points. But under certain circumstances much larger units may be viewed as points in time, *eg: The assets of the company at January 1963 were* . . . (see also Sandhagen 1956: 12 for an attested example containing *at 1939*). Similarly, even very small units may be conceived as having an interior. Thus one may say *in that instant* or *in that moment*. On the other hand, an actual point in time apparently never occurs with the preposition *in* – *in 10 o'clock* is not possible.

Like *in*, *at* is neutral as between space and time. Thus the characterization of its meaning in terms of the single component 'locative' (*cf* **1.2.4**) will suffice also as far as its temporal uses are concerned.

The preposition *on* is more problematical. Among the questions that need to be answered are the following:

(a) Do the examples in [114] represent a single sense of *on*, or more than one sense?

on Tuesday	[114a]
on July 4	[114b]
on that occasion	[114c]
On opening the can, I managed to cut myself	[114d]

(b) Does *on* have the same meaning in any (or all) of the examples in [114] that it has in *on the table*?

Sandhagen suggests (1956: 49) that the units of time that occur with *on* are like a 'stage on which activities are placed'. If one were to accept this as being correct, it would be a short step to claiming that 'Tuesday' and 'July 4' have a surface, and that the meaning of *on* is the same in temporal environments as in spatial environments. However, if the only evidence in support of such an analysis is the fact that *Tuesday* and *July 4* occur with *on*, then the reasoning is clearly circular. Whereas one can justifiably claim that units of time have an interior as well as physical objects, the notion 'surface' applies only to the latter. This means that our answer to question (b) is that *on* has a different meaning in temporal environments from its meaning in spatial environments.

The units of time that take *on* do not take *in*, and those that take *in* do not take *on*. There is apparently no way in which one can conceive of the period of time designated by *Tuesday* that would make it appropriate to say *in Tuesday*. Nor can one conceive of the period designated by *August* in such a way as to necessitate saying *on August*. Thus whereas in 1.2.4 we rejected the view that the choice of *at*, *on* and *in* in spatial contexts is determined by the physical characteristics of the object in question, one can make out a rather stronger case for a comparable analysis of the temporal uses of *on* and *in*. There is a complication, however, as we shall see presently.

On Tuesday and *in August* may be regarded as having the semantic representations

[locative [interior of Tuesday] time]
[locative [interior of August] time]

The string 'locative interior' is realized as *on* or *in* depending on the unit of time with which it occurs (days requiring *on*). It was noted above that *in* contrasts with *at* (*cf: in January 1963* versus *at January 1963*).

Similarly, it is not difficult to find contrasts between *on* and *at*. Thus while one is likely to encounter *on December 31* more frequently than *at December 31*, the latter is certainly possible and is different in meaning in that it entails viewing 'December 31' as a point in time. On the other hand, as far as the present type of examples is concerned, *on* and *in* do not contrast.

The complication referred to above consists in observing that in somewhat different temporal environments it is possible to find *on–in* contrasts but no *on–at* contrasts. For instance, there is a difference in meaning between [114d] and

> In opening the can, I managed to cut myself   [115]

This last example can be paraphrased as *In the course of opening the can, . . .* It implies that the accident happened before the can was completely open. In [114d] the accident happened immediately after the can was opened. The event of opening the can is conceived of as having an interior according to [115], in that other events can take place in the middle of it. In [114d], on the other hand, the event of opening the can is regarded as an indivisible whole. With regard to the suggestion that *on* and *at* do not contrast in this kind of environment, the following examples are relevant:

> On seeing so many people, I decided to . . .
> At the sight of so many people, I decided to . . .
> *At seeing so many people, I decided to . . .
> *On the sight of so many people, I decided to . . .

Here, then, it would seem reasonable to regard *on* as realizing simply 'locative'.

In the course of the preceding discussion we have posited two temporal senses of *on*. In [114a and b] its meaning is 'locative interior'. In [114d], and probably also [114c], its meaning is simply 'locative'. Corresponding to the three-way spatial contrast between *at*, *on* and *in*, it seems that there is only a two-way contrast as far as time is concerned. Periods of time, events and states are either thought of as having extent, in which case they have an interior, or they are regarded as punctual and have no interior. In some contexts *on* and *in* occur with things that are thought of as having extent, and they jointly contrast with *at*. In other contexts *at* and *on* occur with things that are treated as having no extent, and they jointly contrast with *in*.

2.2.2 *Before* and *after*

It is customary to regard [116] and [117] as illustrating different uses of *before*, to which Fillmore (1971b) applies the terms 'factive' and 'counter-factive', respectively.

He finished the symphony before he died	[116]
He died before he finished the symphony	[117]

Comparable examples in which *before* functions as a preposition rather than a conjunction can also be found. However, such examples do not require us to posit two distinct senses of *before*, since the difference in meaning resides in the context rather than in *before* itself. Two events are mentioned in each of the above examples. In [116] they both happened. In [117], on the other hand, only the first event occurred; the second was hypothetical. *Before* simply indicates the temporal relationship between the two events in each case; the question of whether the second event was real or hypothetical is not part of its meaning.

As could be inferred from the discussion of 1.2.7, *after* is defined as 'locative posterior time'. Its definition thus differs from that of *behind* in containing the component 'time' where the latter contains 'place'. In view of the fact that *before* has spatial uses as well as temporal (*eg: She set an enormous meal before him, He was ordered to appear before the magistrate*), the component 'time' will be omitted from its definition, which is therefore 'locative anterior'. However, spatial uses of *before* are comparatively rare, and in many contexts it is not an acceptable substitute for *in front of*. I am unable to provide a characterization of the contexts in which the two are interchangeable.

Invoking the components 'anterior' and 'posterior' in defining the meaning of *before* and *after* implies that events and states, periods of time and points in time – like physical objects – have a front and a back. The front is the leading end or side, according to the metaphor that sees time as a kind of conveyor-belt moving past a stationary observer. Or it is the side that the observer first reaches, according to the metaphor that sees time as stationary and the observer as moving through it. The other side is, of course, the back.

2.2.3 *From, to, till* and *until*

With regard to *from* and *to*, nothing needs to be added to what we have already stated above. They express the general notions 'beginning' and 'end' (which we have chosen to refer to as 'source' and 'goal', *cf* 1.1.1). *Till* and *until* also express the notion 'end'. They differ from *to* in being restricted to temporal environments. Accordingly, *till* and *until* are defined as 'goal time'.

We saw in **1.2.10** that 'goal' is often not overtly expressed in spatial environments – *cf: Trevor walked behind the door*. With regard to temporal environments, 'goal' seems to require to be expressed overtly. *The film lasted after 11 o'clock*, meaning the same as *The film lasted until after 11 o'clock*, strikes me as being not totally impossible, but is at any rate not standard English.

2.2.4 *Since* and *by*

The preposition *since* has only one sense. To account for all temporal uses of *by*, however, it may be necessary to set up three distinct senses, illustrated by the sentences *We're travelling there by night*, *He gets stronger day by day* and *It must be finished by next week*. I shall consider only the last of these. Corresponding to this one sense, Sandhagen recognizes two senses (1956: 152–62), which he glosses as 'no later than' (*eg: It must be finished by next week*) and 'as early as' (*eg: By the end of the first week of the month he had spent the whole of his allowance*). This is yet another case where it seems preferable to attribute the apparent difference in meaning to the context of the preposition rather than to the preposition itself.

The first part of our discussion of *since* and *by* will be devoted to supporting the claim that the proportion in [118] is a true reflection of the meaning of the items in question.

since : by ::	[118]
from : to/till/until	

This proportion implies, of course, that *since* and *from* are similar in some respect, and *by* is similar to *to/till/until*; and also that from another point of view *since* is similar to *by*, and *from* is similar to *to/till/until*. We will begin by indicating what is shared by the members of each column, and then examine what the members of each row have in common.

The sentence *John has bought a new car* locates a particular event in a period of time ending at the moment of speaking. In the absence of any temporal adverbial a listener would normally assume that the event had taken place quite recently. Certain kinds of adverbials would indicate that a much longer period of time is involved – *cf: John has bought a new car only once in his life*. What a *since* adverbial does is mark the beginning of the period in question. Thus *John has bought a new car since your last visit* locates the buying of the car in a period which begins at the time of the addressee's last visit and ends at the moment of speaking. What *since* and *from* have in common, then, is that they both express the notion 'beginning' (*ie* 'source'). The sentence *I'm going to return this book* locates the event of my returning a particular book in a period of time extending forward from the moment of speaking. In the absence of a temporal adverbial a listener would probably assume that the event was going to take place fairly soon. The function of a *by* adverbial is to indicate how far forward the period in question extends. *I'm going to return this book by Saturday* locates the event in a period of time beginning at the moment of speaking and ending on Saturday. (*By Saturday* thus covers the two possibilities *before Saturday* and *on Saturday*.) What *by* and *to/till/until* have in common, then, is that they both express the notion 'end' (*ie* 'goal').

We turn now to the rows in [118]. Consider first of all the sentences

Joe was in the army from 1955 until 1957 [119]
Trevor lost his watch from Monday until Friday [120]

The first of these is a quite normal sentence; the second is rather more difficult to interpret. Together they demonstrate that temporal adverbials of the form *from X until Y* mark the fact that the accompanying predication is durative. There is no problem about placing a durative interpretation on Joe's being in the army, since this is a stative predication. On the other hand, *Trevor lost his watch* would normally refer to a single punctual event (an achievement predication, to use Vendler's term). If we are able to interpret [120] at all, it is only by virtue of placing a durative interpretation on the predication. There are two possibilities. Either we are dealing with iterative activity lasting from Monday until Friday, or else it is a state which has the duration in question. In the first case it would be rather more natural to say *Trevor kept on losing his watch from Monday to Friday* or perhaps *Trevor lost his watch every day from Monday to Friday*. In the second case, the state involved would be the state of the watch being lost, *ie* we assume that on Friday or Saturday Trevor recovered the watch. According to neither of these interpretations is [120] a very acceptable sentence as it stands. The point of the discussion was simply to demonstrate that temporal adverbials of the form *from X until Y* force us to place a durative interpretation on the accompanying predication. They necessarily indicate the beginning and end of activities and states. The period of time in question is thus entirely occupied by some activity or state.

As we have seen, *since* and *by* (like *from* and *to/till/until*) express the notions 'beginning' and 'end'. But whereas *from* and *to/till/until* mark the beginning and end of activities and states, *since* and *by* mark the beginning and end of periods of time. Let us consider first of all two examples containing *since*:

Jack has been in the army since 1968   [121]
John has bought a new car since your last visit   [122]

According to Leech 1969 (132–3), *since* would have two different meanings in these two sentences. The meaning he would ascribe to it in [121] could be glossed as 'throughout the period beginning . . .'. The [122] sense, on the other hand, would be glossed as 'in the period beginning . . .'. If we accept this as being correct, it means that a *since*-phrase is a durational adverbial when it accompanies a stative predication, but a locative adverbial when it accompanies a telic (*ie* accomplishment or achievement) predication. This looks, again, suspiciously like ascribing a particular difference in meaning to a preposition, which is more appropriately attributed to its environment. My own view is that *since* means 'in the period beginning . . .' not only in [122] but also in [121]. It is because it occurs with a durative predication in [121] that it appears to mean 'throughout the period beginning . . .'. In support of this view, notice the effect of placing the main intonational prominence in [121] on the word *since*. In this case the sentence might be said in order to correct the view that Jack had been in the army only BEFORE 1968. But Jack would not need to have been in the army throughout the period from 1968 till the moment of speaking. It would be quite in order to use the sentence even if Jack had spent only a small fraction of the period in the army. We see, then, that a stative predication accompanied by a *since*-phrase does not necessarily occupy the whole of the time in question. The situation is different if *since* is preceded by *ever*. In this case the whole of the period is occupied, but this is because *ever* means 'all the time' rather than because of the meaning of *since*.

Just as *since* means 'in the period beginning . . .', *by* means 'in the period ending . . .'. Stative predications accompanied by a *by*-phrase are comparatively rare. In my own idiolect I can say *They'll still be here by next Thursday*, but some speakers of standard English regard such a sentence as unacceptable. The sentence does imply that the 'being here' will occupy the whole of the period in question, but this seems to be determined by the presence of the word *still* rather than by the meaning of *by*. *By*-phrases occur more frequently in sentences such as *I'm going to*

return this book by Saturday, where there is, of course, no question of the
event occupying the whole of the available period.

Repeating our findings on the subject of the meaning of the items that
feature in [118], whereas *from* and *to/till/until* mark the beginning and
end of activities and states, *since* and *by* mark the beginning and end of
periods of time irrespective of what is located in them. In formalizing
the distinction, I shall treat *from* and *to/till/until* adverbials as occupying
a relatively more central position within propositions. *Since* and *by* adverbials, on the other hand, will be assigned a relatively more peripheral
position. The details will be described in **3.2.3**. In conclusion, we need
still to propose a componential definition of *since* and *by*. With regard to
since, *Fig* **17** shows the relevant part of the semantic representation of

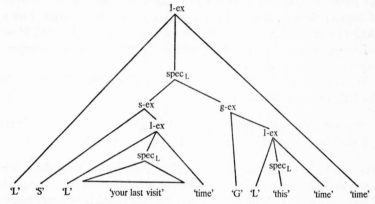

Fig 17 Relevant part of the semantic representation of [122]

sentence [122]. Comparing this diagram with that of *Fig* 14, our representation of the present perfect, we see that in *Fig* 17 the specifier slot of
the highest locative expression contains not only a goal expression but
also a source expression. Two possibilities that suggest themselves as the
componential definition of *since* are (i) 'locative source locative time',
and (ii) 'locative source time'. In deciding between these, phrases such
as *since before 1960* are relevant. The semantic representation of this
phrase would be:

[locative [source [locative [anterior of 1960] time]] time]

Before would be mapped onto 'locative anterior', and *since* onto the
initial 'locative source' and the final occurrence of 'time' (the first

occurrence of 'time' has no overt realization in this instance). Thus possibility (ii) is to be preferred. The second occurrence of the element 'locative' in *Fig* 17 has no overt realization – like the corresponding occurrence of 'locative' in the semantic representation of *from 1960 (to 1970)* or *from the door (to the window)*. *By* receives an exactly parallel definition as 'locative goal time'.

2.2.5 *Through* and *throughout*

Any activity or state that lasts from X until Y lasts throughout the period bounded by X and Y. Like *from* and *to/till/until, throughout* requires the listener to place a durative interpretation on the predication with which it occurs. There is no problem if we invent sentences in which a *throughout*-phrase occurs with a stative predication, *eg: Jim was in the army throughout the war*. But we have the same trouble interpreting *Trevor lost his watch throughout the week* that we had with example [120]. If we can interpret it at all, it is only by virtue of placing a durative interpretation on the predication.

We need to account for two distinct uses of *through*, as illustrated in the following two examples:

She was writing letters all through the night	[123]
I shall be in Cambridge from Monday through Friday	[124]

The word *all* in [123] has the same effect as the *out* of *throughout, ie* it states explicitly that the whole of the period in question was occupied. *Through the night* without *all* is also possible, but seems to be less common than *all through* or *throughout*. The componential definition of *through* proposed in **1.2.8** – 'path locative interior' – covers also the temporal use of [123]. In other words, *through* is regarded as having the same meaning in *through the night* as in *through the forest*.

With regard to *throughout*, we have a perfectly adequate characterization of its meaning if we think of it as consisting of *through* plus *out*. It will be recalled that *out* was defined in **1.2.5** as 'goal locative exterior'. Attributing the same meaning to *out* also in the present context, *throughout the night* may be said to mean 'via at the interior of the night to at the exterior'. Saying that an activity or state lasts through the night to its exterior is one way of expressing the fact that the whole of the night is occupied. *Throughout* is defined, then, as 'path locative interior goal locative exterior'. It was partly in anticipation of this analysis of *throughout*, and partly also because of the existence of temporal uses of *out of* (*eg: out of season*), that it was decided in 1.2.5 not to ascribe the component 'place' to the meaning of *out*.

The use of *through* in [124] is a feature of American English and the speech of Englishmen whose usage has been enriched (or contaminated, depending on one's attitude) by exposure to American English, but is not otherwise found in standard British English. *From Monday through Friday* means 'from Monday to Friday inclusive of Friday'. It is thus more specific than *from Monday to Friday*, which leaves open the question of whether or not Friday is included. (If it seems more likely that *from Monday to Friday* would be taken to include Friday, this is no doubt for the non-linguistic reason that Friday, like Monday, is a weekday. *From Friday to Monday* is perhaps less likely to be taken as including Monday, since Monday comes immediately after the weekend.) One possible analysis of the [124] use of *through*, then, would be to ascribe to it the two components 'goal' and 'inclusive'. There are two reasons why we should not be in too much of a hurry to accept this analysis. First, it implies that this particular use of *through* has nothing whatsoever in common with other uses of the same preposition. Secondly, it would entail positing a component ('inclusive') which is not used anywhere else in the analysis. A glance at *Tables* 9 and 10 will show that 'inclusive' would not be the only component of which this is true. However, in the present instance there is an alternative analysis which removes the need for positing the component 'inclusive'. It will be recalled that *past his station* in [46d], *The passenger fell asleep and went past his station*, was regarded as meaning 'to a place at the end of a path leading past his station', *ie* the semantic representation was said to contain a level 4 directional expression. *Through Friday* in [124] can be similarly analysed as meaning 'until a time which is at the end of a path leading through Friday'. The semantic representation is:

[G [L [P [L [interior of Friday] time]] time]]

It remains to decide how much of this structure *through* is mapped onto. The policy adopted in Part I for deciding on the componential definition of particular prepositions consisted in identifying such components as are always present in the semantic representation when the particular preposition is used (*cf* 1.2.1). In the present instance, the facts seem to favour departing from this policy. If we were to adopt the same policy, *through* would be regarded also in [124] as being mapped onto 'path locative interior', and the initial 'goal locative' of the above semantic representation would be treated as having zero realization. The reason for

treating 'locative', 'path' and 'goal' as capable of having no overt realization in Part I was that in this way we were able to give a general account of the meaning of the prepositions that were considered. The
alternative would have been to set up many senses of most of the prepositions, considering the occurrences of 'locative', 'path' and 'goal' referred to above as part of their meaning. Such an analysis would have
contained a great deal of duplication, since it would have emerged that
many of the prepositions were polysemous in exactly parallel ways.
Notice now that there is nothing to be gained from treating the initial
'goal locative' of the semantic representation of *through Friday* in [124]
as having zero realization. We cannot point to other temporal prepositions which exhibit a use that exactly parallels this particular use of
through. Thus 'goal locative' will be considered part of the meaning of
through, along with 'path locative interior'. In addition, the component
'time' is included, since it is only in temporal contexts that *through* has
this particular meaning. The componential definition is therefore 'goal
locative path locative interior time'. It will be noticed that although this
constitutes a different sense from the one that occurs in [123] and in
spatial contexts, the two senses are related in meaning in so far as they
both contain the components 'path locative interior'.

2.2.6 *For* and *during*
As in spatial contexts, *for* expresses the meaning 'extent'. The two examples in [106], *Gwyneth stayed in Cardiff for a week* and *Gwyneth went
to Cardiff for a week*, both contain the extent expression

[extent a-week time]

The apparent difference in meaning – between 'duration' and 'intended
duration' – depends on the type of predication with which *for a week*
occurs. 'Staying in Cardiff' is a stative predication, and *for a week* specifies the duration of the state. 'Going to Cardiff' is a telic predication –
specifically, an accomplishment predication with both an activity and a
goal component. We might therefore expect *for a week* to modify the
activity of going to Cardiff, but in fact it would almost invariably be understood as specifying the extent of the subsequent stay in Cardiff, *ie* the
extent of the state which follows the attainment of the goal. Since activity
can also be marked as having a particular extent, *eg: I wrote letters for an
hour*, it ought to be possible to invent examples containing an accomplishment predication modified by a *for*-phrase which would be ambiguous depending on whether the *for*-phrase was taken to indicate the

duration of the activity or of the subsequent state. Possibly this is true of the sentence *She was travelling to Cardiff for a week*. The problem is, however, that even when a sentence in theory has two possible interpretations, it is often the case that one of them would require rather more elaborate contextualization than the other and so would not necessarily occur to a listener when the sentence is presented in isolation.

When we compare two sentences such as those in [125], it is apparent that there is an element of duration in [a] which is absent from [b].

I met a friend of yours during the vacation   [125a]
I met a friend of yours in the vacation   [125b]

However, it is not the event of meeting a friend of the addressee's that is being marked as durative. Rather, it is the vacation. In [125b] the vacation is thought of from a static point of view – as a period of time in which a particular event was located. In [125a], on the other hand, the event is located at a time at which the vacation was lasting, so to speak. *During* entered English on the model of Latin absolute constructions of the kind *vita durante*, meaning literally 'with life lasting' (*cf* Oxford English Dictionary). Its meaning does not appear to have changed in any respect in the intervening time. The correctness of this account of the meaning of *during* is substantiated by the fact that we cannot say **during 10 o'clock*. Points in time cannot last; only a period of time can last. The semantic representation of [125a] is given in *Fig* 18. The temporal locative expression in $prop_1$ – like the corresponding one in *Fig* 16 – represents the past tense. The lowest proposition, $prop_4$, expresses the fact that the vacation extends, *ie* lasts, via some point in time, which we may refer to as T. This same point T features also in $prop_2$ – namely, it is the point at which the event 'I meet a friend of yours' occurs. We need now to propose a componential definition for *during*. One component of its meaning is the notion 'extent', which besides being realized as the preposition *for* may also be realized in temporal contexts as the verb *last*, or even as *last for*. However, *during* is not what I would call a durational preposition. Durational prepositions are those which force us to place a durative interpretation on the accompanying predication; they are the prepositions whose function is to specify the duration of activities and states. In this category we have discussed *from, to, till, until, through, throughout* and *for*. The other prepositions whose temporal uses we have discussed are all locative: *at, on, in, before, after, since* and *by*. *During* belongs in this group. The event described in [125a] is simply located in time; nothing

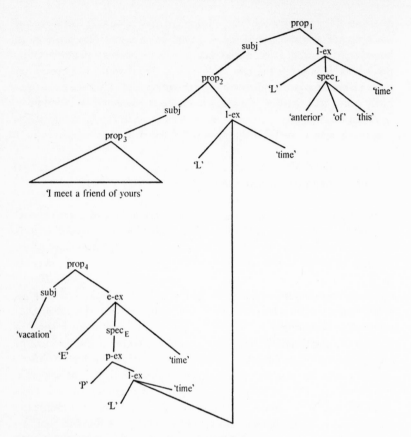

Fig 18 Semantic representation of [125a]

is said about its duration. The element of duration comes in because the event is placed at a point in time which something else is moving past. This means, then, not only that *during* must contain the component 'locative' but also that 'locative' must be its leftmost component. It would seem that prop$_4$ gets expressed in right-to-left order, presumably as a result of the fact that we enter it from prop$_2$ on the right-hand side. If 'locative' and 'extent' are components of *during*, it seems necessary to ascribe the intervening component 'path' also to its meaning. Finally, since *during* is specifically temporal and the notions 'locative', 'path' and 'extent' are neutral as between space and time, it seems desirable to add the component 'time' to the definition. Thus we arrive at 'locative path extent time' as our componential definition of *during*. (The question of the order of these components will be discussed in more detail in 3.2.5.)

2.2.7 Summary of the componential analysis

Tables 11 and 12 summarize the componential analysis not only of the present section but also of 1.2. *Table* 11 contains all the prepositions whose meaning is locative. It should be noted that the second and third senses of *on* – *on₂* and *on₃* – are both temporal, *cf: on Tuesday* and *on opening the can*. The component 'time' was omitted from the two definitions since it would be necessary to state rather more specific contextual conditions to explain when 'locative interior' and 'locative' are realized as *on* rather than *in* and *at*. The remainder of the prepositions are listed in *Table* 12. With the exception of *for*, the leftmost component in each instance is one of the directional cases 'source', 'path' or 'goal'.

above:	'locative higher'
after:	'locative posterior time'
(a)round:	'locative surround'
at:	'locative'
before:	'locative anterior'
behind:	'locative posterior place'
below:	'locative lower'
beyond:	'locative path locative'
by$_1$:	'locative proximity'
by$_2$:	'locative goal time'
during:	'locative path extent time'
in:	'locative interior'
in back of:	'locative posterior place'
in front of:	'locative anterior place'
inside:	'locative interior of side'
on$_1$:	'locative surface'
on$_2$:	'locative interior'
on$_3$:	'locative'
outside:	'locative exterior of side'
over:	'locative superior'
since:	'locative source time'
under:	'locative inferior'

Table 11 Summary of the componential analysis of the locative
prepositions

across:	'path locative transverse'
along:	'path locative length'
away (from):	'goal locative some place'
down:	'goal locative lower'
for:	'extent'
from:	'source'
into:	'goal locative interior'
off:	'goal locative off'
onto:	'goal locative surface'
out (of):	'goal locative exterior'
past:	'path locative proximity'
through$_1$:	'path locative interior'
through$_2$:	'goal locative path locative interior time'
throughout:	'path locative interior goal locative exterior'
till:	'goal time'
to:	'goal'
towards:	'goal wards'
until:	'goal time'
up:	'goal locative higher'
via:	'path'

Table 12 Summary of the componential analysis of the non-locative
      prepositions

Part Three

Towards a formalization of the analysis

3.1 Opening remarks

In the course of Parts I and II we were concerned with two kinds of linguistic elements, as exemplified by *in*, *through* and *arrive*, on the one hand, and 'locative', 'path' and 'superior', on the other. Elements of the first kind have already been referred to as 'lexemes'. Elements of the second kind may be referred to as 'sememes'. Representations of sentences in terms of lexemes may be called 'lexemic representations'. They are similar to what are elsewhere referred to as surface structures. Representations of sentences in terms of sememes may be called 'sememic representations'. I shall draw no distinction here between 'sememic representations' and 'semantic representations'; the two are simply alternative labels. In formalizing the analysis presented in Parts I and II, it is necessary to indicate (i) how the set of well-formed sememic representations can be generated, and (ii) how sememic representations are mapped onto lexemic representations. The part of a stratificational grammar concerned with the first of these two tasks is known as the 'semotactics'. It is a syntax of sememes, *ie* a generative device which specifies what combinations of individual sememes are well-formed. With regard to the second task, two subcomponents of the overall grammar are involved: the 'lexotactics' and the 'semolexemic realizational structure'. The lexotactics is a generative device, exactly comparable to the semotactics, which generates the set of well-formed lexemic representations. The semolexemic realizational structure characterizes the relationship between the sememes and the lexemes of a language. It states how particular sememes and combinations of sememes are realized in terms of lexemes. Without the semolexemic realizational structure, the two 'tactic patterns' (the semotactics and the lexotactics) would generate sememic and lexemic representations independently of each other. The intervening realizational structure ensures that a particular sememic representation is paired with the corresponding lexemic representation.

The semotactics, semolexemic realizational structure and lexotactics are discussed in sections 3.2, 3.3 and 3.4. Then in 3.5 we discuss the way in which these three subcomponents are integrated with one another; and 3.6 is devoted to a number of concluding remarks.

3.2 Semotactics

This section is divided into five parts. In the first, a small fragment of the semotactics is presented, using rewrite rules and also the network notation proposed in Lamb 1966a and b. In 3.2.2 some of the advantages of the network notation are mentioned. The next subsection, 3.2.3, presents more of the semotactics. Then in 3.2.4 a distinction between sememic representations and 'semotactic traces' is discussed. In the final subsection, I draw attention to certain problems relating to the fragments of the semotactics discussed earlier, and indicate ways in which the analysis may profitably be extended.

3.2.1 Initial fragment of the semotactics

To give a detailed account of the semotactic structure that would generate all the semantic representations of Parts I and II would take up a considerable amount of space. Moreover, much of it would make somewhat tedious reading. I have decided, therefore, to present only a relatively small fragment of the semotactics initially, and then in 3.2.3 to indicate some of the most important respects in which this fragment requires augmenting. It was also in an effort to ease the burden on the reader that it was decided to present the semotactics first of all in the form of phrase structure rules (PS rules), rather than in the relatively less familiar form of the network notation. The initial fragment characterizes the basic structure of locative, directional and extent sentences, as discussed in Part I, with the exception in particular of the mechanism for generating sentences such as *The post office is over the hill*, which will be discussed later.

Propositions, it will be recalled, consist of a subject and a predicate. The predicate is of three types: locative, directional or extent. The subject is either a physical object or an embedded proposition. Three examples in which the subject is an embedded proposition are the following: [[*Trevor was sitting on a bench*] *in the park*], [[*Gwyneth sat on her case*] *from London to Manchester*], [[*We walked along the road*] *for three miles*]. In the first, a locative proposition is embedded inside another locative proposition; in the second, a locative proposition is the subject of a directional sentence; and in the third, a directional proposition is the subject of an extent sentence. Certain combinations would seem to be impossible, *eg* a directional proposition embedded inside another directional proposition, but I have made no attempt to incorporate such co-occurrence restrictions into the analysis. This much information is stated in the three PS rules in [R1].

prop → subj pred   [R1]

$$\text{subj} \rightarrow \begin{Bmatrix} \text{p-obj} \\ \text{prop} \end{Bmatrix}$$

$$\text{pred} \rightarrow \begin{Bmatrix} \text{l-pred} \\ \text{e-pred} \\ \text{d-pred} \end{Bmatrix}$$

A locative predicate optionally contains a posture, *eg* 'sit', 'lie', 'stand'. In addition, it contains 'be' and a locative expression. The latter consists of the element 'locative', a specifier and the element 'place'. The specifier consists of a part, *eg* 'interior', 'surface', 'superior', 'posterior', or a physical object, *eg* 'kitchen', 'hill', 'post office', or a part and a physical object. This information is expressed in the rules of [R2].

l-pred → (posture) 'be' l-ex   [R2]
posture → {'sit', 'lie', 'stand', ...}
l-ex → 'locative' spec$_L$ 'place'
spec$_L$ → (part⁂p-obj)
part → {'interior', 'surface', 'superior', 'posterior', ...}
p-obj → {'kitchen', 'hill', 'post office', ...}

The 'linked parentheses' (*cf* Fillmore 1968: 28) used in the fourth of the above rules express the fact that although each constituent is optional, one at least must be selected. Symbols enclosed by quotation marks are terminal symbols. They represent sememes, the ultimate constituents of the semotactics. Symbols not enclosed by quotation marks are non-terminal symbols. As was pointed out in 1.1.1, a number of scholars have suggested that *be* and *go* are 'dummy verbs' which serve to carry tense, and other, distinctions in the surface structure of sentences. Positing two sememes 'be' and 'go' is by no means necessarily in disagreement with such a view, since a distinction is made between determined and non-determined elements at all levels of a stratificational grammar, and 'be' and 'go' are good candidates for being treated as determined sememes (see further 3.5.1). As to why they are sememes at all – even if *be* and *go* are dummy verbs, it is necessary to ensure that the right dummy verb is inserted in a given instance. In the network notation this can be achieved by means of lines leading from the parts of the semotactics that generate locative and directional predicates to the lexemes *be* and *go* respectively. Positing these lines amounts to recognizing the sememes 'be' and 'go'. (An inadequacy of the present approach is indicated in 3.2.5.)

An extent predicate consists simply of what was referred to above as an extent expression. Thus there is in fact no need for both terms. I will retain the former. Accordingly, an extent predicate consists of the sememe 'extent', a specifier and the sememe 'place'. The specifier slot is filled either by a measurement expression or by part of a directional predicate (referred to as d-pred$_1$). A directional predicate consists of an optional means of locomotion constituent – *eg* 'walk', 'run' – and a d-pred$_1$. The latter consists of 'go' and a directional expressions constituent, which in turn contains either a source expression, path expression and goal expression, or any one or two of them (if more than one is selected, the order is: source—path—goal). Each individual directional expression consists of a case – 'source', 'path' or 'goal' – followed by a locative expression. The corresponding PS rules are:

e-pred → 'extent' spec$_E$ 'place'   [R3]

$$\text{spec}_E \rightarrow \left\{ \begin{array}{l} \text{meas-ex} \\ \text{d-pred}_1 \end{array} \right\}$$

meas-ex → {'five miles', 'three inches', . . .}
d-pred → (means) d-pred$_1$
means → {'walk', 'run', . . .}
d-pred$_1$ → 'go' d-exs
d-exs → (s-ex)(p-ex)(g-ex)
s-ex → 'source' l-ex
p-ex → 'path' l-ex
g-ex → 'goal' l-ex

Finally, the sememe 'of' is inserted between a part and a physical ob-

ject whenever both are selected, but not if only one is selected (*cf* 'spec$_L$'
rule in [R2]). This fact is stated in the transformational rule:

part p-obj $\Rightarrow$ part 'of' p-obj [R4]

[R1] illustrates two types of PS rules. The first rule states that a proposition consists of a subject AND a predicate, in that order. The second
rule states that a subject is EITHER a proposition OR a physical object.
The third rule is of the same type as the second: it involves the OR relationship rather than the AND relationship. In the network notation these
two relationships are represented by the two different nodes illustrated
in *Fig* 19. The node in diagram (a) represents the AND relationship;
specifically, it is an ORDERED AND, the left-to-right sequence of the
lines from the bottom of the node reflecting the sequence of the constituents in question. The node in diagrams (b) and (c) is an UNOR-
DERED OR; the lines connecting to the lower side emerge from the same
point. The symbols alongside the lines in *Fig* 19 correspond, of course,
to the symbols occurring in [R1]. We note now that some symbols occur
more than once. For instance, 'pred' occurs in (a) and also in (c). What

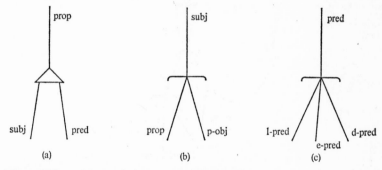

Fig 19 Three 'networks' corresponding to [R1]

this means is that the line at the bottom right of (a) is, in fact, the same
line as the one at the top of (c). This fact can be made explicit by connecting diagram (c) to the appropriate place in diagram (a). Similarly,
the 'subj' line in (b) is the same line as the 'subj' line in (a). Thus (b),
too, needs to be attached to the bottom of (a). The resulting diagram is
given as *Fig* 20. We notice, however, that there are two lines in *Fig* 20
labelled 'prop'. These two lines need to be connected together. *Fig* 21
incorporates the appropriate revision. The part of this diagram below
the line labelled 'prop' states the internal structure of propositions:

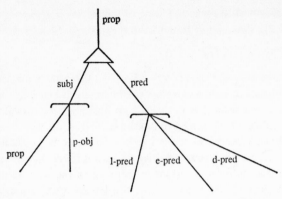

Fig 20 Partially integrated network corresponding to the three diagrams
in *Fig* 19

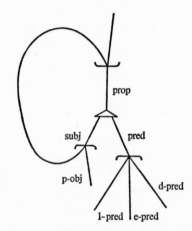

Fig 21 Fully integrated network corresponding to the three diagrams in
Fig 19

each proposition consists of a subject and a predicate. The part of the
diagram above the 'prop' line represents the slots in which a proposition
may occur. We see that there are two possibilities: either it is embedded
inside another proposition (in which case we get to it via the loop), or it is
not embedded inside another proposition (in which case we get to it via
the line at the top of *Fig* 21). *Fig* 21 thus contains two distinct kinds of
UNORDERED OR nodes. The original kind (*cf: Figs* 19 and 20) is the
DOWNWARD kind; the new kind is an UPWARD OR. In each case we are

dealing with alternatives – on the one hand, alternative kinds of subject and predicate; on the other hand, alternative positions in which a proposition may occur.

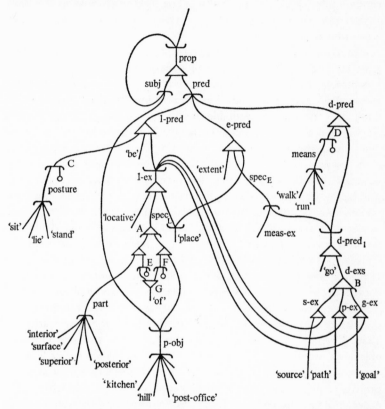

Fig 22 Network grammar corresponding to the rewrite-rule grammar of [R1], [R2], [R3] and [R4]

Applying the same principle according to which *Fig* 19 was converted into *Fig* 20 and then *Fig* 21 (together with certain additional notational conventions that will be explained below), a single network can be constructed corresponding to the rewrite rules of [R1], [R2], [R3] and [R4]. This network is shown in *Fig* 22. The places in *Fig* 22 at which additional notational conventions have been employed are marked by the capital letters A, B, ..., G. The node which occurs at A and B may be called an AND-OR node. It corresponds to the linked parentheses of the

PS rules. The same information that is expressed by such a node can also be expressed by means of a configuration of AND nodes and OR nodes. Thus the AND-OR may be regarded as an abbreviation for a particular configuration of more basic nodes. (For further discussion, see Reich 1970a: 166–76 and 1970b: 103–4 – where, however, the term 'intercatenation element' is used.)

Generating a sememic representation according to the fragment of the semotactics given in *Fig* 22 can be thought of in terms of impulses travelling through the network from top to bottom. When an impulse reaches a downward AND node, impulses are sent out from the bottom of the node along each of the available lines. On the other hand, an impulse reaching a downward OR node results in an impulse being sent out along only one of the available lines connecting to the bottom of the node. (For detailed discussion of the way in which impulses travel through networks, see Reich 1969, 1970a and 1970b.) This brief reference to the question of impulses travelling through a network will make it easier to understand the mechanism for inserting 'of', which involves in particular the three nodes labelled E, F and G, and also the two downward ANDS immediately above E and F. The node at G is an UPWARD ORDERED AND. The sememe 'of' will occur whenever impulses reach G from E and F in that order. This will happen whenever the specifier constituent of a locative expression contains a part and a physical object. The downward AND above E ensures that each time a part is selected, an impulse is sent also to the node at E. Similarly, the downward AND above F ensures that each time a locative expression contains a physical object, an impulse is sent also to the node at F. The nodes at E and F are DOWNWARD ORDERED ORS. The ordering of an OR node is one of priority or preference. The various alternatives are tried in left-to-right order until one succeeds. Nodes E and F are special also in so far as the second of the two alternatives is zero (symbolized by a line ending in a small circle). Let us imagine that a particular locative expression contains a physical object but no part. An impulse will reach F, whereupon an impulse is sent initially along the line leading to node G, but in this instance G will not accept an input from F, since there has been no preceding input from E. Consequently, the second of the two alternatives at F is now taken, *ie* the zero alternative.

Downward OR nodes with one line connecting to zero are used also, at C and D, to express the fact that the posture and means of locomotion constituents are optional – either one selects a member of the category in question or one selects zero. Optionality was represented in Lamb

1966a by means of an unordered OR (with one line ending in zero). While writing computer programmes designed to generate sentences according to relational network grammars, Reich encountered difficulties using Lamb's account of optionality, and was able to overcome them by making the OR ordered rather than unordered. I have followed Reich's treatment (cf 1970a: 166–76, 1970b: 103–4), even though in the present context the issue is rather marginal.

3.2.2 Advantages of the network notation

The network of *Fig* 22 is equivalent, as we have seen, to the rewrite rules of [R1], [R2], [R3] and [R4]. It is relevant to ask, therefore, whether the network notation is in any way to be preferred over rewrite rules. There are, in fact, a number of respects in which the network notation has proved its usefulness. Some of its advantages centre around the question of a simplicity measure. Given two distinct descriptions of the same linguistic data, it is generally agreed that the simpler description is to be preferred. In some cases it may be obvious which description is simpler. In other cases – particularly when the data described are fairly extensive – it is necessary to employ a reliable measure of simplicity. Possible candidates for a simplicity measure are tested on small amounts of data, concerning which there is general agreement on which of the available descriptions is simplest. The most reliable measure arrived at in this way is then applied generally. The network notation is particularly useful in demonstrating the inadequacy of what might otherwise appear to be quite plausible simplicity measures. For instance, one might regard the number of rules occurring in a description as an indication of the complexity of the description. Or, alternatively, one might consider counting the number of symbols rather than the number of rules. In this connection let us compare the three rules of [R1] with the one rule given below:

$$\text{prop} \rightarrow \begin{Bmatrix} \text{prop} \\ \text{p-obj} \end{Bmatrix} \begin{Bmatrix} \text{l-pred} \\ \text{e-pred} \\ \text{d-pred} \end{Bmatrix} \qquad\qquad \text{[R5]}$$

On the basis of counting either the number of rules or the number of symbols, it would seem that [R5] is preferable to [R1]. In fact, however, [R1] and [R5] are not competing descriptions at all. They are merely superficially distinct versions of a single description. Each expresses exactly the same facts as the diagram of *Fig* 21.

The simplicity measure employed in evaluating competing stratificational grammars was worked out in relation to the network notation.
Examples such as that of *Fig* 23 (*cf* Lamb 1966a: 47) are of particular in-

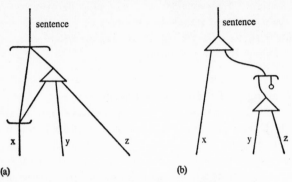

(a)   (b)

Fig 23 Two competing descriptions of a simple language

terest at this point. The two diagrams represent alternative grammars of
a language that has just two sentences, x and xyz. It is generally felt that
(b) is the preferable grammar. It makes the generalization that sentences
in this language begin with x. Grammar (a) makes no such generalization.
It states merely that the sentences of the language are either x or xyz –
ie it simply lists the sentences. An adequate simplicity measure ought,
therefore, to pronounce (b) as being simpler than (a). Notice now that
each diagram contains seven lines and three nodes. Thus neither a line-
count nor a node-count would reflect our intuition that (b) is simpler.
On the other hand, this intuition is reflected if we adopt the simplicity
measure proposed in Reich 1968, which entails counting the number of
nodes and adding 1 for each line in excess of three connecting to any
node (three being the minimum number of lines connecting to a node).
Diagram (a) scores 4 according to this measure – 3 for the number of
nodes and 1 for the extra line coming out of the downward AND. Diagram (b) scores 3 and thus emerges as simpler.

Using Reich's simplicity measure amounts to reducing a network to an
equivalent network containing only minimal nodes (*ie* nodes with just
three connections) and then counting the number of nodes in the modified network. Thus one is counting the number of 'junctions' in the network (Michael Ashby, unpublished paper) – *ie* the number of instances
of binary conjunction or disjunction. Whether the original network contains minimal nodes or not depends entirely on the data being described. This point can be illustrated by reference to *Fig* 22. In specifying

that a locative predicate consists of an optional posture, the sememe 'be' and a locative expression, a single downward AND node was used, with three lines connecting to the bottom. To have used two separate downward ANDS, one above the other, would have entailed claiming that (for instance) 'be' and the locative expression together form one constituent of a locative predicate (which could be referred to as 'l-pred$_1$'). There is no linguistic evidence for recognizing such a constituent. On the other hand, directional predicates (according to *Fig* 22) consist of an optional means of locomotion followed by a d-pred$_1$, which in turn consists of 'go' followed by a directional expressions constituent. It was necessary to recognize a d-pred$_1$ constituent, since precisely this much of a directional predicate may be embedded inside an extent expression. Thus we posit a d-pred$_1$ line in *Fig* 22 in order to be able to connect the extent part of the diagram to the directional part at just that point, thereby expressing two facts – (i) directional expressions may be accompanied by 'go' even when embedded inside an extent expression, *cf: The Mall goes from Buckingham Palace to Trafalgar Square*; and (ii) directional expressions embedded inside an extent expression may not be accompanied by a means of locomotion constituent, *cf: *The Mall drives from Buckingham Palace to Trafalgar Square* (*run* occurs in such sentences, but it is perhaps not unreasonable to claim that a different sense is involved from that which occurs in *The dog ran away*).

In theory one could count the number of junctions (in Ashby's sense) that occur in a rewrite-rule grammar. In practice, however, it is difficult – in particular, because the upward OR relationship is not explicitly expressed in PS rules. Consider, for instance, the upward OR on the line labelled 'l-ex' in *Fig* 22. The four lines leading into the top of this node express the fact that there are four different slots in which a locative expression may occur. If we inspect the rewrite-rule version of the semotactics, we see that there are four separate occurrences of the symbol 'l-ex' on the right-hand side of the rules (one in [R2] and three in [R3]). Thus the same information is available; but to locate it, it is necessary to scan the right-hand side of all the rules, counting the number of occurrences of the symbol in question. (The algebraic notation described in Lamb 1966a: 9–10 and Lockwood 1972: 59–64 does not suffer from this deficiency. Moreover, it provides an explicit means of representing all three of the distinctions: upward versus downward, ordered versus unordered, and AND versus OR.)

Linguists working within the framework of transformational grammar have sometimes been uncertain whether a simplification in one part of a grammar outweighs or is outweighed by a resulting complication in some other part of the grammar (*cf*, for instance, Bach 1967: 463–4 and Stanley 1967: 431). The problem is that quite distinct notational conventions are employed in, say, PS rules, transformational rules, phonological rules and morpheme structure conditions. This problem does not exist in relation to stratificational descriptions, since the same notation is used in all parts of a grammar. Thus the same measure of simplicity is employed irrespective of whether the descriptions that are being evaluated involve a single subcomponent of the overall grammar or several distinct subcomponents.

Lockwood points out (1972: 59), with regard to Reich's measure of simplicity, that 'although this procedure has been found to be the most generally useful measure . . . yet proposed, further research may result in its refinement'. It is relevant to mention the AND-OR node in this connection. It will be recalled that this node was said to be an abbreviation for a particular configuration of AND and OR nodes. This means that an AND-OR with three lines connecting to it is not a minimal node in the same sense that, say, an AND with three connections is minimal. Thus in calculating the complexity of a particular network, it is necessary to take into account the fact that an AND-OR node is more complex than an AND or an OR. In this instance, the difficulty can be overcome by reducing the AND-OR to the configuration of more basic nodes that it represents. A rather more tricky question is whether or not ordered and unordered nodes should contribute equally to the complexity count. (For further discussion of the simplicity measure, *cf* Lockwood 1972: 58–9.)

The only advantages of the network notation mentioned so far have centred around the issue of a simplicity measure. On a completely different note, it may be pointed out that Reich's (1969) 'breadth hypothesis' concerning short-term memory as used in the production and understanding of sentences arose out of a study of the way in which impulses need to be allowed to travel through networks. Reich's 'breadth hypothesis' is an alternative to Yngve's (1960) 'depth hypothesis'. Yngve had postulated a central short-term memory with a depth of about seven items, possibly identical to the memory which is used in the immediate recall of random digits and unconnected words (Yngve 1960: 452, 465). His model predicted that speakers should have no difficulty producing 'progressive', *ie* right-branching, structures (*cf: Fig* 24a), since they impose no burden on short-term memory. This prediction is correct: sentences such as *This is the cow that tossed the dog that worried the cat that killed the rat* . . . can be extended indefinitely. The model predicted that 'regressive', *ie* left-branching, structures (*cf: Fig* 24b) would be more difficult to process, since they require items to be held in

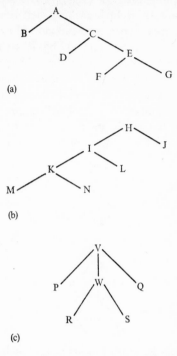

(a)

(b)

(c)

Fig 24 Tree diagrams representing (a) right-branching, (b) left-branching and (c) nested structures

short-term memory for a time before being processed. For instance, while K is being expanded as M + N, one has to remember (according to Yngve's model) to return both to L and to J. In view of the fact that left-branching structures such as *John's brother's father's uncle* can be extended indefinitely, this second prediction is apparently false. This and other deficiencies of Yngve's model were pointed out by Chomsky and Miller (1963: 474–5) and Chomsky (1965: 13, 197–8). In particular, they noted that nested structures – a type not specifically recognized by Yngve – are more difficult to process than either right-branching or left-branching, and that self-embedding is even more difficult than other nesting. (In *Fig* 24c, W is nested inside V; and the example is, in addition, a case of self-embedding if W is a phrase of the same type as V.)

According to Reich's breadth hypothesis, short-term memory is distributed over all the nodes of the network of the grammar. Nowhere, however, does its depth exceed one (1969) or two (1970c). The crucial feature of his account of right-branching, left-branching and self-embedding is a distinction between 'recursion' (already well known in linguistics) and 'iteration'. Self-embedding is treated as involving recursion, but right-branching and left-branching involve iteration. Both recursion and iteration require impulses to travel round a loop. The difference is that whereas in the case of recursion it is necessary to keep track of the number of times one has gone round the loop, this is unnecessary in the case of iteration. To clarify this point, let us consider the diagrams of *Fig* 25. Each of the three structures would re-

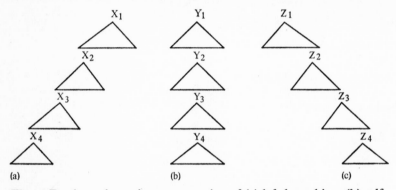

Fig 25 Further schematic representation of (a) left-branching, (b) self-embedding and (c) right-branching

quire going round some loop three times (to produce the second, third and fourth instance of the constituent in question). With regard to (b), the self-embedded structure, if this structure is to be produced correctly, it is essential to keep track of the fact that Y_4 is indeed the fourth Y that one has embarked upon, since one ultimately has to complete Y_3, Y_2 and Y_1. Contrast this situation with that which obtains in the case of Z_4 in the right-branching structure (c). By the time one embarks upon Z_4, the first three Zs are otherwise complete. Thus after completing Z_4, it is unnecessary to return to Z_3, Z_2 and Z_1. Consequently, it is irrelevant that Z_4 happens to be the fourth Z. It could just as well be the fourteenth or the forty-fourth. Similarly, with regard to (a), by the time one embarks upon X_3 proper (as opposed to the X_4 part of X_3), X_4 is already complete; by the time one embarks upon X_2 proper, X_4 and X_3 are both complete; and so on. Thus, as in (c), it is irrelevant that X_3 happens to be X_3 rather than some other X. (It might be preferable to number the Xs from the bottom up rather than from the top down, but of course this in no way affects the point at issue.)

In view of the fact that it is unnecessary to keep track of the number of times one goes round the loop in producing right-branching and left-branching structures, such structures can be generated to any desired depth by means of a network in which each of the nodes is a finite-state device (their exact nature is described in detail in Reich 1969 and 1970a). This would not be true of self-embedded structures, since it is necessary in this case to keep track of the number of times a loop is used. However, the number of self-embeddings that speakers can actually produce and understand is very limited. The first of the following examples, containing just one self-embedding, is perfectly acceptable; the second, containing two self-embeddings, is already barely acceptable; and the third, containing three self-embeddings, seems quite unacceptable.

[The cat [that the dog worried] killed the rat]
[The cat [that the dog [that the cow tossed] worried] killed the rat]
[The cat [that the dog [that the cow [that the farmer shot] tossed]
    worried] killed the rat]

Admittedly other factors are involved in determining acceptability besides merely the depth of self-embedding – as is clear from the fact that

[The cat [that the dog [that ran away] worried] killed the rat]

is more acceptable than the second of the above examples even though it contains the same number of self-embeddings. Nevertheless self-embedding – unlike right-branching and left-branching – appears to involve a relatively sharp cut-off point. Reich builds such a cut-off point into his model – which is, of course, a model of the production and understanding of sentences. As a result, each of the nodes in the network of his grammar remains a finite-state device; and since the grammar as a whole contains a finite number of such devices, Reich considers it to be a finite-state grammar. Thus Reich concludes that natural language is, after all, describable by means of a finite-state grammar (despite Chapter 3 of Chomsky's *Syntactic Structures*). Chomsky's position has been that, although an indefinite amount of self-embedding is unacceptable (*ie* not part of the 'performance' of speakers of a language), multiply self-embedded sentences are nevertheless grammatical (*ie* part of the 'competence' of speakers of a language). Moreover, Chomsky regards the linguist as being concerned in the first place with describing competence rather than performance. Therefore grammars should be capable of generating sentences containing an indefinite amount of self-embedding. Therefore natural languages are not describable by means of finite-state grammars. It might be claimed that there is no real conflict between Reich and Chomsky on this issue, since Reich is concerned with performance whereas Chomsky's remarks relate to competence. Nevertheless, it seems a little odd to assign priority (as Chomsky appears to do) to the set of sentences that could be produced with the help of such aids to memory as paper and pencils, rather than to the set of sentences that might actually be uttered.

In pointing out the advantages of using a network notation, I have not claimed that it is capable of representing facts that could not be expressed by means of, say, rewrite rules. Rather, I have adopted a standpoint that is somewhat analogous to a weak version of the Sapir-Whorf hypothesis. The suggestion underlying the preceding discussion is, namely, that through using the network notation one may be led to particular conceptions of linguistic structure which one might otherwise not arrive at.

In conclusion, I will comment briefly on the status of the symbols which occur in rewrite rules, in the light of the network notation. The symbols occurring in rewrite rules serve the function of pointing (back or forward) to other rules. For instance, 'subj' on the left-hand side of the second rule in [R1] points back to the first rule; and the occurrence of the same symbol in the right-hand side of the first rule points forward to the second rule. Constructing the equivalent network grammar (*cf: Fig* 21) consists in joining up all the rules. As soon as this is done, the symbol 'subj' becomes redundant. It could be omitted from *Fig* 21 without in any way affecting the description embodied in the diagram. In practice, we tend to supply labels for many of the intermediate lines in a network as well as the lines at the edge of the network. This is done in order to make the diagram more easily readable. But what really matters is the network of relationships itself.

3.2.3 Elaborating the initial fragment

In indicating how our initial fragment of the semotactics (*Fig* 22) can be elaborated, I will concentrate on three topics: coordination, sentences of the kind *The post office is over the hill*, and temporal adverbials.

The account of coordination given in 1.1.1 recognized two types of coordination: appositive and conjoined; and demonstrated that this distinction applies to sequences of locative expressions, to sequences of individual directional expressions (whether source, path or goal), and to sequences of d-exs constituents (each of which comprises one or more individual directional expressions and defines one 'journey'). Sequences of these various constituents can be generated by inserting loops into the semotactics at the appropriate places. *Fig* 26a shows the loop that might

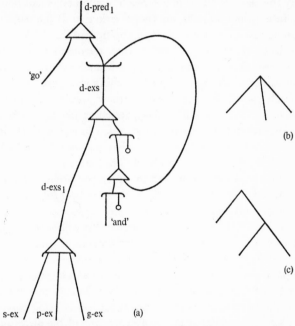

Fig 26 Modifying the semotactics to account for coordination

be inserted on the line labelled 'd-exs' in *Fig* 22. The higher of the two optionality nodes indicates that taking the loop is optional. The lower optionality node states that if the loop is taken there is a further option of selecting 'and'. The corresponding modification of the PS rules in [R3] consists in replacing the rule

d-exs → (s-ex◊p-ex◊g-ex)

by the two rules

d-exs → d-exs₁ (('and') d-exs)
d-exs₁ → (s-ex◊p-ex◊g-ex)

In giving the PS rule version it is necessary to introduce an additional symbol. The constituent in question is labelled 'd-exs$_1$', and this label is included also at the appropriate place in *Fig* 26a. Similar loops to that of *Fig* 26a could be inserted on the l-ex, s-ex, p-ex and g-ex lines in *Fig* 22.

It will be realized that this account of coordination would require expanding in a number of respects. It implies that the distinction between appositive and conjoined coordination depends on whether or not 'and' is selected, but does not express the fact that *and* is usually inserted between only the last two items in a series of conjoined constituents. The brief but interesting remarks on coordination in Reich 1969: 840-1 should also be taken into account. Reich points out that by handling coordination in terms of iteration rather than recursion a series of coordinate items would be assigned a multiple-branching structure like that in *Fig* 26b rather than, say, a right-branching structure as in *Fig* 26c. (It is generally agreed that the latter treatment ascribes too much structure to what is essentially a list.) Also, Reich argues from intonational evidence that coordination should be handled in terms of left-iteration rather than right-iteration. The conjunction *and* would then be selected not before taking the loop (as in *Fig* 26a) but after the loop.

In 1.1.3 two ways were indicated in which the preliminary semantic structure proposed for *The post office is over the hill (from here)* in 1.1.1 might be revised. Of these the second (*cf: Fig* 11) seems more promising, and it is this that will be discussed further here. It will be recalled that we treated the sentence as having two propositions in its underlying representation: a directional proposition defining a journey leading from the speaker's position over the hill to some place; and a locative proposition indicating that the post office is at some place. Moreover, the place that features in the locative proposition was regarded as being coreferential with the place that occurs in the goal expression of the directional proposition. The method most commonly employed within present-day linguistics of indicating that two items are coreferential is to assign to them the same referential index. For instance, a sentence such as *Fred admires himself* might be derived from something like 'Fred$_1$ admire Fred$_1$', containing two instances of 'Fred', each accompanied by the same subscript. (And the underlying representation 'Fred$_1$ admire Fred$_1$' would indicate that two different Freds were involved, so that reflexivization would not be possible in this case.) A somewhat different proposal was made by Bach (1968: 110), according to which the underlying representation of *Fred admires himself* would be something more like 'Fred$_1$ admire i'. The method employed in *Fig* 11 for showing that the two places are coreferential does not make use of referential indices. Instead, the specifier constituent of one locative expression is shown to be identical to the specifier of another locative expression by allowing the two lines in question to merge. This means that the resulting semantic representation is no longer a tree in the usual sense of this term. We need now to consider how such a semantic representation might be generated by the semotactics. The germ of a solution is actually already present in another part of the semotactics. The diagram in *Fig 27* rep-

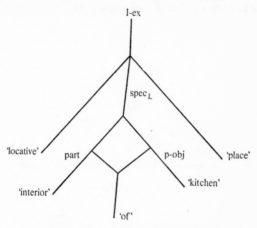

Fig 27 The route taken by impulses during the production of the semantic representation of *in the kitchen*

resents the route that impulses would take during the production of the locative expression underlying *in the kitchen*. It will be seen that there is a place in the diagram at which two lines merge (immediately above the sememe 'of'). This feature of the diagram depends on the presence in the semotactics of an upward AND node (at G in *Fig 22*). Impulses have to come together from two different parts of the tactics before it is appropriate to insert 'of'. The solution to our present problem also entails using an upward AND node. The main respect in which it will differ from the one at G in *Fig 22* is that the line from the bottom of the node will not connect to any sememe (comparable to 'of'). Instead, it will be allowed to terminate in a zero – *cf: Fig* 28. Thus the function of the node is simply to link the two propositions together.

The next thing to determine is the place in the semotactics to which the lines x and y of *Fig 28* connect. The corresponding lines in the semantic representation given in *Fig 11* come from the specifier slot of two separate locative expressions. Now in the semotactics itself there is only one locative expression construction (which is used two or more times in the generation of sentences that contain two or more locative expressions). This means that there is only one place in the semotactics corresponding to the specifier slot of a locative expression. But to allow the lines x and y of *Fig 28* to connect to the same place in the semotactics would have rather drastic consequences as far as the network notation is concerned. There is no sense in positing two separate lines which connect from the same point on one node to the same point on another

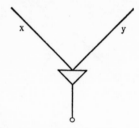

Fig 28 An upward unordered AND terminating in a zero

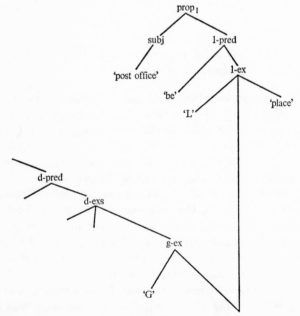

Fig 29 Revised version of part of *Fig* 11

node. We would be dealing, in fact, with a single line. Moreover, if there is only one line, there is no justification for inserting an upward AND node. We can get round this problem by making a small modification to the semantic representation we want the semotactics to generate. *Fig* 29 shows the revised portion of *Fig* 11. It will be seen that the line from the specifier slot of the locative expression in $prop_1$ merges with a line corresponding to the second constituent of the goal expression in $prop_2$ (which would otherwise be filled by a locative expression of the usual kind). Thus when we modify the semotactics, we need to specify that the second slot in a goal expression may be occupied either by a locative expression of the usual kind or by what occurs in *Fig* 29. If we were simply presenting the network notation, there would be no need to give any name to the second constituent of the goal expression in *Fig* 29, but in order to be able to give a corresponding rewrite-rule version it is necessary to call it something. I will use the label '$l\text{-ex}_{CR}$', in which 'CR' stands for 'coreferential'. Similarly, there are now two possibilities for filling the specifier slot of a locative expression – either what was stated in the '$spec_L$' rule in [R2] (*cf* also *Fig* 22); or what occurs in *Fig* 29. The original kind of specifier will be referred to as '$spec_{L-1}$' and the kind illustrated by *Fig* 29 as '$spec_{L-CR}$'. The label '$spec_L$' will be used from now on as a cover symbol representing either type. *Fig* 30 shows the revised version of the relevant portion of *Fig* 22. The added structure consists of two downward OR nodes, at P and Q, the upward AND at R, and the two lines leading from P and Q to R. I have ordered the two downward ORS, in such a way that the 'normal' specifier (now called '$spec_{L-1}$') and the 'usual' locative expression constituent of a goal expression constitute the 'otherwise' possibilities.

As one would expect, the corresponding changes in the rewrite-rule version are also relatively minor. The rule

$$\text{spec}_L \rightarrow (\text{part}\emptyset\text{p-obj})$$

in [R2] is replaced by the two rules

$$\text{spec}_L \rightarrow \left\{ \begin{array}{l} \text{spec}_{L-1} \\ \text{spec}_{L-CR} \end{array} \right\}$$
$$\text{spec}_{L-1} \rightarrow (\text{part}\emptyset\text{p-obj})$$

It should be noted, however, that the first of these rules is less specific than the node at P in *Fig* 30, in so far as it does not reflect the fact that the OR is ordered. Similarly, the rule

$$\text{g-ex} \rightarrow \text{'goal' l-ex}$$

in [R3] needs to be replaced by the rule

$$g\text{-}ex \rightarrow \text{`goal'} \begin{Bmatrix} l\text{-}ex \\ l\text{-}ex_{CR} \end{Bmatrix}$$

– which, again, is less specific than the ordered OR at Q in *Fig* 30. The work of the upward AND at R in *Fig* 30 would be done by a transforma-

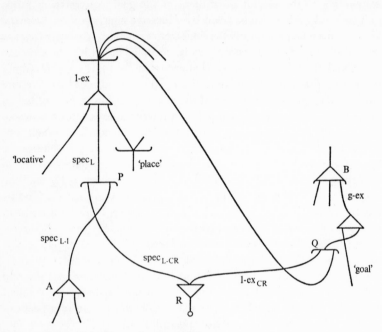

Fig 30 Revised version of part of *Fig* 22

tional rule within the rewrite-rule framework. However, it would be a little unrealistic at this point to attempt to translate the network solution literally into the form of a transformational rule, since an independently proposed transformational treatment would probably take a rather different form in a number of respects. I shall therefore propose no transformational equivalent of the upward AND at R in *Fig* 30.

As yet nothing has been said concerning the way in which the upward AND of *Fig* 30 would function in the course of producing the sememic representation of *The post office is over the hill* (*from here*). The exact details are, in fact, unclear to me. However, there are certain general issues that merit discussion. Two separate approaches can be distinguished.

According to one approach, the locative and directional propositions would be generated independently of each other and would be linked together by virtue of the fact that an impulse reaches the upward AND at R both along the 'spec$_{L-CR}$' line and along the '1-ex$_{CR}$' line. This approach has a number of problems, of which I will mention two. First, it is not clear how it would be shown that prop$_2$ is embedded inside prop$_1$ (*cf:* *Figs* 11 and 29), rather than prop$_1$ inside prop$_2$. Secondly, if a locative and a directional proposition are produced simultaneously, the situation might arise where two separate impulses needed to travel along the same line in the semotactics at the same moment (*eg* the 'prop' line or the 'pred' line in *Fig* 22). According to the alternative approach, which seems more satisfactory, the unordered upward AND of *Fig* 30 would have to be defined in such a way that an impulse reaching the node along either of the two upper lines would immediately cause an impulse to be sent out along the line at the bottom. A feedback signal (*cf* 3.5) returning to the node along this same line would then cause an impulse to be sent out up the other of the two upper lines. With regard to *The post office is over the hill* (*from here*), one would first of all produce the locative proposition, prop$_1$. Then at the appropriate point in prop$_1$ one would embark upon prop$_2$, by way of the locative expression constituent of its goal expression.

As the description stands at present, there would be nothing to prevent the generation of structures such as that shown in *Fig* 31. It is clear that we would want to block the generation of such a structure. It

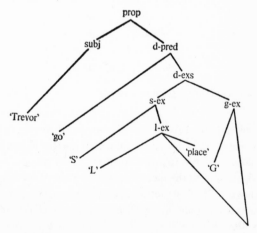

Fig 31 An undesirable semantic representation

represents a directional sentence in which there is no indication of the location functioning as the source and goal, beyond the fact that they are coreferential. We need to ensure that the upward AND that we have been discussing is used only for linking together a locative proposition and a directional proposition, as in the underlying representation of sentences such as *The post office is over the hill (from here)*. This we can do by stipulating that the upward AND may be used only if an impulse reaching it along the 'spec$_{\text{L-CR}}$' line comes from a locative expression that is part of a locative proposition. *Fig 32* is a revised version of part of

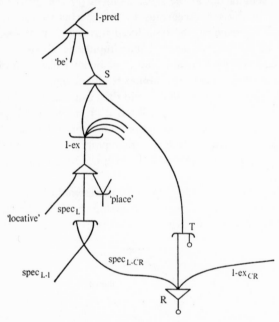

Fig 32 Revised version of part of *Fig 30*

Fig 30 that will achieve this result. Two extra nodes are included, at S and T. The node at S is a downward unordered AND. Its presence means that, in the course of producing a locative predicate, at the same time that an impulse is sent to the locative expression construction an impulse is also sent down to T. A structure such as that in *Fig 31* could now no longer be generated, since no impulse would be available from (S and) T. The zero alternative at T is used whenever the locative expression of a locative proposition contains a spec$_{\text{L-1}}$ rather than a spec$_{\text{L-CR}}$.

Wherever a downward unordered AND (*eg* S in *Fig* 32) dominates a downward ordered AND (*eg* the locative expression construction in *Fig* 32), this configuration of nodes states that something – let us call it p – is simultaneous with something else – call it q – which, in fact, is a sequence of things: r s t. Thus p is simultaneous with r and s and t. Such a configuration can be used in phonology to show that some feature, *eg* nasality, accompanies a sequence of segments. Accordingly, the impulse sent down from S to T (and R) would be simultaneous with all three parts of a locative expression. In the present instance, there is actually another possible solution, which might even be preferable to the one shown in *Fig* 32. Instead of inserting the downward unordered AND at S, we could allow a fourth line to come out of the bottom of the downward ordered AND representing the locative predicate construction. This line would connect to the downward OR at T. According to this solution, an impulse reaching R from T would get there after an impulse along the 'spec$_{L-CR}$' line. This fact would need to be taken into account in defining the upward AND.

More important than the specific details discussed in the preceding paragraph is the general point that emerges from our discussion of *Fig* 32. We know from Part I and 3.2.1 that there are four different slots in which a locative expression may occur. Now in order to permit the generation of structures like *Fig* 29 but prevent the generation of structures like *Fig* 31, it was necessary to single out locative expressions which are part of a locative proposition (as opposed to those which are part of a directional proposition). This is a typical situation in which a transformational rule would be called for. The line in *Fig* 32 that goes via T to R ensures that the transformation is applicable only to such locative expressions as exhibit the appropriate 'derivational history'.

It will be recalled that directional expressions may occur either in directional sentences or in extent sentences. This raises the question whether we ought to specify that the goal expression which features in *Fig* 30 must be part of a directional proposition rather than an extent proposition. It would be an easy matter to incorporate such a condition into the semotactics; the mechanism would be exactly parallel to that which was introduced in converting *Fig* 30 into *Fig* 32. This may not be necessary, however. Perhaps a sentence such as *The post office is over the hill* may be regarded as containing either an embedded directional proposition or an embedded extent proposition. In the one case, the post office would be at the end of a hypothetical journey. In the other case, it would be at the end of a particular stretch of space. (The existence of sentences such as *The post office is three miles from here* is relevant at this point.) These would simply be two equivalent ways of viewing the same situation.

Let us consider now once again sentences such as *The caretaker lives to the right from here*. Here, too, a location is being specified in relation to what might be called a hypothetical journey, but the location is co-referential in this instance with a location in the middle of the hypothetical journey rather than at the end of it. Thus while *The post office is over the hill* can be paraphrased as *The post office is at the end of a path leading over the hill*, *The caretaker lives to the right* would be paraphrased as *The caretaker lives on a path leading to the right*, rather than **The caretaker lives at the end of a path leading to the right*. This is perhaps more obvious in the case of an example such as *I want that lamp to stand well into the corner*. *Into the corner* here does not mean 'at the end of a path leading into the corner' (if the lamp really had to be at the end of the path, we would say simply *I want that lamp to stand in the corner*); instead it means 'on a path leading into the corner', and the adverb *well* indicates how far along the path the lamp is to be situated, namely a considerable distance along it. In both the 'post office' type of example and the 'caretaker' type, two points on a journey are given, and a third has to be inferred since it is functioning as the location of something else. In the 'post office' example, the beginning and middle of the journey are given, we infer where the end is, and that is where the post office is located. In the 'caretaker' example, the beginning and end of the journey are given, we infer where the middle is, and that is where the caretaker lives.

To handle the semantic structure of the 'caretaker' example, it would seem, then, that we simply need to generalize the 'post office' example solution (*cf* especially *Fig* 30) so that it would apply either to the goal expression constituent or to the path expression constituent of a directional predicate.

Finally, it should be noted that an upward AND would be used to generate the sememic representation of *I met a friend of yours during the vacation* (*cf: Fig* 18) and of sentences containing a progressive verb-form, *eg: I was driving to Wales* (*cf: Fig* 16). In this last example an upward AND would also be used to represent the fact that 'I' functions in two separate propositions, prop$_2$ and prop$_4$ (the diagram of *Fig* 16 does not make this explicit).

We turn now to temporal adverbials. The facts are rather complex, and as a result the account that I shall give will be sketchy in a number of respects. At several places I shall make specific mention of unsolved problems; at other similar places I shall simply remain silent. It was pointed out in **2.1.2** that some writers have noted similarities between tenses and articles or pronouns. With regard to the question of how to formalize such an analysis, McCawley writes (1971: 111): 'my suggestion that tenses are pronominal in nature would entail having a reduplication rule which added a pronominal copy of every time adverb'. The term 'copy' has tended not to be used by linguists working within the framework of stratificational grammar, but it seems to me that some exactly analogous mechanism will need to be employed here (and also to handle the insertion of *there* in sentences such as *There's a book on the table*). Since I am unable to specify how the mechanism would work, tense will be omitted from the elaboration of the semotactics presented below. It should be noted that the 'semantic representations' given in *Figs* 16 and 18, which contain a temporal locative expression expressing the meaning of the past tense, will require modification when the mechanism of tense-insertion is better understood.

Fig 33 contains a further fragment of the semotactics. It indicates the slots in the structure of propositions that may be occupied by temporal adverbials. The latter are of two kinds: locative expressions and extent expressions (I have not attempted to include what Huddleston, 1969: 779, calls 'ordinal specifiers' – *eg: for the second time*). In combining *Figs* 22 and 33, the l-pred, e-pred and d-pred parts of *Fig* 22 would need to be connected to the lines bearing those labels in *Fig* 33. I shall discuss the new diagram in small sections, presenting a PS-rule version in the process.

The first rules are:

$$\text{prop} \rightarrow \text{subj pred}_{TR} \qquad\qquad\qquad\qquad\qquad \text{[R6]}$$
$$\text{subj} \rightarrow \ldots$$
$$\text{pred}_{TR} \rightarrow \begin{Bmatrix} \text{pred}_{punct} \\ \text{pred}_{dur} \end{Bmatrix} (\text{l-ex}_T)$$
$$\text{l-ex}_T \rightarrow \text{'locative' spec}_{L-T} \text{'time' ('plur')}$$

As in the first rule of [R1], *cf* **3.2.1**, it seems desirable to state at the outset that all kinds of propositions have a subject, rather than to distinguish the different kinds of propositions and then indicate for each separately that it contains a subject. The second constituent of a proposition is now a 'predicate with time reference (pred_{TR})'. With regard to the possibility of a proposition occupying the subject slot in another proposition (*cf* **3.2.1**), there are now certain problems, centring around the

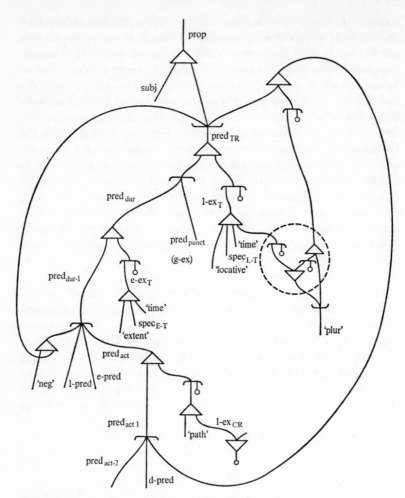

Fig 33 A further fragment of the semotactics

fact that we need to block the generation of ungrammatical utterances such as *[[Trevor was sitting on a bench at 10 o'clock] in the park at 11 o'clock]*. The third rule indicates that any kind of predicate may be accompanied optionally by a temporal locative expression, and at the same time distinguishes two types of predicates: punctual and durative. Punctual predicates correspond to Vendler's achievement class (class 3 – *cf* **2.1.2**). They contain verbs such as *recognize*, *find*, *lose*, *arrive* and *reach* in their surface structure. In our terms, they contain simply a goal expression. (Thus the semantic representation of sentences containing *arrive* and *reach* contains no occurrence of the sememe 'go', which is inserted only in the presence of a directional expressions constituent.) Durative predicates correspond to Vendler's other three classes – activity, accomplishment and state. A temporal locative expression contains the sememe 'locative', a specifier, the sememe 'time' and (optionally) the 'plural' sememe. This last element is included with temporal adverbials such as *on Sundays* in mind. As we shall see, however, the choice of 'plural' in a temporal locative expression will be treated as being determined by a similar choice made elsewhere. Since the set of things that can occupy the specifier slot of a temporal locative expression is different from the set of things that occupy the corresponding position in a spatial locative expression, the subscript 'T' is added to 'spec$_L$'. The various possibilities will be indicated in a further diagram below, but we know already that the prepositions *at, on, in, before, after, since, by* and *during* occur in the surface realization of temporal locative expressions. Sentences such as *Nowadays when it's hot Bill usually takes his shirt off when he's alone* (for similar examples, *cf* Hudson 1971) are probably best analysed as containing several appositive coordinate locative expressions, and are therefore similar to spatial examples such as *The towels are near the bathroom in the cupboard on the shelf*. We would therefore need to allow the possibility of generating sequences of coordinate temporal locative expressions.

The next two rules are:

$$\text{pred}_{dur} \rightarrow \text{pred}_{dur-1} \ (\text{e-ex}_T) \qquad\qquad\qquad\qquad [R7]$$
$$\text{e-ex}_T \rightarrow \text{'extent'} \ \text{spec}_{E-T} \ \text{'time'}$$

The first rule indicates that durative predicates may optionally contain a temporal extent expression, *ie* a durational adverbial. (Punctual predicates, on the other hand, may not take a durational adverbial – unless one of the two loops described below is used, but in this case we are, strictly speaking, no longer dealing with a punctual predicate.) Temporal extent expressions consist of the sememe 'extent', a specifier and the sememe 'time'. We know from earlier sections (*cf*, for instance, 2.2.6) that *from, to, till, until, through, throughout* and *for* occur in durational adverbials. Some details of the structure below the 'spec$_{E-T}$' line in *Fig* 33 will be indicated with the aid of a further diagram.

Speaking informally, there are two kinds of durative predicates. One kind I will call 'actional'. It comprises Vendler's activity and accomplishment classes, *ie* classes 1 and 2. All other durative predicates are

stative. It will be seen, however, that there are four lines coming out of
the bottom of the downward OR below the 'pred$_{dur-1}$' line in *Fig* 33,
rather than just two. One of these lines corresponds to the actional type
of durative predicate; the other three lines represent three kinds of
stative predicates. The reason there is no line in the diagram corresponding to stative predicates as a whole is that there is no positive feature
which unites the three kinds. There is only the negative feature that none
of them is actional. Actional predicates are those that can take the progressive. Suppose we had originally shown a binary breakdown of durative predicates (pred$_{dur-1}$) into actional (pred$_{act}$) and stative (pred$_{stat}$).
Then we would subcategorize the stative predicates by means of a downward OR at the bottom of the 'pred$_{stat}$' line with three lines coming out
of it. Now this would mean that we would have two instances of the
same kind of node (the downward unordered OR), one immediately
above the other. In such a situation, one of the two nodes is redundant,
since it is always possible to collapse them into a single node with correspondingly more lines coming out of it. In the process of collapsing
the two nodes in the present instance, the 'pred$_{stat}$' line would disappear.
What it would mean, in terms of the network notation, to have a positive
reason for setting up a single class of stative predicates, is that it would
be necessary to connect some other line to the 'pred$_{stat}$' line by means of
some other kind of node than a downward OR. In this case there would
be no question of collapsing the two downward ORS, since they would
no longer be one immediately above the other. The same general point
was illustrated by our discussion in 3.2.2 of the 'd-pred$_1$' line in *Fig* 22
and the fact that there is no corresponding 'l-pred$_1$' line.

The PS rule in [R8] expresses the same facts as the downward OR at
the bottom of the 'pred$_{dur-1}$' line:

$$\text{pred}_{dur-1} \rightarrow \begin{Bmatrix} \text{'neg' pred}_{TR} \\ \text{l-pred} \\ \text{e-pred} \\ \text{pred}_{act} \end{Bmatrix} \qquad \text{[R8]}$$

Two of the kinds of stative predicates are locative and extent predicates,
as described in *Fig* 22. The third type consists of the sememe 'neg' – *ie*
'negative' – in construction with any kind of predicate (by way of the
loop to the upward OR on the 'pred$_{TR}$' line). Thus although *recognize* in
a sentence such as *I recognized your sister* would not be accompanied by
a durational adverbial (**I recognized your sister until she took her hat off*/

put her hat on), a durational adverbial is quite in order if the predicate is negated, *eg: I didn't recognize your sister until she took her hat off.*

Actional predicates, as already noted, are those that can be used in the progressive. The semantic representation of *I was driving to Wales* shown in *Fig* 16 (**2.1.2**) and the discussion in the present subsection of the mechanism for generating *The post office is over the hill* make it clear that actional predicates may optionally be accompanied by a path expression, whose locative expression constituent is coreferential with a locative expression in some other proposition. Thus we have the rule:

$$\text{pred}_{act} \rightarrow \text{pred}_{act-1} \; (\text{'path'} \; \text{l-ex}_{CR}) \tag{R9}$$

Directional predicates, as described in *Fig* 22, are one type of actional predicate. The line 'pred_{act-2}' allows the possibility of non-directional actional predicates. A third possibility, as regards actional predicates, is to take the loop at the right of *Fig* 33. Taking this loop is frequently accompanied by selecting the sememe 'plural', as in *I've been recognizing people I know all morning*, which refers to more than one act of recognition. A single act of recognition would involve a punctual predicate (which could not take the progressive), but a predication of any kind may take the progressive when it is in the plural, *ie* iterative, since in this case we are dealing with a kind of activity.

The point at which locative adverbials may be selected in *Fig* 33 is higher up the diagram than the point at which durational adverbials may be selected. This means that locative adverbials are in general more peripheral than durational adverbials. However, if the loop at the right of *Fig* 33 is used, it is possible to generate sememic representations in which a durational adverbial is more peripheral than a locative adverbial, *eg: I was shopping on Saturday throughout June.* The sememic representation of *on Saturday* – like that of *shop* – would be selected after travelling round the loop, as a result of which *on Saturday* is directly in construction with *shop. Throughout June* modifies not simply *shop* but *shop on Saturday.* Thus we have, in effect, a complex verb *to on-Saturday-shop.* When a locative adverbial is selected without going round the loop, it refers to a definite, specific time, and moreover to the same time to which the tense refers. Thus *on Saturday* in *I bought this watch on Saturday* refers to 'last Saturday'. On the other hand, locative adverbials that are selected after travelling round the loop do not refer to a specific time. Taken out of context, *I ate meat on Friday* would be understood as meaning the same as *I ate meat last Friday.* But when placed in a suitable context, the non-specific interpretation of *on Friday* may come to the fore: *I used to be really wicked. For instance, I ate meat on Friday*. In this case we have, in effect, a complex verb *to on-Friday-meat-eat*; *on Friday* is selected after going round the loop. In *I've eaten meat on Friday*, only the non-specific interpretation of *on Friday* is possible. This is because the specific meaning would be incompatible with the meaning of the tense. As a specific temporal adverbial *on Friday* refers either to 'last Friday' or to 'next Friday', but the tense of this sentence is present rather than past or future.

The PS rule which incorporates the loop that we have been discussing, as part of a characterization of actional predicates, is:

$$\text{pred}_{\text{act--1}} \rightarrow \begin{Bmatrix} \text{d-pred} \\ \text{pred}_{\text{act--2}} \\ \text{pred}_{\text{TR}} \, (\text{'plur'}) \end{Bmatrix} \qquad [\text{R10}]$$

It seems necessary to make the 'plural' sememe optional, as shown, in view of the fact that it would be appropriate to say *I've eaten meat on Friday* even if the event in question had occurred only once. In [R10] it appears that 'plur', if selected, follows 'pred$_{\text{TR}}$', but from the network version it will be seen that the two constituents are taken to be simultaneous. The configuration of nodes surrounded by a dotted circle in *Fig* 33 ensures that 'plur' may be selected in a temporal locative expression only if it has been selected also in conjunction with the loop.

Fig 34 gives details of the internal structure of temporal locative expressions and extent expressions. In broad outline it is very similar to the corresponding section of the spatial analysis. Instead of discussing the whole diagram, I will this time simply refer to a number of features of it, pointing out not only things that it can handle but also things that it cannot handle.

As was pointed out in 2.2.6, sentences of the kind *X during Y* mean 'X happened (or existed) at a time which Y was lasting via'. Two separate propositions are linked together by the fact that they share a particular constituent, namely a temporal locative expression. The mechanism for linking the two propositions is exactly comparable to that proposed in *Figs* 30 and 32 for linking together propositions that share a spatial locative expression. It involves the upward unordered AND at the bottom of *Fig* 34 and the three lines connecting to the top of it.

During examples thus represent one of the possible ways in which the specifier slot of a temporal locative expression may be filled. Otherwise, the specifier may be a point in time, *eg: 10 o'clock*, or a period of time, *eg: August*; or it may contain a member of the category labelled 'part$_{\text{P/T}}$'

in *Fig* 34, either with or without an accompanying point or period. There are four members of the category labelled 'part$_{P/T}$': 'anterior', 'posterior', 'interior' and 'exterior'. They constitute the subset of the larger set of parts that occur in both spatial and temporal contexts.

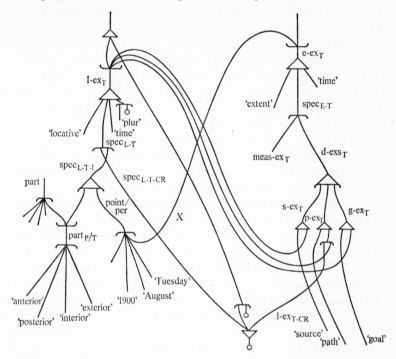

Fig 34 A further fragment of the semotactics

There are two kinds of temporal extent expressions, depending on whether the specifier slot contains a measurement expression (as in *lasted for two hours*) or directional expressions (as in *lasted from seven o'clock until nine o'clock*). Measured extent expressions may be embedded inside a locative expression, as in *I learned French in six weeks* or *We went home after a month*. In generating such sentences, it would be necessary to use the line at X in *Fig* 34, which leads from the downward OR representing the category of points and periods to the upward OR above the extent expression construction. Notice, however, that this line allows any temporal extent expression to be embedded inside a temporal locative expression, rather than just a measured extent expression. *Since* and *by* become relevant at this point. According to the analysis of 2.2.4, a *since*-phrase realizes a source expression embedded inside a locative expression, and a *by*-phrase realizes a goal expression embedded inside a locative expression. It is now clear that we could achieve a simpler semotactics by regarding the source expression or goal expression as being embedded first of all inside an extent expression. In this case, line X would be used also in generating the sememic representation of *since* and *by*. A semotactics containing the one line X would clearly be simpler than one in which there were two separate lines – one going to an extra downward AND characterizing measured extent expressions (used in generating phrases such as *in six weeks*) and one leading to the 'd-exs$_T$' line (used in generating *since*-phrases and *by*-phrases). Moreover, it would then be true of all temporal directional expressions that they are embedded inside an extent expression – *ie* not only of the directional expressions in *lasted from seven o'clock until nine o'clock* (*cf* 2.1.1) but also of those that occur in *since yesterday* and *by tomorrow*. If such a proposal were adopted, we should need to revise our account of the perfect also, inserting an extent expression not only in *Fig* 17 (2.2.4) but also in *Fig* 14 (2.1.2). However, a number of problems involving *since* and *by* would remain. For instance, why is it that *since*-phrases and *by*-phrases do not co-occur (**They've been living in Canada since 1970 by now*)? Also, whether we keep line X or replace it by two separate lines, *Fig* 34 would generate not only *until after 10 o'clock* but also **until since 10 o'clock* and **until by 10 o'clock*. I will therefore retain the componential definition of *since* and *by* given in 2.2.4 – *ie* 'locative source time' and 'locative goal time' – rather than replace them by 'locative extent source time' and 'locative extent goal time', which would contribute nothing further to a solution of the problems mentioned above.

It would be an easy matter to add to *Fig* 34 a mechanism for inserting 'of' between a part and a point or period, exactly parallel to the mechanism for inserting 'of' in spatial locative expressions (*cf: Fig* 22). However, there is a problem concerning the general question of 'of'-insertion – to which we shall devote a certain amount of attention in 3.2.5.

3.2.4 Semotactic traces and sememic representations

It is important to draw a distinction between the route taken by impulses travelling through the semotactics, on the one hand, and the output from the bottom of the semotactics, on the other. A semotactic trace is a record of the route taken by impulses as they pass through the semotactics on a given occasion. *Fig* 27 shows part of a semotactic trace, namely the part corresponding to the locative expression underlying *in the kitchen*. (Adopting a somewhat more precise diagramming convention, Lamb included downward and upward ANDS in traces, *cf* 1966a: 25; see also Lockwood 1972: 37.) All of the 'semantic representations' given in the form of tree diagrams in Part I seem to be more like semotactic traces than they are like what would qualify as a sememic/semantic representation within the framework of stratificational grammar. We may think of a sememic representation as a particular series of impulses leaving the semotactics and entering the semolexemic realizational structure. Each individual impulse corresponds to a sememe, *ie* a terminal element (or ultimate constituent) of the semotactics. From this account, it would appear that sememic representations are ordered, but otherwise unstructured, strings of sememes. This raises the question of what happens to the information about constituent structure that is contained in the tree diagrams of Part I (and which would be reflected equally clearly in a semotactic trace). Is this information simply thrown away? I will make a brief comment, initially, in answer to this question, and then expand on it below. The brief answer is that whatever information about constituent structure is needed by subsequent components of the grammar has to be incorporated in the sememic representation. This means that some sememes apparently have the sole function of marking constituent structure. Constituent structure information that is not needed by any subsequent component of the grammar is not incorporated into the sememic representation. Thus it is not the case that all constituent structure information is automatically passed on into subsequent components of the grammar.

Within the framework of transformational grammar no distinction has ever been drawn, as far as I am aware, that is analogous to the distinction between semotactic traces and sememic representations. Just as a semotactic trace is a record of one particular route through the semotactics, so also a phrase marker may be thought of as a record of one particular route through a set of PS rules. But, at the same time, the phrase marker itself constitutes the underlying representation of a sentence. Thus, in effect, the view is held that a semotactic trace and a sememic representation are one and the same thing.

In the hope of giving a clearer picture of the present issue, I intend to set it against the background of the notion of 'tree-pruning' (Ross 1966) and one proposal for eliminating the need for tree-pruning (Robinson 1970). Ross (1966: 1–2) regards the noun phrase *his yellow cat* as being derived from the same structure as that which underlies *the cat which he*

has which is yellow, by means of two applications of a relative clause reduction transformation. After the application of this rule, *his yellow cat*
has the structure shown in *Fig* 35. Ross observes, in relation to this struc-

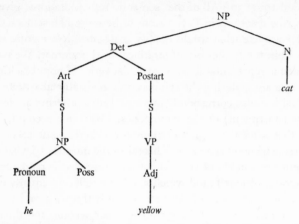

Fig 35 The structure of *his yellow cat* after the application of relative
clause reduction (according to Ross 1966)

ture, that it is counterintuitive to assert that the possessive pronoun *his*
and the adjective *yellow* are both sentences. Thus it seems desirable to
provide some mechanism for removing the S nodes from *Fig* 35. Furthermore, Ross points out that in some cases unless such S nodes are deleted, further transformations will be allowed to apply which ought not
to apply. For instance, the structure underlying *A jug which was from
India got broken* may undergo extraposition, giving *A jug got broken
which was from India*. However, if relative clause reduction has applied,
extraposition is impossible – *ie* there is no *A jug got broken from India*
corresponding to *A jug from India got broken*. Ross argues, therefore,
that the S node dominating *from India* has to be deleted in order to block
the application of the extraposition transformation in this instance. His
proposed tree-pruning convention deletes any embedded S node which
does not branch (*ie* which directly dominates only NP or VP), at whatever point in a derivation such a situation arises.

Robinson argues that there would be no need for tree-pruning conventions if the base component of a transformational grammar were to
contain a dependency grammar in place of the customary phrase structure grammar. The reason for this is that dependency grammar recognizes only terminal nodes (*eg* N, V, Adj); non-terminal nodes (*eg* S, NP,

VP) do not occur. Dependency markers representing the structure of *a yellow cat*, before and after relative clause reduction, are given in *Fig* 36

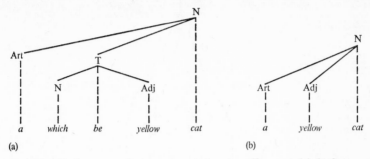

Fig 36 Dependency markers representing *a yellow cat* (a) before and (b) after relative clause reduction (according to Robinson 1970)

(*cf* Robinson 1970: 284). The category T in *Fig* 36a is the 'governor' of a sentence, *ie* the element on which all other elements in the sentence directly or indirectly depend. It carries distinctions of sentence type (*eg* declarative versus interrogative), tense and intonation (Robinson 1970: 282). The relative clause reduction transformation deletes the N (*which*) and the T (*be*) of *which be yellow* – whereupon the Adj (*yellow*), having lost its governor, is attached directly to the N node representing *cat*.

On the face of it, stratificational grammar seems to adopt a position that is distinct both from that of Ross and from that of Robinson. I shall attempt to characterize the stratificational approach on the basis of some extremely simple hypothetical data. I leave it to others to judge to what extent this approach resembles that of Ross or that of Robinson.

The semotactics of our hypothetical language is shown in *Fig* 37, and an equivalent phrase structure grammar is given below:

$$S \rightarrow P \,(\text{'c'}) \,\text{'d'} \qquad\qquad\qquad\qquad [R11]$$
$$P \rightarrow \begin{Bmatrix} \text{'a'} \\ Q \end{Bmatrix}$$
$$Q \rightarrow \text{'b'} \,(\text{'c'})$$

Fig 38 contains the full set of phrase markers generated by [R11]. It will be noticed that the string 'b c d' is generated in two distinct ways – *cf* (d) and (e). What concerns us in particular is the nature of the set of sememic representations generated by *Fig* 37, *ie* the set of possible outputs from the bottom of the semotactics. In its present form, there are five possible outputs: 'a d', 'a c d', 'b d', 'b c d' and 'b c c d'. These

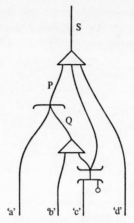

Fig 37 The semotactics of a simple hypothetical language

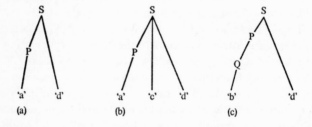

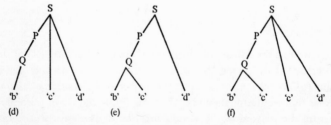

Fig 38 The set of phrase markers generated by [R11]

sememic representations contain none of the higher structure shown in the trees of *Fig* 38. Such structure would be present in the corresponding semotactic traces, but is absent from the sememic representations. The question now arises whether such sememic representations are adequate. The answer is that they are indeed adequate, provided that later components of the grammar do not require access to any of the higher structure shown in the trees of *Fig* 38. On the other hand, if later components of the grammar did need access to information about any of the higher structure, it would be necessary to modify the semotactics so that the information in question would be available in its output.

Let us suppose, for instance, that the sememe 'd' is expressed either as *m* or as *n*, depending on whether or not it occurs in the environment of 'c' selected in the Q construction – *ie* 'd' is realized as *m* in *Fig* 38e and f, but as *n* otherwise. *Fig* 39a includes this information about the re-

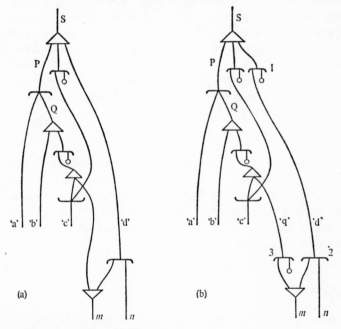

Fig 39 Two extensions of *Fig* 37

alization of 'd', together with the necessary modifications to the semo-tactics. Whenever 'c' is selected in the Q construction, an impulse is sent simultaneously to the upward AND above *m* to signal the fact that the condition for realizing 'd' as *m* is satisfied. *Fig* 39a differs from *Fig* 37 also in relation to the optionality of 'c'. In *Fig* 37 we stated once only that 'c' is optional; and allowed this statement to apply to either of the two positions in which 'c' may occur, by means of an upward OR. If we had maintained this feature in *Fig* 39a, it would have been possible to send a signal to trigger off the *m* realization of 'd' and then nevertheless not select 'c'. This problem is avoided if we express the optionality of 'c' separately for each of the two positions in which it can occur. The downward unordered AND which sends a signal to *m* is situated below the relevant optionality node, so that a signal is sent to *m* only if 'c' is in fact selected (in the Q construction).

When we now reconsider the question of the possible outputs from the semotactics, we realize that there is an additional line – as yet un-labelled – along which impulses may leave the semotactics. Since the lines at the bottom of the semotactics represent sememes, it is clear that our extension of *Fig* 37 has entailed positing an additional sememe. But it is a sememe of a different kind from 'a', 'b', 'c' and 'd', in that its presence is determined by the selection of one of these other sememes in a particular construction. To draw attention to this difference, and to re-flect the fact that its function is to signal that 'c' has been selected in the Q construction, we may label it 'q'. There are now six possible outputs from the semotactics:

$$\text{'a d', 'a c d', 'b d', 'b c d', 'b } {\overset{c}{\underset{q}{}}} \text{ d' and 'b } {\overset{c}{\underset{q}{}}} \text{ c d'}$$

The modification of the semotactics that we have discussed has had the effect of incorporating into the sememic representations just enough of the tree structure shown in *Fig* 38 to achieve the desired result in later components of the grammar. To emphasize the relationship between the last two of the above sememic representations and *Fig* 38e and f, we may restate the sememic representations as:

$$\begin{array}{ccc} \text{Q} & & \text{Q} \\ | & & | \\ \text{'b c d'} & \text{and} & \text{'b c c d'} \end{array}$$

Let us summarize the main points that have emerged so far concerning the sememic representations generated by the semotactics of our hypo-thetical language. Notice, first of all, that we did not assume that the phrase markers of *Fig* 38 ARE sememic representations. Instead, we asked how much of the tree structure in *Fig* 38 has to be incorporated into the sememic representations. The general answer to this question is that any information that is used elsewhere in the grammar must be available in the sememic representations. In the case of our simple example, we saw that information about the constituent Q is sometimes needed, namely whenever Q contains 'c'. Therefore we build precisely this much information into the sememic representations. We do not express the fact that 'b' is part of Q, either when Q contains no 'c' or even when 'c' has also been selected – because this information is unimportant from the point of view of the rest of the grammar.

We have reached the point at which we can begin to indicate where stratificational grammar stands on the question of tree-pruning conventions. Let us consider in this connection the nodes P and Q occurring in the phrase markers of *Fig* 38. As far as P is concerned, there is no need to prune it from any of the sememic representations generated by our semotactics, since it would not be incorporated into them in the first place. The same is true of the Q node of *Fig* 38c and d. On the other hand, the sememic representations corresponding to *Fig* 38e and f would, in effect, contain a Q node, as we have seen. But here, too, we need no tree-pruning convention as such. Rather, the Q node would be deleted in the process of being used to trigger off the *m* realization of 'd'. That is to say,

$$\text{'b } \overset{c}{q} \text{ d'}$$

would be realized as

b c m

in which not only 'd' but also 'q' is no longer present.

On the basis of the preceding discussion, it would seem that stratificational grammar lacks anything corresponding to tree-pruning conventions. The picture is incomplete, however, owing to the oversimplified nature of the data we have considered so far. To remedy the situation, let us consider a slightly different language in which the sememe 'd' is optionally present in each S, rather than obligatorily present. Such a language is represented in *Fig* 39b (I have refrained from collapsing nodes 1 and 2 into a single node – *cf* 3.2.3 – in view of the fact that, strictly speaking, they should be separated by a 'diamond' node – *cf* 3.5). As before, the sememic representation

$$\text{'b } \overset{c}{q} \text{ d'}$$

would be realized as

b c m

Notice, however, that it is now possible to produce the sememic representation

'b $\begin{smallmatrix} c \\ q \end{smallmatrix}$'

The sememe 'q' indicates (as before) that the 'c' in question is an immediate constituent of Q rather than S, but in this instance we have no need for this information since the sememic representation contains no occurrence of 'd'. In such a case the zero alternative at node 3 in *Fig* 39b permits us to discard the information that 'c' is part of Q. As such, it is in effect a Q-pruning convention. It appears, then, that there is some equivalent of tree-pruning conventions in stratificational grammar after all.

Returning now to the tree diagrams that were presented in Part I as the 'semantic representations' of locative, directional and extent sentences – it is relevant to ask how much of the information about constituent structure contained in those trees is required by other parts of the grammar. I am unable to give a very definite answer to this question at the present time. One reason why this is a difficult question to answer is that the distinction between sememes whose function is to convey information about constituent structure – *eg* 'q' in our simple example – and other sememes – 'a', 'b', 'c' and 'd' – is not as clear-cut as was implied above. For instance, the sememes 'time' and 'place', which featured in the analysis of Parts I and II, were treated as though they were similar to 'a', 'b', etc, in the above example. However, it would also be possible to regard them as having the same function as 'q'. (For further discussion, see 3.2.5.) In 3.2.3 we saw that the mechanism for linking together a locative and a directional proposition to produce the sememic representation of a sentence such as *The post office is over the hill* makes use of information about constituent structure – specifically, whether or not a particular locative expression is part of a locative predicate. However, that information was used within the semotactics rather than in some other component of the grammar. One fairly clear case where semotactic constituency information is used in some other component of the grammar is provided by a pair of examples discussed in 1.2.4:

The student went into the library   [62a]

The student went in to the library   [62b]

As was pointed out earlier – while [62a] contains only one goal expression, [62b] contains two. Thus in producing the sememic representation of [62b] it would be necessary to use a loop in the semotactics (*cf* the discussion of coordination in 3.2.3). It seems quite feasible, therefore, to allow the fact of using the loop in [62b] to trigger off the insertion of a phonological boundary after *in* in this example. The phonological distinction between [62a] and [62b] would be shown in this way to be determined by a difference in sememic structure.

On the whole, however, it seems unnecessary to make use of much of the constituency information contained in the tree diagrams of the earlier sections of this book in characterizing the meaning of the prepositions that were investigated. Thus, as was stated at the beginning of the present subsection, those tree diagrams seem to correspond more to semotactic traces than to sememic representations. The sememic representations presupposed by our account of the semolexemic realizational structure (*cf* 3.3) will be nothing more than strings of sememes corresponding to the terminal elements of the earlier tree diagrams. In conclusion, it should be stressed, however, that it remains an open question how much semotactic constituency information is relevant at other levels of the description. It is quite conceivable that if the scope of the present analysis were widened, it would be necessary to incorporate rather more of the constituent structure into the sememic representations themselves.

3.2.5 Problems and prospects

In the present subsection brief mention is made of a number of problems in the analysis outlined above, and several suggestions are advanced concerning ways in which the analysis might profitably be extended. We will begin by considering the schematic semantic representation given in [126], together with some of the surface structures that express the meaning in question (*cf* [127]).

'X goal locative Y'	[126]
X arrives at Y	[127a]
X ends at Y	[127b]
The end of X is at Y	[127c]
Y is at the end of X	[127d]

Since [126] contains the directional case 'goal', it would be regarded as a directional proposition according to the way in which this term was used above. Yet two of the surface structures which realize [126] – *ie* [127c and d] – contain the verb *be*, which we associated with locative sentences. If terms such as 'directional sentence' are to be used at all, it would seem that in applying them one needs to give consideration not merely to properties of the semantic structure but also to the way in which it is expressed in a given instance. Similarly, the insertion of *be* seems to depend not so much on properties of the semantic structure as on the way in which the structure is expressed.

The occurrence of the preposition *of* between *end* and *X* in [127c and d] reminds us of 'semantic representations' such as

[locative [interior of kitchen] place]

which have appeared from time to time in the earlier sections of this book. We see, then, that the notions 'goal' and 'interior' are similar at least to the extent that *of*-insertion applies to each of them. This similarity was not given recognition above. The sememe 'goal' was referred to as a directional case, whereas 'interior' was said to be a member of the category of parts. Comparing [127c and d] with [127a and b], it would seem also that the insertion of *of* depends as much on the way in which a semantic structure is realized as on the semantic structure itself.

The difference between [127b] and [127d] draws attention to the important fact that semantic structures can typically be expressed starting from either end. The factors which determine the order in which a semantic structure is realized in a given instance fall largely under the heading of information structure – *ie* they involve distinctions such as that between 'theme' and 'rheme', and between 'given' and 'new' information. Definiteness is also involved, in so far as the theme is usually definite.

In relation to *I met a friend of yours during the vacation* (*cf: Fig* 18, **2.2.**6) and *The post office is over the hill from here* (*cf: Fig* 11, **1.1.**3, and *Fig* 29, **3.2.**3), it was suggested that the order in which an embedded proposition is realized depends upon the place at which one enters it from the higher proposition. There was a problem with regard to the order of the sememes in terms of which *during* was defined. The first three of the components assigned to *during*, *ie* 'locative path extent', occur in right-to-left order in *Fig* 18. However, the fourth component – 'time' – occurs to the right of 'locative', rather than to the left of 'extent'. A possible solution to this problem will now be indicated. It invokes the distinction drawn in 3.2.4 between sememes whose function is to convey information about constituent structure (which I will refer to as 'type 2 sememes') and other sememes (referred to as 'type 1 sememes'). In the example discussed in 3.2.4, 'q' was a type 2 sememe, and 'a', 'b', etc, were type 1 sememes. The difference between the two types was emphasized there in so far as our analysis allowed 'q' to co-occur simultaneously with 'c', which could well give the impression that the relationship between type 1 and type 2 sememes is analogous to that between segmental and suprasegmental phonemes. Such an impression would be enhanced by the observation that it might be desirable in some instances to allow a particular type 2 sememe to extend over a sequence of type 1 sememes. Notice, however, with regard to the example of 3.2.4, that we could have achieved the desired result also by allowing 'q' to be inserted AFTER relevant occurrences of 'c'. The sememic structure underlying *b c m* would in that case have been 'b c q d'. According to such an analysis, the distinction between type 1 and type 2 sememes would be somewhat less sharply drawn than according to the original analysis. The sememes 'source' and 'interior' are good examples of type 1 sememes. Whenever they occur in a sememic representation, they are overtly expressed in the surface structure, either separately or together with other sememes in a semantically complex lexical item. An equally clear-cut example of a type 2 sememe would be a sememe which is never realized separately in the surface structure and whose function is solely to determine the way in which other neighbouring sememes are realized. When we examine more data, however, it becomes clear that many sememes can be regarded as a cross between a type 1 and a type 2 sememe. This is true, for instance, of the sememes 'place' and 'time'. If we think of them as type 1 sememes, their status is exactly comparable to that of 'locative' and 'posterior'. In this case, the meaning of *behind* and *after* is defined in terms of three exactly comparable components: 'locative posterior place', 'locative posterior time'. Alternatively, we may think of 'place' and 'time' as providing the conditioning environment in which 'posteriority' – *ie* 'locative posterior' – is realized either as *behind* or as *after*. In this case, *behind* and *after* would be regarded as having the same meaning, defined in terms of the two components 'locative posterior'. As far as our network description is concerned, it makes no difference whether 'place' and 'time' are thought of as components of the meaning of *behind* and *after* in their own right or simply as the conditioning environments in which 'posteriority' is realized in one way or the other. The facts would be represented by the same configuration of nodes and lines in either case. However, the possibility of regarding 'place' and 'time' simply as conditioning environments suggests a way in which the semotactics might be modified in order to solve the problem of the order of the components of the preposition *during*. The modification would be quite minor. It would consist in removing the 'place' and 'time' lines from the locative expression and extent expression constructions (together with the 'plural' sememe in the case of temporal locative expressions, *cf: Fig* 33) and attaching them by means of a downward unordered AND to the line above the construction from which they originally emanated. The result would be that 'place' and 'time' would no longer follow the specifier constituent of locative and extent expressions; rather, they would be simultaneous with both the case – 'locative' or 'extent' – and the specifier.

In conclusion, we will consider once again the tree diagrams proposed in *Fig* 11 (**1.1.3**) and *Fig* 29 (**3.2.3**) to represent the semantic structure of *The post office is over the hill from here*. It was suggested that the directional predicate occurring in those diagrams is realized in right-to-left order in view of the fact that one enters it from $prop_1$ at the right-hand side. This account of the facts presupposes, however, that $prop_2$ is embedded inside $prop_1$. It is worth asking, therefore, whether a semantic structure of the kind in question could be realized in such a way that $prop_1$ would be embedded inside $prop_2$. The fact that we were uncertain as to exactly what constitutes the subject of $prop_2$ presents a minor problem in this connection, but we can get out of this difficulty by making 'John' the subject of $prop_2$. It then becomes clear that *John went over the hill to where the post office is* would be an example of what we had in mind. Moreover, since this sentence is obviously closely related to *John went over the hill to the post office*, the possibility emerges that it might be desirable to posit embedded propositions also in the last example and all comparable examples. *To the post office* would then mean 'to at a place which the post office is at'. A decision on this question will have to await the results of further work.

3.3 Semolexemic realizational structure

The main task in this section is to present our componential analysis of English prepositions in network form, discussing various general points in the process. Thereafter we turn our attention to the question of stratificational terminology; and the final subsection is devoted to a discussion of synonymy and polysemy.

3.3.1 Network version of the componential analysis

Componential definitions such as those of *Tables* 11 and 12 (**2.2.7**) involve the AND relationship and also the OR relationship. For instance, to define *through* as 'path locative interior' is to say that its meaning contains the notions 'path' AND 'locative' AND 'interior'; and to attribute the component 'interior' to both *through* and *in* and other lexemes means that whenever the sememe 'interior' occurs, it is a component EITHER of *through* OR of *in* OR of some other lexeme. In representing parts of the realizational structure in network form, the convention is adopted that the top of the diagram points towards the meaning end of language, and the bottom towards the sound end. This convention perpetuates the well-established metaphor according to which the phonetic level is the lowest level of language. Unfortunately this metaphor conflicts with another one, which sees the phonetic facts as being on the surface and treats syntax and semantics as being deeper. The word *underlie* (as in *underlying representation*), which I have used from time to time above, reflects the second metaphor. (In a tactic pattern 'upward' and 'downward' do not mean 'towards meaning' and 'towards sound'. As one progresses through a tactic pattern in a downward direction, so the units represented by the lines along which one travels become progressively smaller, until one reaches the ultimate constituents at the bottom. If the realizational structure is thought of as extending in a vertical dimension, each tactic pattern is horizontal and intersects with the realizational structure at a particular level. The top of the tactics, representing the largest unit generated by that particular tactic pattern, is in that case furthest out to the side, in that it is furthest removed from the ultimate constituents. We shall return to the question of the relationship between realizational structure and tactic patterns in **3.5**.)

Fig 40 is a provisional fragment of the semolexemic realizational structure. It represents the meaning of the lexemes *by*, *past*, *beyond*, *through* and *in*, invoking for this purpose the sememes 'proximity', 'path', 'locative' and 'interior'. In addition, the diagram indicates that the sememes 'path' and 'locative' may have zero realization. (It does not specify the conditions under which the zero possibility is selected; and I shall not be able to remedy this defect, since the facts are not clear to me – *cf* **1.2.10**.) The diagram can be modified in order to express certain generalizations, as we shall see presently. But even at this stage one important advantage of the network format is apparent. *Tables* 11 and 12 represent a fragment of a lexeme-sememe dictionary. It is easy to use them to find out the meaning or meanings of a given lexeme. On the other

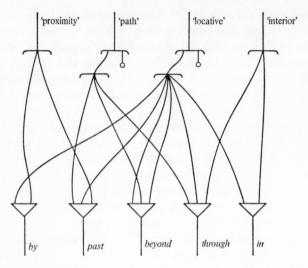

Fig 40 Provisional fragment of the semolexemic realizational structure

hand, they are considerably less easy to use if we want to find out how a particular sememe can be expressed. In fact, we would need to scan the whole dictionary looking for occurrences of the sememe in question. *Fig* 40 is at one and the same time a lexeme-sememe dictionary and a sememe-lexeme dictionary. (This feature of the network notation thus needs to be added to the advantages mentioned in 3.2.2.)

By consulting *Fig* 40 one can see to what extent the various prepositions are related in meaning. For instance, one can see that *past* and *through* share the components 'path locative' and that *through* and *in* share the components 'locative interior'. However, the diagram as it stands does not make these generalizations explicit. *Fig* 41 is a revised version of *Fig* 40, in which the generalization is explicitly made that 'path locative' is part of the meaning of *past*, *beyond* and *through*. The diagram recognizes a component of meaning – represented by the line at A – which is part of the meaning either of *past* or of *beyond* or of *through*, and which itself contains the two components 'path' and 'locative'. Notice now also that *Fig* 41 is simpler than *Fig* 40. Using Reich's measure of simplicity (*cf* 3.2.2), *Fig* 40 scores 19 (11 for the number of nodes and 8 for lines in excess of 3 coming out of any node), and *Fig* 41 scores 15 (12 plus 3). The 'effective information' of the two diagrams is, of course, the same (since they both incorporate the same componential

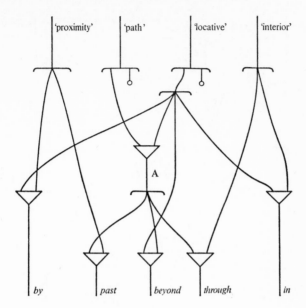

Fig 41 Revised version of *Fig* 40

definition of the same five prepositions), but they differ in 'surface information' (Lamb 1966a: 41–54). Moreover, the diagram which specifically makes a particular generalization is simpler than the one which does not.

Although it specifically makes one generalization, there are two other generalizations that are not explicitly represented in *Fig* 41, namely that *by* and *past* share the components 'locative proximity' and that *in* and *through* share the components 'locative interior'. These two generalizations are incorporated into *Fig* 42 (at B and C). Like the previous diagram, *Fig* 42 scores 15 according to the simplicity measure (11 plus 4). However, in one respect *Fig* 42 is to be preferred. As was noted in **1.2.8**, the two pairs of prepositions *by*/*past* and *in*/*through* are not alike in distribution. Both *by* and *past* may occur in the realization of a path expression (*cf: Table* 6, **1.2.3**). Consequently, the same meaning that is conveyed by the sentence *We drove past the church* can also be expressed as *We drove by the church*. Of the second pair, only *through* can occur in the realization of a path expression (*cf: Table* 8, **1.2.8**). Consequently, *I had to fight my way through the crowd at the entrance* cannot be paraphrased as *I had to fight my way in the crowd at the entrance*. *Fig* 42 gives

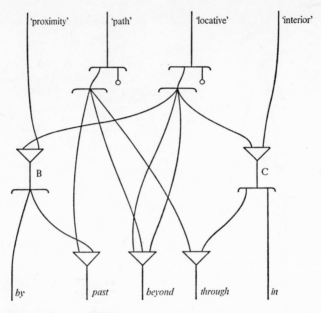

Fig 42 Alternative revision of *Fig* 40

recognition to this difference, in the form of the distinction between an unordered OR (below B) and an ordered OR (below C). The ordered OR below C says the following: in trying to express the notions 'locative interior', first of all check to see whether they are preceded by 'path' and, if so, express all three notions simultaneously by means of the preposition *through*; otherwise, use the preposition *in*. With regard to the unordered OR below B, if 'locative proximity' is preceded by 'path' the three notions may be expressed simultaneously as *past*. However, we are not obliged to use *past*; 'locative proximity' may still be expressed as *by* even when preceded by 'path' (which in this case would have zero realization). *Through* takes precedence over *in* if 'path' is present, but under the same circumstances *past* does not take precedence over *by*.

While *Fig* 42 makes two generalizations not made in *Fig* 41, it is also true that *Fig* 41 makes a generalization not made in *Fig* 42 (namely, the generalization that *past*, *beyond* and *through* contain the components 'path locative'). It is impossible to incorporate all three generalizations into a single diagram – unless we are prepared to accept a diagram that states some information more than once. A similar phenomenon has been observed already by Reich. He writes (1970c):

I now have several examples of areas in English morphology in which there are apparently two equivalent networks which are almost identical in complexity but which are organized along different lines. Essentially the organization division is one of primacy being given to the initial portion of a word versus primacy being given to the final portion of a word. I felt that this double solution meant that there was a problem with the relational network notational system. However, if Brown and McNeill's results hold, perhaps there is a better interpretation of this double solution.

The results Reich refers to at this point are described in Brown and McNeill 1966, a study of the 'tip of the tongue' phenomenon. By presenting definitions of rare English words, Brown and McNeill frequently succeeded in bringing about the situation in which a subject could remember certain details of a particular word even though he was unable to recall the word itself. The results of the experiment showed, among other things, that the beginning of a word is remembered better than the middle, and also that the end of a word is remembered better than the middle. Relating the results to his own work, Reich sets up two alternative hypotheses, each capable of being tested. First, it may be that the internal structure of particular vocabulary items is organized from the front to the back as far as some speakers are concerned, but from the back to the front as far as other speakers are concerned. Secondly, it may be that vocabulary items are stored in the brain with a certain amount of redundancy, and that their internal structure is organized both from the front to the back and from the back to the front. Reich's two hypotheses relate to the way in which the phonological, graphological and morphological structure of vocabulary items might conceivably be stored in the brain. In view of the fact that networks representing the semological structure of vocabulary items can also be simplified in two distinct but roughly equivalent ways, it is worth considering whether in this area, too, there might not be possible behavioural correlates. For instance, is there any set of facts that would be more consistent with one or other of the following two ways in which the structure of the meaning of *through* might be organized?

[[path locative] interior]
[path [locative interior]]

In any event, however, the process of simplifying networks occupies a central position in a model of language acquisition proposed by Reich, according to which

the child organizes the information he takes in by continuously making small incremental improvements to the developing linguistic structure (Reich 1970a: 108).

Fig 43 shows a further fragment of semolexemic realizational structure illustrating four additional points. First, wherever a lexeme has two or more alternative senses, this fact is represented by means of an upward OR node. The upward OR in *Fig* 43 expresses the fact that our description has identified two distinct senses of the preposition *by*. Wherever a particular sense of a lexeme is semantically complex, the line in question connects (directly or indirectly) to an upward AND. Thus the

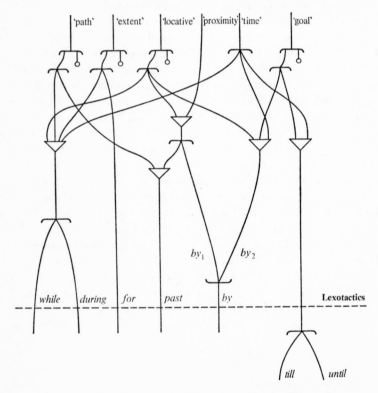

Fig 43 A further fragment of semolexemic realizational structure

upward AND on the by_2 line expresses the fact that this sense of *by* contains the components 'locative goal time'. In the case of by_1, there is an intervening downward OR, expressing the fact that the meaning of by_1 – *ie* 'locative proximity' – is also part of the meaning of *past*.

Secondly, wherever two or more vocabulary items have the same componential definition, the lines corresponding to the separate items connect to a downward OR node. This allows us to state their meaning just once, rather than separately for each individual item. There are two relevant examples in *Fig* 43, one involving *till* and *until*, each of which was defined as 'goal time' (*cf: Table* 12), and the other involving *during* and *while*, which are regarded as being mapped onto 'locative path extent time'. That *during* and *while* have the same meaning is suggested by the similarity in meaning between [128] and [129].

The phone rang during dinner [128]

The phone rang while we were having dinner [129]

It is relevant also that the unacceptability of **during 10 o'clock* is paralleled by that of **The phone rang while I dropped my fork*; and that the German word *während* translates both *during* and *while* (being capable of functioning either as a preposition or as a conjunction).

The third point of interest in *Fig* 43 is related to the last one. It needs to be explained why the downward OR stating that *while* and *during* have the same meaning has been placed at a higher level of the diagram than the *till/until* node – specifically, why the first of these nodes is located above the dotted line and the second below it. The dotted line indicates the level at which the lexotactics will be connected to the realizational structure. Each of the lines at that level corresponds to a lexeme. Lines connecting from the realizational structure into the lexotactics specify the class or classes to which each lexeme belongs; and then the higher structure of the lexotactics characterizes the ways in which members of the various classes can be combined to form phrases, clauses and sentences. The somewhat different treatment of *till/until*, compared with *while/during*, is determined by a concern for stating the facts as simply as possible. This can be demonstrated by reference to *Fig* 44. (The diamond-shaped nodes at the points where the lexotactics is connected to the realizational structure will be discussed in 3.5.) In the (a) diagram, the two examples have been given a comparable treatment, *ie* the downward OR in the realizational structure is above the level of the lexotactics in each case. Lines leading into the lexotactics corresponding to *while*

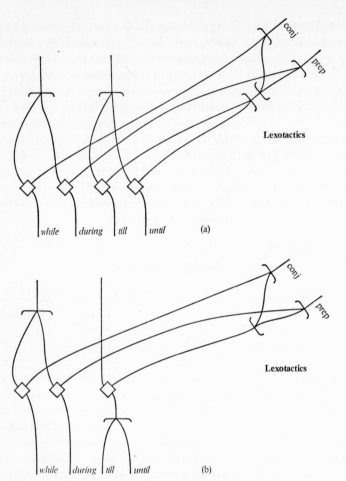

Fig 44 An example of network simplification

and *during* connect to downward ORS representing the classes of conjunctions and prepositions, respectively. In the case of *till* and *until*, the
diagram states that each of them can function either as a conjunction or
as a preposition. Applying the simplicity measure to *Fig* 44a, we see that
it scores 10 (there are ten nodes and they each have just three connections). *Fig* 44b has the same effective information. *Till* and *until* are
shown to have the same meaning by means of the downward OR in the
realizational structure, and the connection into the lexotactics states that
they may function either as a conjunction or as a preposition. But

whereas *till* and *until* were separate lexemes according to diagram (a), in (b) they are alternative realizations of a single lexeme. The simplicity measure gives a count of 8 for (b), which thus contains less surface information and is therefore to be preferred. The possibility of simplifying the *till/until* part of diagram (a) does not depend on the fact that *till* and *until* belong to more than one lexotactic class. What is crucial is that they have an identical lexotactic distribution. This is why we can state their distribution just once rather than separately for each item. The reason the downward OR in the realizational structure corresponding to *while* and *during* has to be above the lexotactics is that these two items have a different distribution as far as the lexotactics is concerned.

There is still one feature of *Fig* 43 on which we need to comment. If we follow the line corresponding to the lexeme *for* in an upward direction from the level of the lexotactics, it will be seen that we encounter no upward AND node. This, of course, reflects the fact that *for* was considered to express the single notion 'extent'. (An upward AND is used wherever an item is ascribed two or more components of meaning.) Nor is there any upward OR on the line in question, in view of the fact that our analysis covered only one sense of the preposition *for*. This means that the part of the semolexemic realizational structure that characterizes the meaning of *for* (according to our analysis) comes closer to showing a one-to-one correspondence between the sememic and lexemic levels than any other part of the network represented so far. We do not have a one-to-one correspondence, however, even in this case, since the sememe 'extent' may be realized in other ways than merely as the preposition *for* – eg as part of the meaning of *during* and *while*, or as zero (*cf* 1.2.10). *To*, *via* and *at* are exactly comparable to *for*. *From* is slightly different in that there is no possibility of realizing 'source' as zero. However, there are other ways in which 'source' can be realized than merely as the preposition *from*, eg as part of the meaning of *since*.

From the fragments of the semolexemic realizational structure presented above it is clear how one would go about converting the whole of *Tables* 11 and 12 into the form of a single network. Some parts of the network would be of little interest, in so far as they would be only loosely integrated with the parts we have discussed above. For instance, the only generalization that can be made about the meaning of *over* ('locative superior') and *under* ('locative inferior'), by way of relating them to other prepositions, is that they both contain the component 'locative'. Additional portions of the network that are of more interest will come up for discussion in 3.3.2, 3.3.3 and 3.5.

3.3.2 Stratificational terminology

The fragments of English semotactics discussed in 3.2.1 and 3.2.3 provide examples of the use in a tactic pattern of AND and OR nodes of both the downward and the upward variety. Owing to the difference in the role of a tactic pattern and the realizational structure (*cf* 3.1 and 3.5.1), these nodes appear to have a somewhat different function in the two parts of the grammar. Additional terms are available to designate the various possible realizational relationships – 'portmanteau realization', 'composite realization', 'diversification', 'neutralization', 'zero realization' and 'empty realization'. These terms may be thought of as alternative labels for 'upward AND', 'downward AND', etc – providing one is discussing the realizational structure (they are not applied to tactic relationships). Before illustrating what is meant by each of these terms, it is worth recalling how upward and downward ANDS and ORS function in a tactic pattern. A downward AND in a tactic pattern represents a construction, *eg* the 'locative expression' construction in the semotactics. A downward OR represents a class, *eg* the semotactic class of 'parts' ('interior', 'anterior', etc) or the lexotactic class of prepositions. An upward OR indicates that a particular constituent may occupy more than one position in the structure of some larger unit, or may occur inside the structure of different larger units; for instance, a locative expression may occur inside a source, path or goal expression within a directional predicate, or may be part of a locative predicate. Sometimes the two or more lines coming out of the top of an upward OR connect directly to downward ANDS; this is true of the four lines indicating the positions in which a locative expression may occur (*cf: Fig* 22, 3.2.1). Sometimes there are intervening downward ORS. An example of the latter kind is provided by *Fig* 44 (3.3.1). *Till* and *until* may function either as a conjunction or as a preposition, *ie* they belong both to the class of conjunctions and to the class of prepositions. The positions in which they can occur are specified not separately for *till* and *until* but for the classes of conjunctions and prepositions as a whole. Finally, an upward AND indicates that a constituent functions at one and the same time in two or more different positions. For instance, in the semantic structure of *The post office is over the hill* there is a locative expression which occupies a slot in both a locative and a directional proposition.

Portmanteau realization is the upward AND relationship as it applies to the realizational structure. An element at one level of the realizational structure is the realization of a particular combination of higher-level elements, *eg* the preposition *past* is the lexemic realization of the sememes 'path locative proximity'. Componential analysis consists in identifying cases of portmanteau realization in the semolexemic realizational structure. The upward ANDS representing individual cases of portmanteau realization are always dominated by downward OR nodes, whose function is to specify the set of possible realizations of the individual components. In *Fig* 43 (3.3.1) there is no downward OR on the line labelled 'proximity'. The absence of an OR at that point expresses the fact that (as far as the data represented in this diagram are concerned) 'proximity' occurs only in combination with 'locative'. It is certainly conceivable that one might want to invoke a component which – even in a language as a whole – occurs in only one combination. However, this could never be true of more than one component in a particular combination, since in that case there would be no justification for identifying the components at all.

Composite realization is the converse of portmanteau realization, and therefore involves the downward AND relationship. An element at one level of the realizational structure is realized by a particular combination of lower-level elements. The word *worse* provides an example of both portmanteau and composite realization, *ie* it has both upward and downward components. The upward components are 'bad' and 'comparative'; the downward components are a particular combination of abstract phonological segments (which perhaps differs depending on what dialect one speaks). All of the items whose meaning we have investigated in Parts I and II illustrate composite realization in so far as they are represented by particular combinations of vowels and consonants, but some of them also exhibit composite realization immediately below the lexotactics, *eg* the lexemes *throughout* and *in front* (*cf* 3.4.2) are represented by *through+out* and *in+front*. The downward ANDS representing cases of composite realization always dominate upward ORS, whose function is to specify the set of combinations in which each individual component occurs. For instance, there would be an upward OR on the line representing the element /w/ that occurs at the beginning of *worse*, and as many lines connecting to the top of this node as there are individual combinations in which /w/ occurs. As in the case of upward components, the possibility exists that a particular downward component might occur in only one combination. The *cran* of *cranberry* provides an example (*cf* Lamb 1966a: 3). Notice, however, that if there were no other combinations in which *berry* could occur, there would be no justification for recognizing the separate elements *cran* and *berry* at all. This kind of interdependence between the paradigmatic and the syntagmatic axis was clearly recognized at least as long ago as De Saussure 1916 (177–9).

'Diversification' is the label for the situation in which a higher-level element has two or more alternative realizations lower down. It thus involves the downward OR relationship. However, the downward ORS that dominate upward ANDS representing portmanteau realization have usually not been referred to as instances of diversification. Typical examples of diversification cited in stratificational writings involve downward ORS that do not dominate upward ANDS. (This point will be discussed further below.) Clear examples of diversification in this sense are provided by the *while/during* and *till/until* downward ORS in *Fig* 43 (3.3.1).

'Neutralization' designates the situation in which two or more different higher-level elements may be realized by a single lower-level element. It involves the upward OR relationship. However, the upward ORS that are dominated by downward ANDS representing composite realization have usually not been referred to as cases of neutralization. Typical examples of neutralization cited in the literature involve upward ORS that are not dominated by downward ANDS. A clear case from our analysis of the meaning of English prepositions is the upward OR in *Fig* 43, which expresses the fact that *by* has two alternative meanings.

Our analysis of the meaning of English prepositions also provides examples of zero realization and empty realization. For instance, there is zero realization of the sememe 'path' in the sentence *We drove by the church*, or of 'goal' in *The dog ran under the table* (meaning 'to under'); and the *of* that occurs in example [75], *The bird flew out of the window*, is a case of empty realization (*cf* 1.2.5 and 3.5.3).

Stratificational grammar may be thought of as a specific kind of relational network grammar in which the claim is made not only that languages are networks of relationships but also that they are stratified. (Reich's work has not been overtly concerned with the notion of strata, and so may be thought of as illustrating relational network grammar but not stratificational grammar – *cf* Reich 1970a: 1–2, 1970b: 96–7.) All theories of language recognize levels of some kind. The thing about strata that makes them rather special is that any given stratum – *eg* the lexemic – is regarded as having essentially the same structure as any other stratum – *eg* the phonemic. (It is certainly not claimed, with regard to transformational grammar, that the phonological component has essentially the same structure as, say, the base component or the semantic component.) What makes the various strata resemble each other in particular is the fact that they all have a tactic pattern. Moreover, the only reliable way to decide how many strata there are is by determining how many separate tactic patterns need to be posited – 'The essential property of a stratum is its distinctive tactic pattern' (Lamb 1971a: 119). In addition, however, the view has been held that the various stratal systems resemble each other also in their realizational structure. It is perhaps worth considering the kind of evidence that led to this view.

First of all, it is an easy matter to identify instances of the various realizational relationships – portmanteau and composite realization, etc – at all levels of language. Thus the idiom *to kick the bucket* illustrates composite realization just as much as the fact that *pin* is represented by /p/ followed by /i/ followed by /n/. (Examples of the various relationships from different levels of language are to be found in many of the stratificational writings; see, for instance, Lamb 1966a and Lockwood 1972.) Furthermore, it was apparent that particular configurations of AND and OR nodes occur at different levels. For instance, *Fig* 45 shows two ex-

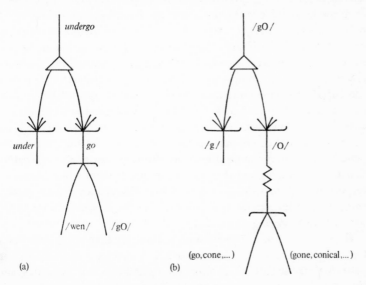

Fig 45 Recurrent configurations of nodes

amples involving a downward AND dominating an upward OR dominating a downward OR. Diagram (a) states that the lexeme *undergo* consists of *under* followed by *go*. Other lines connecting to the top of the two upward ORS correspond to occurrences of *under* and *go* in other combinations than *undergo* (and one line in each case corresponds to occurrences of *under* and *go* as separate lexemes). The downward OR on the *go* line then states that there are two alternative realizations: /gO/ and /wen/ (as in *went*). Diagram (b) states that /gO/ consists of /g/ followed by /O/. Other lines connecting into the two upward ORS from above represent occurrences of /g/ and /O/ in other combinations than /gO/. Finally, the downward OR below the /O/ line represents the vocalic alternation exhibited by pairs of words such as *go/gone* and *cone/conical*. (The zig-zag section of the /O/ line indicates that some structure has been omitted; it would seem, namely, that the alternation ought to be handled in terms of feature-sized rather than segment-sized elements.) It is obvious that *Fig* 45b belongs at a lower level of the realizational part of a grammar than *Fig* 45a, since diagram (b) can, in fact, be attached to the bottom of diagram (a).

Two hypotheses concerning the internal structure of stratal systems are represented in *Fig* 46 (which shows the part of a grammar extending from the lexotactics to the phonotactics). Each hypothesis involves defining what is meant by a 'sign pattern' and an 'alternation pattern', and then specifying the internal structure of a stratal system in terms of patterns. A sign pattern contains instances of portmanteau realization above instances of composite realization (Lamb 1966a: 12), thus involving (from the top downwards) downward ORS, upward ANDS, downward ANDS and upward ORS. An alternation pattern has downward ORS at the top and upward ORS at the bottom (Lamb 1966a: 15), *ie* it contains instances of diversification above instances of neutralization. Sign patterns and alternation patterns constitute places in the realizational structure at which there may be a discrepancy from a one-to-one correspondence. (There does not have to be a discrepancy, however, and in general many lines pass through a particular sign or alternation pattern without encountering any nodes.)

Hypothesis (a) of *Fig* 46 is somewhat simpler than the position adopted in Lamb 1966a. It treats each stratal system as containing three patterns: a tactic pattern, an alternation pattern (above the tactics) and a sign pattern (below the tactics). Owing to the possibility of a discrepancy from a one-to-one correspondence in a sign pattern or alternation pattern, the elements represented by lines above and below any such pattern are considered to be different in kind. Accordingly, different terms are used to refer to them. Two kinds of terms suffice to designate all the various linguistic units that are distinguished under hypothesis

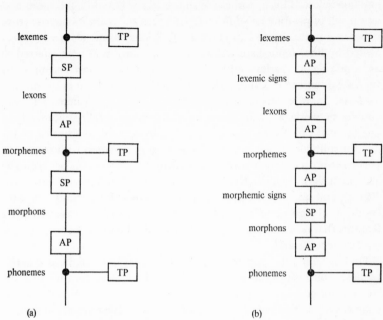

Fig 46 Two hypotheses concerning the structure of stratal systems (S P = 'sign pattern', A P = 'alternation pattern' and T P = 'tactic pattern')

(a). Terms with the suffix *-on* designate units immediately below a sign pattern (and above the alternation pattern of the next lower stratal system). Terms with the suffix *-eme* designate units that are immediately below an alternation pattern (and above a sign pattern). Since (according to this hypothesis) tactic patterns are connected to the realizational structure between an alternation pattern and the next lower sign pattern, the units with the *-eme* suffix are also the ultimate constituents of the tactics.

Soon after the appearance of Lamb 1966a it was realized that networks such as that of *Fig* 44b (3.3.1) are preferable to the alternative network shown in *Fig* 44a. This meant that it was necessary to recognize the possibility of diversification immediately below a tactic pattern. Since neutralization immediately below a tactic pattern had already been recognized (Lamb 1966a: 16–17), it now seemed that stratal systems needed to be attributed two alternation patterns, one above the tactics and one below. This hypothesis is shown in *Fig* 46b. It will be seen that as a result of positing an additional pattern in the realizational structure it became necessary to introduce an additional term: elements represented by lines immediately above a sign pattern were now referred to as '-emic signs'. Various other changes that were proposed around this time are discussed in Lamb 1971a. One of these is relevant to the present analysis. In representing composite realization it became clear that simpler networks are achieved by allowing the possibility not merely of one layer of downward ANDS connecting to upward ORS but of an indefinite number of such layers. The analogous situation with respect to portmanteau realization was illustrated by the distinction between *Fig* 40, which shows just one layer of downward ORS and upward ANDS, and *Figs* 41 and 42, which contain two such layers. Hypothesis (b), with 'multi-level sign patterns', as they were now called, and certain other features that need not concern us here, was proposed in Lamb 1971a as 'the current model'.

On examining the data of the present analysis in the light of this hypothesis concerning the structure of stratal systems, we find that the two do not correspond particularly well. At this point one should, of course, suspect the hypothesis – which is, after all, set up on the basis of observing data – rather than suspect the data! I will briefly indicate the kind of things that strike me as problematical. On the basis of the considerations outlined below, one is led to the view that it might be worthwhile attempting to characterize the structure of stratal systems in terms of two kinds of patterns referred to here as the 'upward componency pattern' and the 'downward componency pattern', rather than in terms of sign patterns and alternation patterns.

The trouble with sign patterns and alternation patterns is that the distinction between the two is sometimes blurred. A given OR node may need to be attributed both to a sign pattern and to an alternation pattern. We will consider two such examples. The downward OR at A in *Fig* 47 represents a typical case of diversification: a particular higher-level element (which we know to consist of 'locative path extent time', *cf: Fig* 43) is realized either as *while* or as *during*. This downward OR would therefore belong inside an alternation pattern. Diagram (b) shows two layers of portmanteau realization. Thus the downward OR at B would belong inside the top half of a sign pattern (according to Lamb 1966a). Consider now the downward OR at C, representing the fact that 'locative proximity' may be realized in two distinct ways. As far as the *by* realization is concerned, C resembles A, and so would appear to belong in an

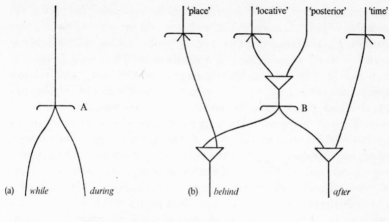

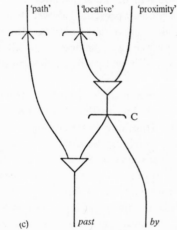

Fig 47 A problematical OR node

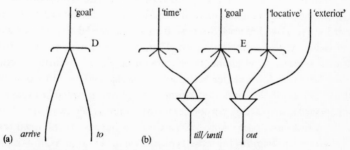

Fig 48 A further example of a problematical OR node

alternation pattern; but as regards the other realization (as part of the meaning of *past*), C resembles B, and so would seem to belong in a sign pattern. *Fig* 48a states that the sememe 'goal' may be realized either as *arrive* or as *to*, a typical case of diversification. Thus node D looks as though it belongs inside an alternation pattern. However, 'goal' is also a component of the meaning of lexemes such as *till/until* and *out*, suggesting that node E belongs in the top half of a sign pattern. But node D and node E are the same node. (In **3.5.3** we shall employ an ordered OR immediately above an unordered OR – *cf: Fig* 43, **3.3.1** – rather than a single node, but this does not affect the point being made here. On a similar note, some readers will know of a proposal to represent portmanteau realization somewhat differently from the method employed in this book – *cf* Lamb 1971a: 116, Ikegami 1970. This proposal entails taking portmanteau realization out of the top half of the sign pattern, and might seem therefore to invalidate the argument presented above. However, an exactly parallel argument can be developed concerning the upward ORS which represent neutralization proper (and belong in an alternation pattern) and those which are involved in composite realization (and belong in a sign pattern).)

To throw out the notion of patterns in the realizational structure altogether would be undesirable. It would imply that there is no regularity at all in the realizational structure from one stratal system to another. Examples such as those of *Fig* 45, which can be extended considerably and are very numerous, argue against such a position. Thus, as indicated above, it seems to me worthwhile trying out a different kind of pattern from the sign pattern and alternation pattern. An 'upward componency pattern' would represent an indefinite number of layers of portmanteau realization, and would contain downward ORS and upward ANDS. A 'downward componency pattern' would be a mirror-image of an 'upward componency pattern'; it would represent an indefinite number of layers of composite realization, and would contain downward ANDS and upward ORS. The downward OR at B in *Fig* 47b and the two upward ANDS below it illustrate the 'normal' upward componency situation: each of the lower-level elements contains more than one upward component. Diagram (c) represents the somewhat special case in which one of the lower-level elements (*by*) contains only one upward component. (It necessarily shares this component with some other lower-level element – in this case, *past* – since there would otherwise be no need for a downward OR.) Diagram (a) – the typical case of diversification – represents the even more special type of upward componency in which each of the lower-level elements contains only one upward component. (As in the last type, the component in question is necessarily shared, since otherwise there would be no need for a downward OR.) Neutralization would, of course, constitute the equally special case of downward componency in which each of the higher-level elements contains only one downward component. The component would necessarily be shared, since otherwise there would be no need for an upward OR.

The main advantage of componency patterns over sign patterns and alternation patterns is that there would never be any question of whether to assign a given node to one type of pattern or the other, since no node would be capable of occurring in both types of pattern. The obvious possibility as a first revised hypothesis concerning the structure of stratal systems is that each stratal system contains a tactic pattern, an upward componency pattern and a downward componency pattern. The semolexemic data of *Fig* 43 (3.3.1) would suggest that the upward componency pattern belongs immediately below the tactics (and the downward componency pattern immediately above the tactics). However, this hypothesis would need to be tested on a large amount of data from all levels and may well prove inadequate.

Since no attempt was made in 3.3.1 to fit the data into the existing scheme of sign and alternation patterns, the only labels for linguistic elements that we have had occasion to use are 'sememe' (designating the ultimate constituents of the semotactics) and 'lexeme' (designating the ultimate constituents of the lexotactics – *cf* 3.4). We have had no occasion to use 'semon', 'sememic sign', 'lexon' and 'lexemic sign'. In view of the confusion these and other terms (*eg* 'basic -eme') seem to have caused, it is perhaps a good thing that we have not used them. Postal writes (1968: 201):

> instead of a single lexical item 'man' consisting of an association of unpredictably combined properties of different sorts, Lamb is committed to having a basic sememe, a rule (rules?) to realize this as a sememe proper, a rule to realize this as a basic lexeme, a rule to realize this as a lexeme proper, a rule to realize this as a basic morpheme, and finally rules to realize the basic morpheme as a sequence of morphons. In cases like 'man', all of these intermediate stages are completely useless and contribute no information since the representations are simply arbitrary symbols. They are entirely artifacts of the underlying assumptions which they disconfirm.

If the facts concerning the item *man* (as described by Postal) were

represented in a network alongside an item such as *go*, it would be seen
that over a large portion of the *man* network there would be a simple one-
to-one correspondence, *ie* a single line encountering no nodes at all. In the
go network, on the other hand, there would be far less of a one-to-one
correspondence – *ie: go* would easily be seen to be more complex than
man. For convenience I have spoken above of linguistic elements, but
Lamb insists that there are no elements – only relationships:

> the entire linguistic system consists just of relationships – not symbols
> and relationships, just relationships, which may be diagrammed in a
> network of lines and nodes. Symbols are needed only at the end points
> of a diagram. In a network diagram of the whole of a linguistic struc-
> ture . . ., symbols would be needed only for phonetic features, at the
> bottom, and concepts, at the top. (Lamb 1971b: 204–5).

Labels such as 'sememe', 'lexeme', etc, serve the purpose of indicating
what part of linguistic structure a given network represents. Moreover,
it would seem that these labels become less important the more one is
concerned with describing a relatively large body of data. In a reasonably
extensive description the relationship between the different parts of the
description is apparent from their position in the overall network. On
the other hand, if isolated examples are discussed (to illustrate a particular point), labels such as 'sememe' and 'lexeme' are needed in order
to give some idea how the fragment in question would be integrated with
other parts of a grammar. Having recently re-read an earlier article
(Bennett 1968) in which there were rather many occurrences of terms
such as 'hypersemon' and 'sememic sign', the policy I would now ad-
vocate is that one should concentrate on representing the facts and allow
the terminology to sort itself out afterwards.

3.3.3 Synonymy and polysemy
The first thing to note, on the subject of synonymy and polysemy, is that
they involve the downward OR and upward OR relationships, respectively. For instance, the lines in *Fig* 43 (3.3.1) corresponding to *till* and
until – which most people would be prepared to regard as synonymous –
connect to the bottom of a downward OR. Similarly, the fact that *by* has
two distinct meanings (in *She was sitting by the fire* and *Return it to me by
Monday*) is represented in *Fig* 43 by means of an upward OR. Secondly,
it needs to be realized at the outset that synonymy and polysemy are very
much interrelated phenomena, so that whatever approach one decides to
adopt on the one issue will determine one's approach to the other issue

also. To illustrate this point, let us consider the prepositions *by* and *past*. If we had accepted the account of the meaning of *by* given in some dictionaries, we would have recognized three distinct senses of this preposition in

My car is by the post office [45a]
We drove by the post office [45c]
I've put the book by the telephone [45d]

– perhaps glossing them as 'near', 'via near' and 'to near'. The upward OR in *Fig* 43 would then have had four lines coming out of it rather than just two. One of these lines would correspond specifically to the 'via near' sense, and could be labelled 'by_{via}' accordingly. Now to represent the fact that *by* and *past* are synonymous (in [45c] and *We drove past the post office*), we would allow the 'by_{via}' line from the *by* node to connect to a downward OR dominating not only *by* but also *past*. According to the analysis we have adopted, however, there is no sense of *by* that means specifically 'via near', and consequently no line labelled 'by_{via}' at any place in the network representing the semolexemic realizational structure. This means that the synonymy of *by* and *past* will need to be represented in some other way (see below). The consequences of the interrelatedness of synonymy and polysemy for a stratificational description may be stated in general terms as follows: if we were to posit considerably more neutralization than has been posited, it would be necessary also to posit correspondingly more diversification. In other words, by recognizing relatively little neutralization, we have avoided having to recognize much diversification. It is obvious that the resulting network is considerably simpler than it would otherwise have been. Of course, we need to demonstrate that the same data have been accounted for. I shall do this below by showing how the present analysis expresses the synonymy of *by* and *past*. The general format of the treatment described will apply to all comparable examples.

Just as one's approach to synonymy is intimately related to one's approach to polysemy, so also the latter is intimately related to one's approach to componential analysis. In an explicit description everything hangs together. Thus in attempting to characterize our position on polysemy, in 0.2, and our position on componential analysis, in 1.2.1, we were in fact saying the same thing but in somewhat different ways. Nothing further needs to be said here. I will therefore devote the major part of the remainder of this subsection to a discussion of synonymy, returning to polysemy only at the end (in order to draw a distinction between two levels at which polysemy occurs).

It was stated above that synonymy involves the downward OR relation. It is possible to refine this statement in a number of respects. I shall adopt the following procedure. First, I shall characterize a widely-held view of synonymy. Then I shall ask whether all downward OR nodes in the realizational structure correspond to instances of synonymy (in the adopted sense of the term). Three situations will be distinguished in which a downward OR does not correspond to an instance of synonymy (in the adopted sense). In the process we shall identify the additional conditions that need to be satisfied by a downward OR and its immediate environment in a network before the node corresponds to an instance of synonymy. Finally, I shall ask whether all examples of synonymy are represented by a downward OR.

The view of synonymy that we will adopt may be stated as follows: two lexical items are synonymous if they have the same cognitive meaning in some context. 'Lexical item' is chosen in preference to, say, 'lexeme' for reasons that will be made clear below. Among the kinds of meaning one can think of that would not be 'cognitive' (in the sense linguists usually ascribe to the term) would be connotations of various kinds (including emotive connotations) and stylistic factors. Such kinds of meaning have been disregarded in the present description, which attempts to account for only cognitive meaning. Thus the only kind of synonymy that is expressed in the description is cognitive synonymy.

Consider, first of all, the downward OR representing the *while/during* diversification. Even though these two items have the same meaning according to our analysis, they would not normally be regarded as synonyms, since they are not substitutable for each other. There is no context in which they have the same cognitive meaning, because there is no context in which they may both occur. If one wanted to broaden the above definition of synonymy (which is, in any case, rather liberal), one obvious direction in which to do it would be to relax the condition of substitutability. In this case, *while* and *during* would be synonyms. According to normal usage, however, synonyms are substitutable for each other; and the above definition set out to reflect the normal usage. Thus *while* and *during* do not qualify as synonyms. The fact that they are not substitutable for each other is stated in the lexotactics: conjunctions and prepositions occupy different positions in surface structures, and *while* is a conjunction and not a preposition, whereas *during* is a preposition and not a conjunction.

For the second example we need to consult *Fig* 41 (3.3.1), and specifically the part of the network that expresses the meaning of *past* and *through*. The question we will ask is whether the downward OR below A in that diagram represents an instance of synonymy. The generalization made by this downward OR and the upward AND above it is that *past* and *through* (and *beyond*) share part of their meaning, namely 'path locative'. What the downward OR says, then, is that part of the meaning of *past* is synonymous with part of the meaning of *through*. But this statement contains a rather unusual application of the term 'synonymous'. Cognitive synonymy is usually taken to involve the entire cognitive meaning of the items in question, rather than just part of it. It would be pointless to allow the term 'synonymy' to be applied to individual components of the cognitive meaning of lexical items – *ie* there is absolutely nothing to be gained from taking a statement such as '*behind* and *through* have a component of their meaning in common' and rephrasing it as 'part of the meaning of *behind* is synonymous with part of the meaning of *through*'. And it would be quite ridiculous to regard lexical items themselves as synonymous if they have some part of their cognitive meaning in common, since this would mean that (for instance) *above* and *below* are synonymous. Thus the downward OR below A in *Fig* 41 does not represent an instance of synonymy. To generalize from this example, we may say that downward ORS that are involved in cases of portmanteau realization do not correspond to instances of synonymy. Only downward ORS that represent cases of diversification correspond to instances of synonymy. Of course, this is just one of the conditions that have to be satisfied. Another condition was stated above: the lexical items have to share some lexotactic environment. A third condition will be stated immediately below.

The word *economics* may be pronounced either with the vowel of *eat* or with that of *etch* in its first syllable; and although most speakers would favour one pronunciation or the other, there are some who fluctuate. This variation would be represented, in the network notation, by a downward OR node. Moreover, it would be a case of diversification proper. But to suggest that the vowels $/i{:}/$ and $/e/$ are synonymous in the environment *-conomics* would involve placing a far too broad interpretation on the term 'synonymy'. The definition of synonymy adopted above would exclude such a case by virtue of the fact that $/i{:}/$ and $/e/$ are not lexical items. With regard to the question of what lexical items are (in this connection), it would seem that they are elements corresponding to the lines in the middle portion of the realizational structure. Below a certain level the lines would not represent what we would be prepared to call 'lexical items', eg /iː/ and /e/ are not lexical items; and the same would be true above a certain level – eg although there is a noun *interior*, which we would be prepared to regard as a lexical item, we would not consider the sememe 'interior' to be a lexical item. The possibility suggests itself, of course, that lexical items are the elements represented by the set of lines AT A PARTICULAR LEVEL of the realizational structure. This may be so, but in that case the level in question would be below that of the lexotactics – and therefore lexical items would not be the same as lexemes. This conclusion is dictated by the facts of the following example.

Till and *until* count as genuine synonyms according to our definition of synonymy. They are substitutable for each other, since they have an identical lexotactic distribution; and the whole of the cognitive meaning of *till* is the same as the whole of the cognitive meaning of *until* – ie the downward OR is an example of diversification proper rather than part of a case of portmanteau realization. But *till* and *until* are not separate lexemes (as we have seen); they are alternative realizations of a single lexeme. Thus if we refer to *till* and *until* as lexical items, the latter are not the same thing as lexemes.

Before taking up the question of whether all instances of synonymy involve a downward OR, I will refer briefly to diagram (b) in *Fig* 47 (3.3.2), representing the meaning of *behind* and *after*. It would generally be agreed that these two items are not synonymous, but it is of interest to establish why they are not synonymous. Is it because they differ in cognitive meaning, or is it because they are not substitutable for each other? In Bennett 1968 (160) it was suggested that *behind* and *after* have the same cognitive meaning, designated there as 'posteriority', and that the reason they are not synonymous is that they are in complementary distribution as far as the semotactics is concerned, and therefore not substitutable for one another. One could still defend such a position (with appropriate modifications to accommodate the fact that 'posteriority' is a complex notion). According to such a view, substitutability would depend on having not only a common lexotactic environment but also a common semotactic environment. The alternative view (adopted here) is that the elements 'place' and 'time' are part of the cognitive meaning of *behind* and *after*, which therefore differ in cognitive meaning. It is clear that the two accounts of the facts are really simply superficially distinct ways of saying the same thing: the relationships involved are the same in either case. The example has interesting implications as far as the overall structure of the network is concerned – *eg* the fact that according to the earlier proposal the downward OR at B in *Fig* 47 would be a genuine case of diversification situated above the semotactics – but I will not pursue the matter here.

The question that remains to be answered is whether all generally recognized cases of synonymy involve a downward OR. It turns out that some cases of synonymy – *eg* the *by/past* example discussed above – involve more than one downward OR in the semolexemic realizational structure. *Fig* 49 contains the essential details from *Fig* 47 (and C in the

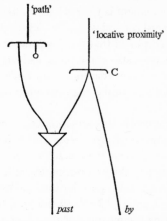

Fig 49 An example of synonymy involving two downward ORs

new diagram corresponds to C in the earlier diagram), together with the information that the sememe 'path' can be realized as zero. The sememic representation of *We drove by/past the post office* contains the string of sememes 'path locative proximity'. *Fig* 49 specifies the two ways in which this string may be realized: either as *past* or as $\varnothing_{path}$ *by*. *Past* is seen to be synonymous with a string of two items, in much the same way as *collect* is synonymous with *gather together*. The present example is special in that one of the items in the string is zero. It should be noted, however, that this zero is not just any old zero; rather, it is the zero realization of the sememe 'path'. The important thing is that in the network notation this particular instance of synonymy involves two separate downward ORs. If we want to make a statement about synonymous items which is based solely on the presence of a downward OR at C, all we can say is that *by* is synonymous with part of the meaning of *past*. Such a pronouncement is not much of an improvement on the statement that part of the meaning of *behind* is synonymous with part of the meaning of *through* (discussed above).

In the light of this example we need to modify an earlier remark. It was said above that the only downward ORS that correspond to instances of synonymy are those that represent cases of diversification (as opposed to those that combine with upward ANDS in representing cases of portmanteau realization). This was an attempt at a stratificational reformulation of the observation that cognitive synonymy involves identity of the whole of the cognitive meaning of the items in question, rather than just part of it. The statement is true as long as one restricts one's attention to single downward OR nodes. But in view of the facts of the *by* and *past* example, we need to add that the downward ORS involved in portmanteau realization may also correspond to instances of synonymy – providing that there is more than one such node and that collectively they account for the whole of the cognitive meaning of the synonymous items.

Finally, I will comment briefly on the question of the levels in the realizational structure at which synonymy and polysemy may be recognized, considering polysemy first. In 2.2.5 we decided that it is desirable to recognize two senses of the preposition *through*. The two componential definitions proposed were 'path locative interior' and 'goal locative path locative interior time' (*cf: Table* 12, 2.2.7). A first approximation to a network representing the meaning of *through* is shown in *Fig* 50. The upward OR representing the polysemy of *by* (*cf: Fig* 43, 3.3.1) is included in the diagram by way of indicating whereabouts in the realizational structure the *through* network belongs. It should be noted also that the line at X corresponds to the *through* that occurs in the lexeme *throughout*. One point of interest in the diagram is that there are three layers of upward ANDS and downward ORS (previously we had encountered only two). What is unsatisfactory about the diagram is the fact that it states twice – once for each sense – that *through* contains the components 'path locative interior'. It is worth considering whether it would not be possible to omit one of these two statements, thereby applying something like the elementary principle of algebra which permits $pqr + pqs$ to be simplified to $pq(r + s)$. In the meaning of *through*, 'path locative interior' combines either with nothing (in *through$_1$*) or with 'goal locative . . . time' (in *through$_2$*). In the latter case, it would seem that 'path locative interior' combines with a discontinuous constituent. This makes the question of simplifying our account of the meaning of *through* somewhat less straightforward than if the meaning of *through$_2$* were 'goal locative time path locative interior'. However, the ambivalent status of the sememes 'place' and 'time' – to which we referred in 3.2.5 and earlier in the present sub-section – is again relevant here. To solve the problem of the order of the component 'time' in the definition of *during*, it was suggested that the semotactics might be modified to allow 'time' (and 'place') to occur simultaneously with the sememe 'locative' and the specifier of a locative expression. The same modification of the semotactics might solve the present problem also, permitting us to regard the meaning of *through*₂ as 'goal locative time path locative interior', which would make it possible to present a simpler diagram than that of *Fig* 50. It should be noted,

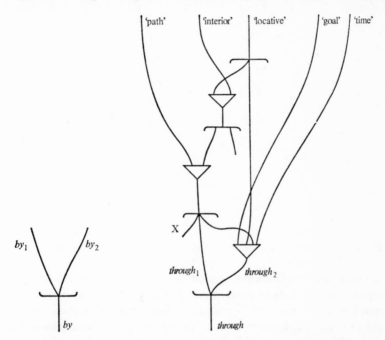

Fig 50 First approximation to a network representing the meaning of *through*

however, that the exact details remain to be worked out. The alternative representation of the meaning of *through* would be as in *Fig* 51. This diagram is slightly simpler than the original one, scoring 9 rather than 10. The main difference between the two networks resides in the position of the upward OR relative to other nodes. In *Fig* 50 the upward OR is the lowest node, implying that the meaning of *through* involves either one

set of components or some other set of components. In *Fig* 51 there is an
upward AND below the upward OR, indicating that the disjunction in the
meaning of *through* involves only part of its meaning: 'path locative interior' is present whichever sense occurs. In view of the fact that there

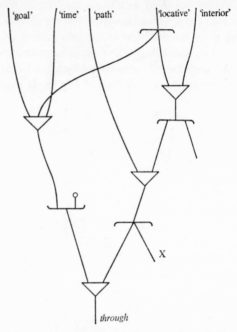

Fig 51 Alternative representation of the meaning of *through*

is an upward AND below the upward OR of *Fig* 51, it seems reasonable to
regard this example of polysemy as belonging higher up the realizational structure than the *by* example. Although no such cases occur in
the present data, it ought to be relatively easy to find examples of lexemes which exhibit both kinds of polysemy. They would be the mirror
image in the content plane of examples such as *go* in the expression
plane, which (as we saw in *Fig* 45, **3.3.2**) exhibits diversification at two
different levels.

In Bennett 1968 (157–65) four levels of synonymy were distinguished,
but at that time it seemed necessary to recognize a 'hypersemotactics'
above the semotactics, *ie* we were operating with three tactic patterns
from the level of the lexemes upwards. It now seems preferable to collapse the top two into one tactic pattern and call it the 'semotactics'.

This reduces the number of levels at which synonymy is recognized. Probably it is sufficient to distinguish just two levels at which synonymy occurs: below the lexotactics (*ie* in the lexomorphemic realizational structure) and between the lexotactics and semotactics (*ie* in the semolexemic realizational structure).

3.4 Lexotactics

3.4.1 General remarks

Classes of linguistic elements can be identified at various levels of language. We have already mentioned classes such as those of 'parts' (comprising 'interior', 'anterior', 'superior', etc) and prepositions (*to, at, through*, etc). As further examples, we may consider the classes of verbal prefixes (*eg: con-, ex-, per-, trans-*) and consonants (*eg* /p, t, k/). Each of these classes is represented in the same way in a stratificational grammar: by means of a downward OR in the tactic part of the grammar. Moreover, the distribution of the members of the various classes, relative to other similar classes, is specified by means of downward ANDS representing constructions. Since elements such as /p/ and 'interior' are so different in nature, it would seem that languages must have separate tactic patterns at different levels of the realizational structure, rather than one tactic pattern in which all of the classes feature. Language has as many strata as there are separate tactic patterns. At the moment a four-stratum model seems to be the most satisfactory, the four strata being the sememic, lexemic, morphemic and phonemic. The way to decide how many strata there are is by representing a large amount of data according to different hunches as to how many strata there might be and then choosing the alternative which results in the simplest overall network. For instance, one might divide the distributional information expressed by the semotactics described in 3.2 between two separate tactic patterns, making corresponding changes in the realizational structure. Then one would carry out a complexity count on the overall network resulting from each of the two hypotheses, and choose the simpler description. As far as I can tell, the one-stratum description would emerge as simpler than the two-stratum description. At the present time, the number of people who are sufficiently familiar with the network notation to carry out such a project is rather small. There needs to be considerably more description of data in stratificational terms, at all levels of language, before one can be really confident about a particular claim as to how many strata there are.

The lexotactics characterizes the ways in which members of the various lexeme-classes (*eg* prepositions, nouns, verbs) can be combined. It is connected to the realizational structure below the level at which our componential analysis of the meaning of English prepositions belongs. It is only below that level that units such as verbs, nouns and prepositions exist. The lines above that level of the realizational structure correspond to components of the meaning of items such as *in, through, arrive* and *enter*, rather than to these items themselves.

3.4.2 Prepositional phrases

As was indicated in the preceding subsection, the total set of distributional information in a stratificational grammar – the facts about what combinations of elements are well-formed – is divided between a small number of separate tactic patterns. It is important to realize that any given distributional fact should be stated in just one tactic pattern, *ie* there should be no unnecessary repetition of information. With this principle in mind, we shall now consider some of the distributional facts about English prepositions that need to be stated in the lexotactics.

We need to specify what prepositional phrases are. This information is not expressed anywhere else in the grammar. For instance, there is no prepositional phrase construction in the semotactics. Various semotactic constituents may be realized as a prepositional phrase, *eg* goal expressions and locative expressions, but they may be realized in other ways as well (and goal expressions differ from locative expressions both in internal structure and as regards where they can occur in larger semotactic constituents). Thus it would be wrong to think that goal expressions and locative expressions ARE prepositional phrases. The amount of information that needs to be given in the lexotactics about the internal structure of a prepositional phrase is minimal. It needs to be stated that a prepositional phrase consists of a preposition followed by a noun phrase, *eg: at the post office*, or of a preposition followed by a prepositional phrase, *eg: from behind the door*. But there is no need to include any information about co-occurrence restrictions between particular subclasses of prepositions and particular noun phrases, since this kind of information is stated in the semotactics. For instance, there is no need to distinguish between spatial and temporal prepositional phrases, in view of the fact that the semotactics distinguishes between spatial and temporal locative and extent expressions. This means that if operating as an independent generative device, the lexotactics would generate not only *under the bookcase* and *since the first week in June* but also *since the bookcase* and **under the first week in June*. But when integrated with other components of the overall grammar, the lexotactics does not generate strings of lexemes randomly; it generates in accordance with whatever signals reach it from elsewhere in the grammar (*cf* 3.5). Assuming, then, that the semotactics would not be able to generate a sememic representation corresponding to **since the bookcase* and **under the first week in June* (but *cf* the discussion of the distinction between *the street behind the church* and *the street after the church* in Bennett 1968: 160), the lexotactics would never be called upon by the semotactics to produce these particular prepositional phrases.

With regard to prepositional phrases such as *from behind the door*, many combinations of prepositions are ungrammatical, *eg: *to from the door*. But, again, it is unnecessary to exclude the non-occurring combinations specifically in the lexotactics, since they are blocked in any case, in the context of the grammar as a whole, by virtue of the fact that they have no corresponding sememic representation. Thus while

source locative posterior of door place

(the sememic representation of *from behind the door*) is a possible output from the semotactics, none of the following strings (which might conceivably underlie **to from the door*) is well-formed:

*goal source door place
*goal source locative door place
*goal locative source door place
*goal locative source locative door place

We shall need to provide a mechanism for generating sequences of prepositional phrases in order to account for examples such as:

from Manchester over the Pennines to Sheffield
on a bench under a tree in the park
in the park under a tree on a bench

All that is required is an iterative loop, permitting an indefinite number of prepositional phrases to be generated at any point where a single prepositional phrase may occur. There is no need for the lexotactics to state the differences in structure between the above sequences, since these are stated in the semotactics.

Consider now the question of 'prepositional phrases inside the verb phrase', as in *John keeps his car in the garage*, and 'prepositional phrases outside the verb phrase', as in *John washes his car in the garage* (*cf* Fillmore 1968: 26). Following Lakoff (1970b: 154–7), I would want to analyse a sentence such as *Goldwater won in the West* as containing an embedded sentence *Goldwater won*. In our terms, the sememic analysis would show an embedded proposition (realized lexemically as *Goldwater won*) functioning as the subject of a higher proposition. *In the West* is the lexemic realization of the predicate of the higher proposition. Similarly, the sememic representation of the second of the 'garage' examples would result from embedding the proposition underlying *John washes his car* inside a locative proposition – as is indicated by the bracketing [[*John washes his car*] *in the garage*]. Without going into details of how the sememic representation of the other 'garage' example would be produced, it is clear that it would not contain an embedded proposition corresponding to *John keeps his car* – *ie* the bracketing *[[*John keeps his car*] *in the garage*] is inappropriate. This means that the sememic representations of the two sentences would be generated quite differently. In consequence, it is unnecessary to invoke a distinction (at the lexemic level) between prepositional phrases inside and outside the verb phrase by way of characterizing the difference in structure between the two examples. Now one reason for having a verb phrase constituent containing not only the main verb and accompanying auxiliaries but also other constituents was so that prepositional phrases might occur either inside or outside it. But if the distinction between these two kinds of prepositional phrases does not need to be made at this level, then this reason for having a verb phrase of the kind indicated disappears. It seems likely that the lexotactics ought to be set up in such a way that a given route through the network would resemble the sort of diagram one might draw to represent 'string constituent analysis', as employed in tagmemics (*cf* Longacre 1960) or systemic grammar (*cf* Hudson 1967), rather than immediate constituent analysis (Wells 1947). A verb phrase would consist of a main verb together with its accompanying auxiliaries; and each of the 'garage' examples would have four constituents at the first level of 'cutting', *ie* NP VP NP PP. It is of interest that there is room in a stratificational grammar for both SC analysis and IC analysis. The lexotactics (as I conceive of it) would be closer to SC analysis, but the semotactics with its many-layered structure would be closer to IC analysis.

A further set of examples relevant to the lexotactics (already briefly mentioned in 1.2.5) is given in [130].

Trevor walked across to the post office   [130a]
*Trevor walked to the post office across   [130b]
The bird flew in through the window   [130c]
*The bird flew through the window in   [130d]

In [130a] *across* realizes a path expression and *to the post office* a goal expression. In [130c] *in* realizes a goal expression and *through the window* a path expression. Thus the unacceptability of [b] and [d] has nothing to do with the particular directional expressions that they contain. It may be that the order of adverbs and prepositional phrases in such sentences is determined by their information structure, the more prominent position at the end being reserved for a prepositional phrase, if available, because it represents a more important part of the message. In the absence of a more satisfactory account of [130], I will assume that it is a fact about the surface structure of English that adverbs such as *across* and *in* have to precede prepositional phrases.

It is appropriate at this point to consider the status of *away from, out of* and *in front of*. According to our informal use of the term 'lexeme' in **0.2**, each of the items in *Table* 1 (**0.1**) was a lexeme, but the fact that *away, out* and *in front* can occur on their own (*She's gone away, We're going out, John's car is in front*) suggests that *away from*, etc, are sequences of two lexemes rather than single lexemes. In this case, *away, out* and *in front* would be treated as adverbs, which may or may not be followed by a prepositional phrase. American English *in back of* would receive a similar analysis. On the other hand, *throughout* would need to be analysed as a complex lexeme rather than as a sequence of adverb + preposition, owing to the fact that – in the writer's dialect, at least – *out* may not function as a preposition.

3.4.3 A fragment of the lexotactics

Fig 52 contains a highly simplified fragment of the lexotactics, incorporating just one slot for adverbials; and *Fig* 53 shows a tentative version of the adverbial network. According to *Fig* 52, sentences consist of a subject noun phrase followed by a verb (auxiliaries are omitted), followed optionally by an object noun phrase and an adverbial. Noun phrases are shown as containing a noun, and other details are omitted. This information is summarized in the following PS rules:

sentence → NP V (NP) (adverbial)
NP → ...N...
N → {*post office, hill, door*, ...}
V → {*go, walk, arrive, enter, be*, ...}

In describing *Fig* 53, I will ignore the loop at the top until after

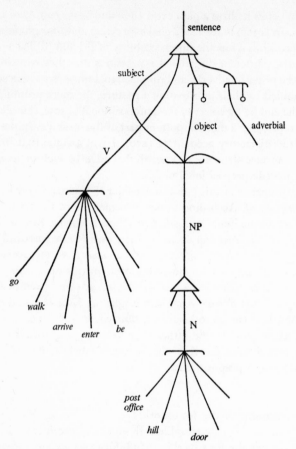

Fig 52　A fragment of the lexotactics

discussing the remainder of the diagram. A PS-rule version (also omitting details of the loop) is given below:

adverbial → (prep) advl
advl → (adv⋄PP)
adv → {prep/adv, *away, out, in front,* ...}
PP → prep NP
prep → {prep/adv, *of, at, from,* ...}
prep/adv → {*in, over, past, behind, through,* ...}

The optional preposition in the first rule accounts not only for examples

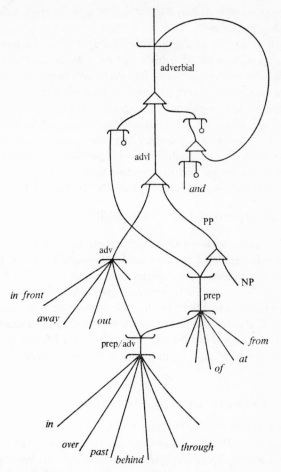

Fig 53 A network representing adverbials

such as *from behind the door* (in which a preposition precedes a prepositional phrase) but also for cases where a preposition precedes an adverb, *eg: from behind*. Otherwise, an adverbial contains either an adverb or a prepositional phrase or an adverb followed by a prepositional phrase. A prepositional phrase consists of a preposition followed by a noun phrase. The remainder of the rules serve to list some of the members of the classes of adverbs and prepositions. Some items, *eg: away, out* and *in front* function only as adverbs. Others function only as prepositions, *eg: of, at* and *from*. But the majority of the lexemes whose meaning was investigated in Parts I and II may function either as adverbs or as prepositions.

The loop at the top of *Fig* 53 is included to allow the possibility of generating sequences of adverbials, *eg: on a bench under a tree in the park*. This loop creates problems, however, with regard to sequences of adverbials containing adverbs as well as prepositional phrases. *Fig* 53 ensures that an adverb precedes a prepositional phrase – *cf* [130] – only within a single adverbial. There is nothing to prevent an adverb being placed after a prepositional phrase, giving the unwanted [130b and d], if the loop is used. The only solution to this problem that occurs to me at present is rather *ad hoc* and there seems little point in describing the details. When the loop is included, the adverbial rule becomes:

adverbial → (prep) advl ((*and*) adverbial)

The distinction between semotactic traces and sememic representations (3.2.4) is paralleled by a distinction between lexotactic traces and lexemic representations. Any information about higher-level lexotactic constituents that is needed by other components of the grammar would have to be made available in the lexemic representations themselves. It seems very likely that the phonology would need to have access to quite a lot of information about lexotactic constituency. However, not having investigated such matters, I am unable to be more specific.

3.5 Integrating realization and tactics

3.5.1 Realization *versus* tactics

A lexeme such as *through* has connections to the upper part of the realizational structure, representing its meaning, and to the lower part of the realizational structure, corresponding to its pronunciation. In addition, it has a connection into the lexotactics, representing its lexotactic distribution. We need now to consider how the lexotactics is attached to the realizational structure; and, more generally, how any tactic pattern is attached to the realizational structure. Since *through* has a meaning AND a pronunciation AND a particular lexotactic distribution, it is clear that we shall need to use some kind of AND node in connecting the lines at the bottom of the lexotactics to the realizational structure. However, neither an upward AND nor a downward AND is appropriate, since there is no compelling reason for regarding the lexotactics as being either above or below the level of the lexemes. Rather, it is at that level. Each tactic pattern may be thought of as occupying a horizontal plane and inter-secting with the realizational structure at a particular level. A diamond-shaped node is used at all points where a line in a tactic pattern is con-nected to a line in the realizational structure. It is a more complex kind of AND node than either an upward AND or a downward AND. The most commonly used type of diamond node is shown in *Fig* 54a. It has con-

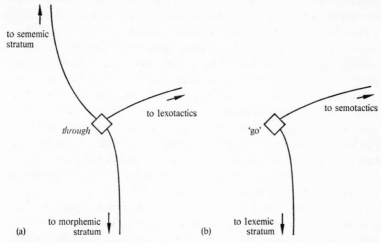

Fig 54 Two types of diamond nodes

nections to higher in the realizational structure (at top left) and lower in the realizational structure (bottom right), and also into a tactic pattern (top right). In the case of the lexeme *through*, there is a connection to-wards the sememic stratum and one towards the morphemic stratum (whose tactic pattern characterizes the internal structure of words); and also a connection into the lexotactics. A second type of diamond is shown in *Fig* 54b. The sememe 'go' has a connection into the semo-tactics and one towards the lexemic stratum, but no connection towards the top of the realizational structure. Such a diamond corresponds to the view that 'go' is a determined element, inserted whenever a directional predicate is produced. It would be possible to omit the node in *Fig* 54b altogether, since a node with only two connections is not really a node at all. In this case, a line from the semotactics would connect straight into the semolexemic realizational structure. However, since the realizational and tactic portions of the grammar are thought of as being at right-angles to each other, such a line would have to turn a corner, so to speak.

To draw attention to this fact, it is customary to use two-way diamonds in such a situation.

3.5.2 A dynamic model

When tactic patterns are integrated with the realizational structure, impulses moving through the combined network enter the linguistic system either at the top or at the bottom of the realizational structure – depending on whether the grammar is being used as a model of encoding or decoding. In the case of the encoding process, the order in which the various subcomponents of the grammar are brought into play is: suprasememic realizational structure—semotactics—semolexemic realizational structure—lexotactics—lexomorphemic realizational structure, and so on. In the case of decoding, the order is: subphonemic realizational structure—phonotactics—morphophonemic realizational structure—morphotactics—lexomorphemic realizational structure, and so on. The output from a particular tactic pattern is determined in a given instance by the set of impulses reaching it from higher or lower in the realizational structure. For instance, with regard to the encoding process, the output from the lexotactics in a given instance is determined by the impulses reaching it from the semolexemic realizational structure, which in turn depend on the output from the semotactics. Thus we need a mechanism, with respect to tactic patterns in general, whereby the route taken by impulses travelling downwards through the network of the tactics is determined by the activation of a particular set of diamond nodes at the place where the tactics intersects with the realizational structure. The solution adopted in the 'Relational Network Simulator', a computer programming system developed by Reich (1969, 1970a) entails treating all the nodes of a network as finite state devices and distinguishing several kinds of signals that may travel through the network. Before 'regular production signals' travel downwards through a tactic pattern, the route that they take is determined by 'anticipatory signals', which travel upwards through the network. Talking in terms of tactic traces, a trace is first built up from bottom to top, and then used from top to bottom.

The model outlined above by no means constitutes the only conceivable way of integrating tactic patterns with the realizational structure. An alternative model currently being developed by Lamb (Lamb forthcoming) makes no use of anticipatory signals. In this model interconnections exist among the higher levels of the various tactic patterns, so that, for example, when an impulse enters the semotactics, it activates a line connecting to an appropriate location high in the lexotactics. Such a model promises to overcome certain defects of the model described in the preceding paragraph. However, since the newer model has not yet been described in any detail in print, I have preferred to presuppose the earlier model in the discussion of 3.5.3.

3.5.3 Specific descriptive problems

One way of showing how a model containing several generative devices (*ie* tactic patterns) works out in practice is by considering a particular sentence at a number of levels. This I attempted to do, on a modest scale, in Bennett forthcoming, taking the sentence *The girl went into the kitchen* and indicating how its sememic representation would trigger off the corresponding lexemic representation. Rather than undertake something similar here, I will briefly discuss four particular problems involving the semotactics, semolexemic realizational structure and lexotactics: first, the relationship between the sememe 'of' and the lexeme *of*; secondly, the mechanism for converting 'goal locative interior' and 'goal locative surface' into *into* and *onto*; thirdly, the circumstances under which 'goal' is realized as *arrive* rather than, say, *to*; and lastly, the relationship between pairs of items such as *in* and *contain*, or *in front of* and *face*.

Although the mechanism of 'of'-insertion remains problematical in certain respects (*cf* 3.2.5), two facts concerning 'of' and *of* seem certain: (i) the sememe 'of' is frequently realized as zero; and (ii) it is necessary to recognize two different *ofs* in British English *out of the house* and *out of the window*, only the former being semantically justified (*cf* 1.2.5). It is these two facts on which we shall concentrate here.

Examples [131] and [132], in which 'of' is realized as *of*, may be contrasted with [133] and [134], in which 'of' is realized as zero.

'locative anterior of house place'	[131]
in front of the house	
'goal locative exterior of house place'	[132]
out of the house	
'locative posterior of house place'	[133]
behind the house	
'locative interior of house place'	[134]
in the house	

(I have encountered *behind of* in American English, but believe it to be uncommon. In standard British English, phrases such as *behind of the house* and *in of the house* do not occur at all.) There is no obvious reason why 'anterior' and 'exterior' should behave differently from 'posterior' and 'interior'. Thus it would seem to be an idiosyncratic fact about the surface structure of English that *of* appears in [131] and [132] but not in [133] and [134]. With regard to the relationship between the absence of *of* and the prepositional status of items such as *behind* and *in*, probably the most reasonable way of stating the relationship is by saying that *behind* and *in* owe their prepositional status to the fact that the *of* which might otherwise be expected to follow them is deleted. But in attempting to formalize the details of [131]–[134], it is convenient to reverse

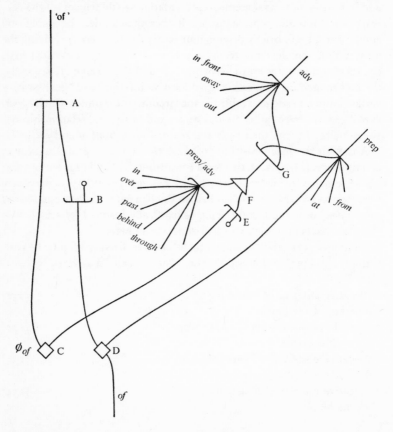

Fig 55 The two realizations of the sememe 'of'

this statement and say that 'of' is realized as zero following any member of the class of lexemes labelled 'prep/adv' in *Fig* 53 (3.4.3). *Fig* 55 contains the relevant portions of the realizational structure and the lexotactics. (The lexotactics differs from the fragment shown in *Fig* 53 as a result of the insertion of two extra nodes, at E and F, and the modification of the upward OR at G.) We will consider how this structure would be used in the course of producing the phrases *behind the house* and *in front of the house*.

A particular set of lines in the semolexemic realizational structure has been activated in response to a particular sememic structure produced by the semotactics. Impulses reach the level of the lexotactics in a particular sequence. There the aim is to build up a well-formed lexotactic trace. If this aim is achieved, a corresponding set of impulses will enter the lexomorphemic realizational structure from the lexotactics. The sememic representation of *behind the house* contains the sememe 'of'. Thus at a particular moment an impulse reaches node A in *Fig* 55. This node – a downward ordered OR – expresses the fact that $\emptyset_{of}$ (*ie* zero) is the preferred realization of 'of'; the *of* alternative is selected only if the condition for choosing $\emptyset_{of}$ is not satisfied. From node A an impulse is sent first of all to node C. From C an impulse is sent up into the lexotactics to node E, and then further to F. An impulse will proceed from F to G only if the other line connecting to the bottom of F has already been activated (F is an ordered AND). In the case of the phrase *behind the house*, the line in question would have been activated, since *behind* belongs to the 'prep/adv' class. The effect of making the upward OR at G ordered is that the lexotactics will try first of all to interpret *behind* as a preposition, *ie* it will check to see if it is followed by a noun phrase. In the present instance, there is a following noun phrase; thus *behind the house* will be interpreted as a prepositional phrase. If there were no following noun phrase, the left-most line out of G would fail, and *behind* would be interpreted instead as an adverb. (In this case, the sememic representation would not contain the sememe 'of' – which means that the zero alternative at E would be used, rather than the line from C.) We see, then, how 'anticipatory signals' are able to form a lexotactic trace from the bottom upwards. When 'regular production signals' travel downwards through the tactic pattern, they usually encounter a number of downward OR nodes. The choice of which line to take out of such a node is determined by the state the node happens to be in at the time; but this is determined by which line was used on the way up. Thus the nodes of a tactic pattern are able to 'remember' the route taken by anticipatory signals. The input to the lexomorphemic realizational structure in the present instance would contain impulses corresponding to *behind* and *the* and *house*. In addition, the diamond at C would be activated (immediately after the *behind* node); but $\varnothing_{of}$ is a zero lexeme, with no connection into the lexomorphemic realizational structure, and consequently the impulse at C would die. (Node C illustrates a third type of diamond node – *cf Fig* 54.)

In producing the phrase *behind the house*, the first alternative at node A succeeds. On the other hand, in producing *in front of the house*, the first alternative would fail: an impulse reaching node F from C would not be able to send a signal up to G, because there would have been no prior signal along the 'prep/adv' line. A 'negative feedback signal' would therefore be sent from F back to A, whereupon an impulse would be sent down the second line at A. It would travel via D to the 'prep' node, and then further to the prepositional phrase construction. When a signal returns down this line to the node at D, an impulse is sent into the lexomorphemic realizational structure corresponding to the lexeme *of*. The input to the lexomorphemic realizational structure would thus contain impulses representing *in front* followed by *of* followed by *the* followed by *house*.

With regard to *The bird flew out of the window*, whose sememic representation contains no occurrence of the sememe 'of' (*cf* 1.2.5), the lexotactics would not accept *out the window* as well-formed, since *out* functions only as an adverb (in British English). However, using the zero possibility at node B, the lexotactics can insert the lexeme *of*, thereby producing the well-formed string *out of the window*. In this case, then, the *of* originates at node B, rather than being the lexemic realization of the sememe 'of'. We have now encountered two different ways in which empty realization may be symbolized in the network notation – by means of a diamond of the type shown in *Fig* 54b or an upward OR with one line connecting to a zero. The two are not equivalent; they represent somewhat different cases of empty realization. The diamond of *Fig* 54b is used whenever the element in question is always empty. On the other hand, an upward OR such as that at B in *Fig* 55 indicates that the element in question is sometimes empty but sometimes not.

This last example also draws attention to a number of respects in which the present analysis is in need of elaboration. The sememic representation of *out of the window* contains a path expression (meaning 'via the window') and a goal expression (meaning 'to the exterior'). Moreover, according to the account of directional expressions given in

Part I, the path expression would precede the goal expression. Now if we disregard the problem of the loop that was mentioned in 3.4.3, the lexotactics would certainly be capable of delaying a prepositional phrase until after the adverb *out*. However, it would be necessary to explain why 'path' is realized in this instance as zero; and, in particular, why *of* has to be inserted in *The bird flew out of the window* but not in *She's sorting out old clothes*. This last question seems to indicate the need for incorporating rather more information about semotactic constituents into the sememic representations themselves than was implied above (*eg* in 3.2.4). Nevertheless, it remains true that we insert only such structure as is actually needed.

The easiest way to handle *into* and *onto* would be to treat them as portmanteau realizations (of 'goal locative interior' and 'goal locative surface'). However, such an analysis – which is entirely appropriate in a case such as *worse*, realizing 'bad' and 'comparative' – would obscure the fact that *into* and *onto* can be segmented into a morpheme that means 'locative interior' or 'locative surface' and a morpheme that means 'goal'. Moreover, before treating the facts of *into* and *onto* as being quite unique, we should ask whether they can be related to anything else in the description as a whole. Now if *into* and *onto* are analysed as consisting of an adverb (*in* or *on*) followed by the preposition *to*, examples such as *into the house* are thereby attributed a surface structure parallel to that of *out of the house*. This would mean, of course, that *The student went into the library* would have the same surface structure as *The student went in to the library*. But since these two sentences are semotactically distinct, and since the phonological difference between them can be treated as being determined by the semological distinction, there is no need to distinguish them also at the lexemic level. If it is true that *to* may function only as a preposition – *ie* if examples such as *Has he come to yet?* can be disposed of in some way – then the structure shown in *Fig* 56 might bring about the necessary reordering of *to* and *in* or *on*. Whenever either 'locative interior' or 'locative surface' is preceded by 'goal', this fact is noted at node C and an impulse is sent to the diamond at E. This particular diamond represents a fourth type of diamond node. It is situated on a line in the middle of the tactic pattern (the 'adv' line) rather than at the bottom, and consequently has connections to higher and lower in the tactics, in addition to its connection to higher in the realizational structure. Whenever E is activated, it forces the lexotactics to produce an adverb. If *to* cannot function as an adverb, *in* or *on* will be selected instead, and *to* will be delayed to fill the following preposition slot. The zero alternative at A allows *in* and *on* to occur unaccompanied by *to*; the one at B allows *to* to occur unaccompanied by *in* or *on*; and the one at D allows the lexotactics to select adverbs other than *in* and *on*.

Fig 57 gives some idea how one might solve the problem of when 'goal' is realized as *arrive* rather than in some other way. This diagram

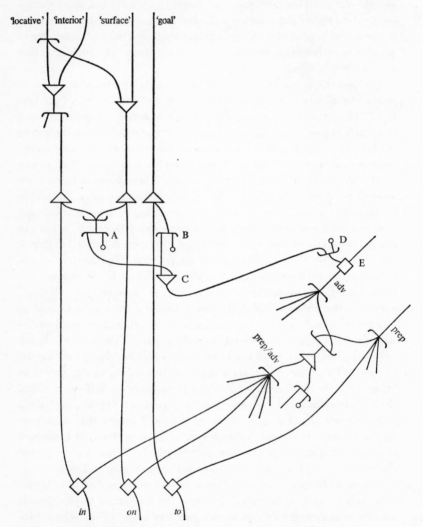

Fig 56 A possible mechanism for handling *into* and *onto*

would need to be elaborated in several ways, but the crucial feature of it is that *arrive* is shown as the first alternative amongst the possible realizations of 'goal'. The *arrive* realization will succeed, however, in a given instance only if the verb slot has not yet been filled. Now if every instance of 'goal' within a d-exs constituent is necessarily preceded by the

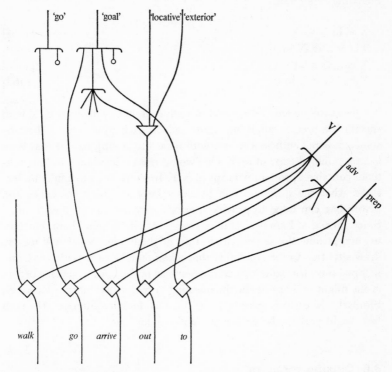

Fig 57 Alternative realizations of the sememe 'goal'

sememe 'go', then the verb slot will always have been filled already by the time that 'goal' is realized – either by the verb *go*, or by a verb such as *walk*, which would pre-empt the verb slot in advance even of *go*. The only time that the *arrive* realization will succeed is when the sememic representation contains a goal expression which is not part of a d-exs constituent. Such a possibility was allowed for during the discussion of punctual predicates in **3.2.3**.

In commenting on the relationship between *in* and *contain*, and *in front of* and *face*, it is convenient to refer to the schematic semantic representation shown below:

'X locative interior Y'   [135]

Presumably [135] is part of the semantic representation of each of the following sentences:

X is in Y	[136a]
There's an X in Y	[136b]
Y contains (an) X	[136c]
Y has (an) X in it	[136d]

To give a fully adequate account of such sentences, one must be able to specify the precise conditions under which each would occur. For instance, it is not sufficient to say, with regard to [136b], merely that *there* is a pronominal copy of *in* Y. One would need to explain why this sentence contains a pronominal copy of *in* Y. In short, one must fully understand what the differences in meaning between these sentences are, before one can hope to provide a satisfactory account of their syntax. Since I feel that I am not yet in possession of all the facts, I am reluctant to suggest how the sentences of [136] might be derived. I will merely draw attention to the possibility that *contain* might be regarded as being mapped onto the same two components as *in*, but in the reverse order; *ie* one might perhaps define the meaning of *contain* as 'interior locative'. Similarly, whereas *in front (of)* is defined as 'locative anterior', the verb *face* might perhaps be defined as 'anterior locative'.

3.6 Closing remarks

Some of the topics touched upon in this book have been treated less adequately than others. This is, no doubt, inevitable. I hope, however, to have achieved some measure of success in shedding light on the meaning of English prepositions, and also in conveying an understanding of stratificational grammar by applying it to an extended body of data.

Each of the existing linguistic theories has its weak points as well as its strong points. Moreover, it is often hard for those working within the framework of any theory to be sure that the issues with which they concern themselves are real issues about the nature of language as opposed to pseudo-issues dictated by the formalism that they happen to be working with. One important reason, therefore, for encouraging the development of a variety of theories and notations is that it is always easier to spot pseudo-issues from the vantage-point of an alternative approach. Genuine issues remain issues when translated into the terms of an alternative theory; pseudo-issues frequently disappear in the process. Thus linguistics can profit considerably from detailed comparison of various alternative theoretical and notational frameworks. But in making such comparisons we need to be prepared to recognize positive features in an approach that we are not actively pursuing ourselves, as opposed to concentrating simply on identifying its weak points – especially since the latter sometimes turn out to reside more in the critic's understanding of the approach than in the approach itself.

References

Allen, R. L. (1966), *The Verb System of Present-day American English*. The Hague: Mouton

Anderson, J. M. (1971), *The Grammar of Case: Towards a Localistic Theory*. Cambridge: Cambridge University Press

Bach, E. (1967), '*Have* and *Be* in English Syntax', *Language*, 43, *pp* 462–85

Bach, E. (1968), 'Nouns and Noun Phrases', in Bach and Harms (1968), *pp* 91–122

Bach, E. and Harms, R. T. (eds) (1968), *Universals in Linguistic Theory*. New York: Holt, Rinehart & Winston

Bauer, G. (1970), 'The English "Perfect" Reconsidered', *Journal of Linguistics*, 6, *pp* 189–98

Bennett, D. C. (1968), 'English Prepositions: a Stratificational Approach', *Journal of Linguistics*, 4, *pp* 153–72. Reprinted in Makkai and Lockwood (1973), *pp* 277–96

Bennett, D. C. (1970), *Spatial and Temporal Uses of English Prepositions*, Yale University PHD Dissertation

Bennett, D. C. (forthcoming), 'English Semotactics and Lexotactics', *Proceedings of the XIth International Congress of Linguists, Bologna, 1972*

Bierwisch, M. (1967), 'Some Semantic Universals of German Adjectivals', *Foundations of Language*, 3, *pp* 1–36

Bloomfield, L. (1933), *Language*. New York: Holt, Rinehart & Winston

Brown R. and McNeill, D. (1966), 'The "Tip of the Tongue" Phenomenon', *Journal of Verbal Learning and Verbal Behavior*, 5, *pp* 325–7

Bugarski, R. (1968), 'On the Interrelatedness of Grammar and Lexis in the Structure of English', *Lingua*, 19, *pp* 233–63

Carvell, H. T. and Svartvik, J. (1969), *Computational Experiments in Grammatical Classification*. The Hague: Mouton

Chomsky, N. (1965), *Aspects of the Theory of Syntax*. Cambridge, Mass: MIT Press

Chomsky, N. and Miller, G. A. (1963), 'Finitary Models of Language Users', in R. D. Luce, R. R. Bush and E. Galanter (eds), *Handbook of Mathematical Psychology*, Vol II (New York: Wiley), *pp* 419–92

Clark, H. H. (1968), 'On the Use and Meaning of Prepositions', *Journal of Verbal Learning and Verbal Behavior*, 7, *pp* 421–31

Close, R. A. (1959), 'Concerning the Present Tense', *English Language Teaching*, 13, *pp* 57–66

Close, R. A. (1962), *English as a Foreign Language*. London: George Allen & Unwin

Fillmore, C. J. (1968), 'The Case for Case', in Bach and Harms (1968), *pp* 1–88

Fillmore, C. J. (1971a), 'Some Problems for Case Grammar', in O'Brien (1971), *pp* 35–56

Fillmore, C. J. (1971b), Lectures on 'Space, Time and Deixis', delivered in Copenhagen in Summer 1971

Garey, H. B. (1955), *The Historical Development of Tenses from Late Latin to Old French*, *Language Dissertation* 51

Garey, H. B. (1957), 'Verbal Aspect in French', *Language*, 33, *pp* 91–110

Gross, M. (1967), 'Sur une Règle de "Cacophonie"', *Langages*, 7, *pp* 105–19

Gruber, J. S. (1965), *Studies in Lexical Relations*, MIT PHD Dissertation

Halliday, M. A. K. (1966), 'The English Verbal Group: a Specimen of a Manual of Analysis', mimeographed. University College London

Halliday, M. A. K. (1967–68), 'Notes on Transitivity and Theme in English', *Journal of Linguistics*, 3, *pp* 37–81, 199–244; 4, *pp* 179–216

Hamp, E. P., Householder, F. W. and Austerlitz, R. (eds) (1966), *Readings in Linguistics II*. Chicago: University of Chicago Press

Huddleston, R. D. (1969), 'Some Observations on Tense and Deixis in English', *Language*, 45, *pp* 777–806

Hudson, R. A. (1967), 'Constituency in a Systemic Description of the English Clause', *Lingua*, 18, *pp* 225–50

Hudson, R. A. (1971), 'How Many Times can a Sentence Mean?', unpublished paper. University College London

Ikegami, Y. (1970), *The Semological Structure of the English Verbs of Motion: a Stratificational Approach*. Tokyo: Sanseido

Jakobson, R. (1932), 'Zur Struktur des russischen Verbums', *Charisteria V. Mathesio Oblata* (Prague: Cercle Linguistique de Prague), *pp* 74–83. Reprinted in Hamp, Householder and Austerlitz (1966), *pp* 22–30

Jakobson, R. (1936), 'Beitrag zur allgemeinen Kasuslehre: Gesamtbedeutungen der russischen Kasus', *Travaux du Cercle Linguistique de Prague*, 6, *pp* 240–88. Reprinted in Hamp, Householder and Austerlitz (1966), *pp* 51–89 (page references to this version)

Joos, M. (1964), *The English Verb*. Madison and Milwaukee: University of Wisconsin Press

Lakoff, G. (1970a), 'A Note on Vagueness and Ambiguity', *Linguistic Inquiry*, 1, *pp* 357–9

Lakoff, G. (1970b), 'Pronominalization, Negation, and the Analysis of Adverbs', in R. A. Jacobs and P. S. Rosenbaum (eds) (1970), *Readings in English Transformational Grammar* (Waltham, Mass: Ginn), *pp* 145–65

Lamb, S. M. (1966a), *Outline of Stratificational Grammar*. Washington, DC: Georgetown University Press

Lamb, S. M. (1966b), 'Prolegomena to a Theory of Phonology', *Language*, 42, *pp* 536–73. Reprinted in Makkai and Lockwood (1973), *pp* 128–65

Lamb, S. M. (1971a), 'The Crooked Path of Progress in Cognitive Linguistics', in O'Brien (1971), *pp* 99–123. Reprinted in Makkai and Lockwood (1973), *pp* 12–33

Lamb, S. M. (1971b), 'Linguistic and Cognitive Networks', in P. Garvin (ed) (1971), *Cognition: a Multiple View* (New York: Spartan Books), *pp* 195–222. Reprinted in Makkai and Lockwood (1973), *pp* 60–83

Lamb, S. M. (forthcoming), *Language, Thought and Knowledge*

Leech, G. N. (1969), *Towards a Semantic Description of English*. London: Longman

Lindkvist, K.-G. (1950), *Studies on the Local Sense of the Prepositions IN, AT, ON and TO in Modern English, Lund Series in English*, 22. Lund and Copenhagen: Munksgaard

Lockwood, D. G. (1972), *Introduction to Stratificational Linguistics*. New York: Harcourt Brace Jovanovich

Longacre, R. E. (1960), 'String Constituent Analysis', *Language*, 36, *pp* 63–88

Lyons, J. (1968), *Introduction to Theoretical Linguistics*. Cambridge: Cambridge University Press

Makkai, A. and Lockwood, D. G. (eds) (1973), *Readings in Stratificational Linguistics*. University, Ala: University of Alabama Press

McCawley, J. D. (1971), 'Tense and Time Reference in English', in C. J. Fillmore and D. T. Langendoen (eds) (1971), *Studies in Linguistic Semantics* (New York: Holt, Rinehart & Winston) *pp* 96–113

Millington-Ward, J. (1954), *The Use of Tenses in English: a New Approach for Intermediate Students*. London: Longman

O'Brien, R. J. (ed) (1971), *Monograph Series on Languages and Linguistics*, 24 (*Report of the 22nd Annual Round Table Meeting on Linguistics and Language Studies*). Washington, DC: Georgetown University Press

Ota, A. (1963), *Tense and Aspect of Present-day American English*. Tokyo: Kenkyusha

Palmer, F. R. (1965), *A Linguistic Study of the English Verb*. London: Longman

Postal, P. M. (1968), *Aspects of Phonological Theory*. New York: Harper & Row

Quirk, R. and Mulholland, J. (1963), 'Complex Prepositions and Related Sequences', Supplement to *English Studies*, 45, *pp* 64–73

Reich, P. A. (1968), 'Symbols, Relations and Structural Complexity', Report of the Linguistic Automation Project, Yale University. Reprinted in Makkai and Lockwood (1973), *pp* 92–115

Reich, P. A. (1969), 'The Finiteness of Natural Language', *Language*, 45, *pp* 831–43

Reich, P. A. (1970a), *A Relational Network Model of Language Behavior*, University of Michigan PHD Dissertation. To be published by Mouton, The Hague

Reich, P. A. (1970b), 'Relational Networks', *Journal of Canadian Linguistics*, 15, *pp* 95–110

Reich, P. A. (1970c), 'Six Performances in Search of a Competence', paper presented at a Seminar on the Construction of Complex Grammars, Harvard University, June 1970

Robinson, J. J. (1970), 'Dependency Structures and Transformational Rules', *Language*, 46, *pp* 259–85

Ross, J. R. (1966), 'A Proposed Rule of Tree-Pruning', Report No NSF-17 of the Computational Laboratory of Harvard University, *pp* (IV-1)–(IV-18)

Ruwet, N. (1969), 'À propos des Prépositions de Lieu en Français', *Mélanges de Linguistique, de Philologie et de Méthodologie de l'Enseignement des Langues Anciennes Offerts à M. René Fohalle* (Gembloux: Duculot), *pp* 115–35

Sandhagen, H. (1956), *Studies on the Temporal Senses of the Prepositions AT, ON, IN, BY and FOR in Present-day English.* Trelleborg: the author

Saussure, F. de (1916), *Cours de Linguistique Générale*, 1st edition (4th edition, 1949). Paris: Payot

Stanley, R. (1967), 'Redundancy Rules in Phonology', *Language*, 43, *pp* 393–436

Stratton, C. R. (1971), 'The Pathological Case', *Working Papers in Linguistics*, 10 (Columbus, Ohio: The Ohio State University), *pp* 221–30

Vendler, Z. (1957), 'Verbs and Times', *The Philosophical Review*, 66, *pp* 143–60. Reprinted in Vendler (1967), *Linguistics in Philosophy* (Ithaca, NY: Cornell University Press), *pp* 97–121

Weinreich, U. (1966a), 'On the Semantic Structure of Language', in J. H. Greenberg (ed) (1966), *Universals of Language*, 2nd edition (Cambridge, Mass: MIT Press) *pp* 142–216

Weinreich, U. (1966b), 'Explorations in Semantic Theory', in T. A. Sebeok (ed) (1966), *Current Trends in Linguistics, Volume 3: Theoretical Foundations* (The Hague: Mouton), *pp* 395–477

Wells, R. S. (1947), 'Immediate Constituents', *Language*, 23, *pp* 81–117. Reprinted in M. Joos (ed) (1957), *Readings in Linguistics* (Washington, DC: American Council of Learned Societies), *pp* 186–207

Wood, F. T. (1967), *English Prepositional Idioms.* London: Macmillan

Yngve, V. (1960), 'A Model and an Hypothesis for Language Structure', *Proceedings of the American Philosophical Society*, 104, *pp* 444–66

Index

Semantic elements are enclosed between single quotation marks; lexical items are italicized.

order
   of directional expressions 38–9,
      46–7, 49, 78, 134, 176
   of semantic components 128–9,
      165, 174, 222
   of surface constituents 38–9,
      46–7, 49, 78, 176, 209, 219
Ota, A. 9, 105, 108–10
out 77–80, 130, 209, 211, 218–19
out of 23–5, 29, 33, 72–80, 124–5,
      130, 209, 215, 218–19
outside 54, 80–1, 129
over 18–19, 35–8, 46–57, 129, 148–
      154, 185
Oxford English Dictionary 5, 127

Palmer, F. R. 105
paradigm 19, 29, 38, 62, 65
paradigmatic axis of language 187
parts 16–17, 37, 53, 60–1, 81, 85,
      133, 162–3
past 36, 58–63, 84, 130, 177–80,
      197, 201–2
'path' 18–19, 21, 29–30, 38, 49,
      51–4, 61–2, 65, 85, 87, 94, 112,
      134, 177–80, 201–4
path expression 18–21, 27–8, 94,
      110–12
patterns 190, 192, 194–5
   alternation 190–2, 194–5
   componency 192, 194–5
   sign 190–2, 194–5
      multi-level 192
   tactic, *see* tactics
perfect 8, 100, 107–9, 123, 164
performance 145–6
phoneme 9–10, 175
phrase marker 3, 38–9, 165, 167,
      170–1
phrase structure grammar 166–7
phrase structure rules 132–5, 138,
      141–2, 147–8, 157, 162, 165,
      209–10
physical object 16–17, 53, 82–3,
      132–3, 138
'place' 15–16, 43, 82, 119, 133–4,
      172, 175–6, 200, 203
point of observation 38, 83

polysemy 4–8, 27, 196–8
   levels of 202–4
portmanteau realization 186–90,
      192–4, 199–202, 219
Postal, P. M. 195
'posterior' 17, 75–6, 82–3, 107,
      119, 163, 175, 215–16
'posteriority' 105, 107, 175, 200
posture 34, 133, 138, 141
precedence 56, 68, 90, 180, 221
predicate 15, 132, 157–8
   directional 21, 134, 161, 176
   durative 158–60
      actional 159–62
      stative 159–60
   extent 44, 134, 160
   locative 133, 160
   punctual 158–9, 161, 221
predication (*see also* proposition)
   accomplishment 101–5, 116, 122,
      126, 159
   achievement 101–4, 121–2, 158
   activity 101–5, 110, 116, 121–4,
      126–7, 159, 161
   iterative 103, 110, 121, 161
   stative 101–4, 110–11
prepositional phrases 206–7
   and adverbs 15, 78, 208–9, 212
   and verbs 34
   inside and outside verb phrase 2,
      207–8
   order of 38, 46
presupposed question 40–1
priority 138, 217
production 142, 145, 214
progressive aspect 40, 91, 101–12,
      156, 160–1
progressive structures 142
proportion 29, 72–5, 78, 86, 98, 120
proposition 14–15, 17–18, 101,
      132–3, 176
'proximity' 60–2, 86, 177–80
psycholinguistic experiments 5, 17

Quirk, R. 2

Realizational structure 177, 186–94,
      212–14